Toward Empowerment

Toward Empowerment

Women and Movement Politics in India

Leslie J. Calman

BARNARD COLLEGE

Westview Press

BOULDER • SAN FRANCISCO • OXFORD

Copyright © 1992 by Westview Press, Inc.

Published in 1992 in the United States of America by Westview Press, Inc., 5500 Central Avenue, Boulder, Colorado 80301-2877, and in the United Kingdom by Westview Press, 36 Lonsdale Road, Summertown, Oxford OX2 7EW

Library of Congress Cataloging-in-Publication Data
Calman, Leslie J.
    Toward empowerment : women and movement politics in India / Leslie J. Calman.
        p.   cm.
    Includes bibliographical references and index.
    ISBN 0-8133-8103-7—ISBN 0-8133-1695-2 (pbk.)
    1. Feminism—India.   2. Women in politics—India.   3. Women—India—Social conditions.—I. Title.
HQ1743.C35   1992
305.42'0954—dc20   92-6420
                                                                                          CIP

Printed and bound in the United States of America

The paper used in this publication meets the requirements
of the American National Standard for Permanence of Paper
for Printed Library Materials Z39.48-1984.

10   9   8   7   6   5   4   3   2   1

To Carole Christie

Contents

The Indian Women's Movement and
  Theories of New Social Movements, 196
Notes, 198

Acknowledgments

Although writing a book is in many respects a solitary enterprise, it can only be done with the help of a great many people. My debts in this instance are so extensive that I have divided them into two parts. The Preface contains thanks to many women in India whose work this study records. This section acknowledges those whose help was more monetary, editorial, and, not of least importance, personal.

The American Political Science Association and Barnard College provided the financial assistance that helped to make my fieldwork possible.

Demetrios Caraley and Rosalind Rosenberg cut, red-pencilled, and cajoled with the firmness of true and good friends. Many others read all or parts of the manuscript and helped, as much as I would let them, to whip it into final shape. My thanks go to Thomas Bernstein, Douglas Chalmers, Dennis Dalton, Neera Desai, Jana Everett, Martha Howell, Peter Juviler, Temma Kaplan, Mary F. Katzenstein, Morton Klass, Jane Mansbridge, Vina Mazumdar, Hanna Papanek, Barnett Rubin, Kathleen Staudt, and Marcia Wright. My editor at Westview, Rebecca Ritke, has been an exacting and remarkably patient reader, and Amrita Basu and Manisha Desai generously shared valuable resources and thoughts.

Research and production were enhanced by the able and generous assistance of Goteh Nzidee, Valerie Green, Pat Karpen, Judith Aks, and Rachel Gibson. Paul Franklin baby-sat to perfection.

I am lucky indeed to enjoy the friendship of two families in India whose caring and generosity surpass even the warm hospitality for which India is rightly known. My thanks to Shukla, Kailash, Meenakshi, and Vinita Nath of New Delhi; and to Sonal, Haresh, and Kabir Shah of Bombay.

Finally, writing this book has meant far too many hours away from my loving family at home. Deepest thanks to Carole and to Benjamin for making it so difficult to leave and so very joyful to return.

Leslie J. Calman

Preface

This book documents the existence of a vital, dynamic women's movement in India. Part One explores the political and structural crises that inspired the movement and the resources that made it possible. Part Two looks at the accomplishments and failings of the movement and seeks to project what promises and problems the future holds.

My decision to write a book on the women's movement in India grew out of my interests in political movements, India, and women in politics. Scholarly work on these topics has rarely overlapped in the past. Western theorists of movements focus largely on those in the United States and Europe, creating generalizations about movement politics—particularly movement politics in democratic states—with nary a glance at the developing world, including the world's largest democracy.[1] By the same token, although scholars of India may read the broad comparative politics literature, the favor is not generally returned; scholarship on India tends to be ghettoized and read mostly by those who are students of South Asia *per se*. When it comes to studying women, there is a large body of literature about women's movements in the West, particularly in the United States and Great Britain. But with regard to women in the developing world, books on the historical development of women's status and on women's roles in economic development far outnumber any on women's collective action or the special problems that gender poses to political organization.[2]

Through my examination of the Indian women's movement, I hope first, then, to inform movement theory. Particularly, I will explore the issue of what women in the developing world can hope to achieve through movement participation. Do women's movements serve valuable functions for women in the developing world that other, more traditional political institutions and processes do not? Social movement theory in the West has been long on the questions of *why* and *how* movements emerge, but short on the question of *what* movements accomplish; to the extent it has addressed the last question, it has done so in terms of advanced capitalist societies, not developing ones. I hope to help correct this imbalance.

The presence of political movements reveals something about the health and capacity of the political system in which they occur. When people choose to participate in movements, it may signify that other channels of political participation are closed to them. Or, it may mean that they face problems that are beyond the capacity of the state to solve, either because the state lacks commitment or resources, or because the problems lie in a social arena, such as the family, that is not wholly within the state's control. Thus, this examination of the causes of the emergence of the women's movement, and of how it has since fared in relation to the state, should reveal something of the capacities and limitations not only of this particular movement but of the Indian state as well.

Finally, I write also for those whose interest is in women in developing areas, and I think that the Indian case has much to teach. Scholars of women in developing areas have grown rightly wary of overgeneralizing about the problems and prospects of women in areas as vast and as distinct as the nations of Asia, Latin America, the Middle East, and Africa. Within the confines of the case study that follows, I have tried to be specific about which groups of Indian women are affected by and react to different social, economic, and political circumstances.

And yet, while it is necessary to be precise about the differences among women in developing areas, it is useful to note and explore their commonalities. Only in this way can the distinct experiences of one group of women illuminate pitfalls and promises for another. Commonalities among women in developing areas do exist in the conditions of day-to-day life.[3] While not all women in the developing world are poor, most of them are; and in the last several decades, with the growing impact of capitalist production and despite economic development schemes during the United Nations Decade for the Advancement of Women that aimed to include women, women's relative access to economic resources, remunerative work, and income has declined.[4] In virtually all states in the developing world, women have less access, also, to public resources, such as education and health care, in part because of state policies and in part because of social customs, which dictate that scarce resources go first to men and boys and only later to girls and women. Women enjoy less-than-equal rights in law (either civil or religious law, or both), whether because the law is written so as to limit their rights or because the law is adjudicated and implemented in such a way as to have this effect. They hold less political power than men on national and local levels both in terms of offices held and in terms of influence.[5] They are subject to violence by men (of their own families, or often, by unrelated men who hold economic power over them, such as landlords or moneylenders, or those with state power, like the police) that goes largely unpunished by the state.

Understanding how the Indian women's movement has attacked these problems, and with what degree of success, will help us to understand prospects elsewhere. All the circumstances described in the previous paragraph exist full-blown in India.

As of 1991, India had a population of some 850 million people. One struggles to understand the enormity of the figure. India's population is three and a third times that of the United States. It is 200 million greater than the continent of Africa's, 125 million greater than all of North and South America's, and 75 million greater than that of the United States, Canada, and Europe combined. Apart from China's 1.1 billion people, India contains 27 percent of the population of the entire third world.[6] India is so vast, and its population so multifarious, that it is in some ways a world unto itself, worthy of study if only for the hundreds of millions it includes. However, it is more than that. Certainly, in many respects, it constitutes a microcosm of the problems of developing states; some of these problems are at their most severe in India.

Like many states artificially brought together by the forces of invasion and imperialism, it is today beset by ethnic and religious strife and divided by language.[7] Political organization of any kind—whether by movements or political parties—is hindered by these divisions.[8] In particular, as in other countries of the world, such divisions separate women, whose first allegiance may be, for instance, to their own ethnic or religious group rather than to the women of another. In India, while Hindu women, Muslim women, Sikh women, Christian women, and Parsi women have many problems in common—some of them problems that appear susceptible to legal remedies—common solutions remain hostage to inter-ethnic strife. The particulars are unique to India, but the fact of ethnic division is not.[9]

India is also afflicted by a poverty more crushing than that experienced in most of the developing world. In 1985 (the most recent year for which numbers are available) the World Bank determined that 420 million Indians, 55 percent of the population, were "poor" (having an income of less than $30 a month), while 250 million, 33 percent of the population, were "extremely poor" (with an income of less than $23 a month). This compares unfavorably with the figures for sub-Saharan Africa, in which 47 percent of the population were deemed "poor" and 30 percent "extremely poor."[10]

Women in India, as elsewhere, are particularly poor. They are more likely to be malnourished, starting as a result of the relative deprivation of food and health care for girls as compared to boys (a deprivation which persists into adulthood) and continuing with repeated pregnancies, the process of lactation, and overwork at physically arduous tasks such as the collection of fuel and water (tasks that have been made more time-consuming in recent years by deforestation).[11]

As elsewhere in the developing world, women are more likely, too, to be illiterate. The 1981 census indicates that in India, overall, 24.8 percent of women are literate, compared to 46.9 percent of men. The situation is most dramatic in rural areas, where only 18 percent of women are literate; urban areas are significantly better, with a 47.8 percent female literacy rate.[12] India's female literacy rate compares unfavorably to other regions in the third world: In 1985, the developing world as a whole had a female literacy rate of 50 percent. In sub-Saharan Africa, female literacy stood at 29.5 percent, the Arab States had a rate of 31.5 percent, East Asia's female literacy was 60.7 percent, and Latin America's was 80 percent.[13]

These problems make the organization of women urgent if they are to achieve equality, but also make it that much more difficult. Thus, the problems presented to women, and to the organizing of women, by poverty in India may be instructive for women elsewhere.

But as in other countries in developing areas, the population of India is not all poor. Indeed, the divide between those of middle-class standing and above, with their access to most of the consumer goods the world economy has to offer, and the majority who are desperately poor, is becoming deeper and more painful.[14] Women of different classes experience different problems and of course have different opportunities and political agendas. Greater wealth helps alleviate some problems but creates others. For example, the phenomenon of dowry death—in which a young bride is murdered by her husband and/or his family in a quest for greater dowry—is most common among upwardly mobile members of the lower-middle class.

The Indian women's movement is sufficiently broad based that it tackles problems of different classes of women, but of course its opportunities for unity are limited by precisely these distinctions. In this way, again, the divisions that are deep in India are not unique to it, and India can provide us with instructive material.

Nor is the Indian population unique in being influenced by social and religious mores that limit the activities of women in politics and in the economy. In India, it is the particular effects of Hinduism and Indian-based Islam that must be the focus of analysis, rather than those of Christianity, Judaism, or Islam as practiced and adjudicated in other parts of the world. Still, the fact of having underlying patriarchal socio-religious traditions that relegate women to a secondary status is common to most developing countries and must with specificity in each instance be taken into account in understanding the status of women and the limits of and possibilities for change.[15]

A Note on Methods and Sources,
Some Acknowledgments, and a Caveat

Just as with a political movement, so too the desired outcome of a book shapes the manner in which the goal is pursued. In addition to adding to theoretical insights about the development and outcomes of movements, I have sought to be explicit and detailed about the facts of the Indian case upon which I develop those judgments. As a nationally based overview of the causes, development, and results of the modern Indian women's movement, this book draws together an array of facts not available in other published sources.

There are a number of studies that examine the status of women in India and analyze its causes.[16] Other books document the role of women in the nationalist movement and the effects of that movement on women.[17] There are works that document women's organizations in a particular city[18] or that study one organization in depth.[19]

Since my goal is to give the broadest all-India view possible of the movement, I make use of such secondary sources and of the reports of international organizations and individual scholars on particular movement organizations. In addition, during my fieldwork in New Delhi, Bombay, and Ahmedabad in 1986, I obtained firsthand accounts of movement activity, both in the Indian research centers mentioned below and directly from movement activists.[20] These consist of unpublished papers (often written for meetings of activists); leaflets announcing demonstrations; pamphlets, newsletters, and reports issued by specific organizations about their activities; newspapers published (sometimes quite fleetingly) by women's collectives; and firsthand accounts of rural development projects by "activist researchers." The women's journal *Manushi* also regularly publishes participant reports of urban and rural movement activities throughout India.

Press reports in the national English-language press were especially important for tracking the activities of what I call the "rights wing" of the movement. Since the goal of rights activists is to influence the national government, they seek (and generally receive) coverage from the newspapers with national sweep that most influence officials in the nation's capital. Demonstrations, meetings (or confrontations) with government officials, and announcements by organizations in the rights wing of the movement are generally planned with the national press in mind. In addition, these newspapers employ a number of journalists who are sympathetic to the movement and who report regularly on women's activities in both urban and rural settings. I surveyed reports on the women's movement from the late 1970s onward in *The Times of India, The Statesman, The Indian Express, The Hindu,* and *The Hindustan*

Times. The magazines *Economic and Political Weekly* and *India Today* were also consistently useful sources of information.

But interviews were the most intriguing and valuable part of the research. I was able to talk with nearly forty people closely involved with the women's movement as activists, researchers (most of whom are also activists), government officials, journalists (whose "beat" is women), attorneys and civil liberties leaders, environmentalists (concerned about the effects environmental deterioration has on women), and development experts engaged in projects for women. Most of them are represented in the endnotes of this book.

Among those I would most like to thank for sharing their time and indispensable insights are the leaders of these major women's organizations: Prema Purao, secretary and founder of Annapurna Mahila Mandal; Renana Jhabvala, secretary of the Self Employed Women's Association; Pramila Dandavate, president of Mahila Dakshata Samiti and former member of Parliament; Vimla Farooqui, general secretary of the National Federation of Indian Women; Vimal Ranadive, secretary of the All India Coordinating Committee of Working Women and vice president of the All India Democratic Women's Association; and Ivy Khan, general secretary of the national Young Women's Christian Association. Thanks, too, to Jaya Arunachalam, president of Working Women's Forum, for her correspondence with me.

Activists from Vimochna in Bangalore, the Women's Centre in Bombay, the Delhi unit of the Janvadi Mahila Samiti, Saheli in New Delhi, and the Women's Forum Against Violence in Bombay were especially helpful; particular thanks to Vibhuti Patel, Corinne Kumar d'Souza, and Susie Methai.

C. P. Sujaya, joint secretary, Government of India, Department of Women and Child Development; and Meena Gupta, director, Government of India, Ministry of Labour, were extremely generous. So too were Viji Srinivasan, then the program officer for women in the Ford Foundation, New Delhi; Marty Chen, then field representative of Oxfam America; and Andrea Singh of the International Labour Organisation.

Madhu Kishwar and Ruth Vanita, coeditors and founders of *Manushi*, were each gracious enough to talk with me, despite the onslaught of international feminists who regularly enter their door. Thanks, too, for the tips provided by these journalists who regularly report on women: Shahnaz Anklesaria, Kalpana Sharma, and Neerja Chaudary.

Smitu Kothari, head of the People's Union for Civil Liberties, provided a valuable perspective from outside the women's movement *per se*; so, too, did Sunita Narain of the Centre for Science and Environment, New Delhi.

Finally, I conducted research at several splendid libraries and research institutes. The Centre for Education and Documentation, Bombay, maintains an extensive and user-friendly collection of works on Indian women, including a number of the unpublished materials described above. Even more impressive are the extensive collections of two institutions whose *raison d'être* is research on women: the Centre for Women's Development Studies in New Delhi and the Research Centre on Women's Studies, SNDT University, Bombay. I would like to thank the excellent staffs of all three of these institutions and particularly the patient operators of their photocopying equipment, without whose help, truly, this book would not have been possible.

I was also privileged to talk with a number of scholars at the latter two institutions: Vina Mazumdar, director of the Centre for Women's Development Studies, and Neera Desai, then director of the Research Centre on Women's Studies, have my special thanks. Govind Kelkar and Lotika Sarkar at CWDS and Maithreyi Krishnaraj and Ramala Baxamusa at RCWS were all extremely helpful.

While all the above deserve praise for their generosity of time and spirit, and respect for their wisdom and knowledge, none deserve any blame if the interpretations that follow are flawed; that is mine alone to claim.

L.J.C.

Notes

1. To support this broad generalization, this note refers to several "schools" of movement theory, offering only a few illustrative examples of specific theorists.

The "collective behavior" school, which developed in the wake of Bolshevism and Nazism, saw movements as inherently destructive, as social pathology; ideology was believed to be radical intellectual depravity (Clifford Geertz' characterization of the view prevalent among Western social scientists, in *The Interpretation of Cultures* [New York: Basic Books, 1973], p. 197); and movement participants were labeled deviants and social outcasts. Among the most frequently cited works are Neil Smelser, *The Theory of Collective Behavior* (New York: Free Press, 1962), and Eric Hoffer, *The True Believer* (New York: Harper and Row, 1951). These theorists did not attempt to account for the Indian nationalist movement although it took place in the same historical epoch as Nazism and Bolshevism. In fact, collective behavior theory cannot explain the brilliant organizational triumph of Mohandas Gandhi and the middle-class leadership of the Indian National Congress, who together mobilized masses of people to act purposefully and with discipline. Taking account of the Indian nationalist movement shows much of collective behavior theory to be false.

The explosion of movement activity in the West during the 1960s and 1970s prompted a new acceptance of movements as a rational means of participation in democratic political bargaining, and thus new theorizing. The "resource mobilization" paradigm, which focuses on strategic issues of how best to organize and articulate grievances, became the dominant theoretical influence among U.S. scholars. This school enfolds a split between those who adopt Mancur Olson's market-oriented analogy regarding movements and believe that selective incentives and "issue entrepreneurs" are necessary components of social movements, and those who argue instead that belief is a critical movement resource. In both instances, social movements in the U.S. and Europe provided the cases upon which the theory was developed. Still, because the theory poses questions about what resources are necessary for movement emergence and development, it provides guidance for exploring a democracy in the developing world. See Olson, *The Logic of Collective Action* (New York: Schocken, 1971) and his supporters John D. McCarthy and Meyer N. Zald, "Resource Mobilization and Social Movements," *American Journal of Sociology* 82 (1977), pp. 1212–1239. For the alternative view see Bruce Fireman and William A. Gamson, "Utilitarian Logic in the Resource Mobilization Perspective," and Charles Perrow, "The Sixties Observed," both in *The Dynamics of Social Movements*, ed. Zald and McCarthy (Cambridge, MA: Winthrop, 1979); Ralph H. Turner, "Collective Behavior and Resource Mobilization as Approaches to Social Movements," *Research in Social Movements, Conflicts and Change* 4 (1981), pp. 1–24; Bert Useem, "Solidarity Model, Breakdown Model and the Boston Anti-Busing Movement," *American Sociological Review* 45 (1980), pp. 357–369; Maren Lockwood Carden, "The Proliferation of a Social Movement: Ideology and Individual Incentives in the Contemporary Feminist Movement," *Research in Social Movements Conflict and Change* 1 (1978), pp. 178–196; and Charles Tilly, *From Mobilization to Revolution* (Reading, MA: Addison-Wesley, 1978).

"New social movement" theory developed in 1970s and 1980s Europe in an attempt to explain the meaning of such recently emerged movements as the feminist, human rights, environmental, and peace movements. Its theorists argue that the movements are products of a post-industrial society in which the state has an expanded capacity to penetrate all areas of life, including those formerly thought of as private. See Alberto Melucci, "The Symbolic Challenge of Contemporary Movements," and Claus Offe, "New Social Movements: Challenging the Boundaries of Institutional Politics," both in *Social Research* 52 (1985). Again, this theory provides some useful questions for examining the causes and possible outcomes of movements, but the present study of an Indian movement will show that much of what the new social movement theorists find new, unique, and distinctly postindustrial about the European movements is not so.

2. Although there are anthologies containing articles on the subject, there are few book-length studies of a women's movement anywhere in the third world. The exceptions to this rule mostly concern Latin America. See Sonia E. Alvarez, *Engendering Democracy in Brazil* (Princeton: Princeton Univ. Press, 1990); Jo Fisher, *Mothers of the Disappeared* (Boston: South End Press, 1989), [on Argentina]; and Carol Andreas, *When Women Rebel: The Rise of Popular Feminism in Peru* (Westport, CT: Lawrence Hill and Co., 1985). Khawar Mumtaz and Farida Shaheed, *Women of*

Pakistan (London: Zed Press, 1987) provides a study of an important organization, the Women's Action Forum, by two of its members.

3. Similarities acknowledged in the writings of many third world women concerned about development. See Gita Sen and Caren Grown, *Development, Crises and Alternative Visions: Third World Women's Perspectives* (New York: Monthly Review, 1987).

4. Sen and Grown, pp. 15–16. There is now a large literature on the failings of economic development with regard to women and of the problems capitalist development has posed for women in particular. In 1970, Ester Boserup argued in *Women's Role in Economic Development* (New York: St. Martin's Press) that women had not been included in capitalist development and that their exclusion widened the gap between women's and men's economic power. Since then, many others have argued that capitalist development *per se* is bad for women. See *Women and Development: The Sexual Division of Labor in Rural Societies,* ed. Lourdes Beneria (New York: Praeger/ILO, 1982). Whether or not capitalist development can be reformulated to better include women remains controversial. But there seems to be no disagreement with the once-controversial assertion made by Irene Tinker in "The Adverse Impact of Development on Women," in *Women and World Development,* ed. Irene Tinker and Michele Bo Bramson (Washington, D.C.: Overseas Development Council, 1976), p. 22, that as a result of "development," "In virtually all countries and among all classes, women have lost [economic] ground relative to men." See also Jane S. Jaquette, "Women and Modernization Theory: A Decade of Feminist Criticism," *World Politics* 34:2 (1982), pp. 267–284.

5. A fact not altered by the political achievements of a few women, notably in Asia and Latin America—Indira Gandhi, Benazir Bhutto, Sirimavo Bandaranaike of Sri Lanka, Aung San Suu Kyi of Burma, Corazon Aquino, Isabel Perón, Violeta Chamorro, and others—who have been wives or daughters of male political leaders.

6. That is, Africa, South America, Central America, the Caribbean, East Asia, West Asia (the Middle East), and South Asia. These figures are calculated from population data in *Statistical Abstract of the United States, 1990* (Washington, D.C.: U.S. Dept. of Commerce, Bureau of the Census, 1990).

7. Present-day India was created by a series of invasions, most importantly by the Moguls of central Asia and the British, that eventually consolidated under one rule peoples who spoke many different languages. These distinct languages—over 1,652 "mother tongues" have been identified—remain an important factor in the regionalism that today threatens to divide India. Efforts in the 1950s to declare Hindi the national language of India failed when confronted by violent protests in southern India, where languages of the Dravidian family (Telegu, Tamil, Kannada, Malayalam and others) are spoken, rather than the Indo-Aryan languages of the north. (Hindi, Urdu, Punjabi, Bengali and Marathi are a few of these. Hindi, the most widespread language, is spoken only by some 30 percent of Indians.) In 1956, states were reorganized along linguistic lines, with 14 "major" languages represented in state governmental usage. See Robert L. Hardgrave and Stanley A. Kochanek, *India: Government and Politics in a Developing Nation* 4th ed., (New York: Harcourt Brace Jovanovich, 1986), pp. 128–133.

Because of the plethora of indigenous languages, English remains the language of the national government, the national press, secondary schools, higher education and national commerce. It is the language of India's elites, both in government and out of it.

8. And accounts, in part, for the continuing dominance of the hundred-year-old Indian National Congress, the only party with a legacy in and an outreach to all of India.

9. One need only think of Nigeria, Lebanon, or Brazil as a few examples of developing countries where ethnic, religious and racial differences (which are often related to class differences as well, as in Brazil) divide women even as they pursue rights. See Barbara Callaway and Enid Schildkrout, "Law, Education and Social Change: Implications for Hausa Muslim Women in Nigeria," in *Women in the World*, ed. Lynne B. Iglitzin and Ruth Ross, 2nd ed. (Santa Barbara: ABC-Clio, 1986); Yolla Polity Sharara, "Women and Politics in Lebanon," in *Third World Second Sex*, ed. Miranda Davies (London: Zed, 1983); and Sonia Alvarez, "Women's Movements and Gender Politics in the Brazilian Transition," in *The Women's Movement in Latin America*, ed. Jane Jacquette (Boston: Unwin Hyman, 1989).

10. Figures cited in "Caged: A Survey of India," *The Economist*, 4 May 1991, p. 8.

11. Kamakshi Bhate, et al., *In Search of Our Bodies* (Bombay: Shatkti, 1987); *The State of India's Environment 1984–85: The Second Citizens' Report* (New Delhi: Centre for Science and Environment, 1985); and Bina Agarwal, *Cold Hearths and Barren Slopes: The Woodfuel Crisis in the Third World* (New Delhi: Allied, 1986).

12. See Government of India, Ministry of Social and Women's Welfare, *Women in India: Country Paper* (New Delhi, 1985), pp. 13, 43.

13. In 1985, the literacy rate for women in South Asia (India, Pakistan, Bangladesh, Sri Lanka) was 27.9 percent. The figures are from UNESCO, *Compendium of Statistics on Illiteracy—1990 Edition* (Paris, 1990), pp. 6–7. The figures for 1990 show the same regional rankings as reported in 1985. The figure for female literacy in developed countries in 1990 was 96.1 percent, compared to 55 percent in developing countries.

14. As Anita Desai recently observed, "The aggression and bullying of those who have, and the despair and rage of those who have not, affects the whole fiber of society. . . . To live in India today is to live in a constant state of tension." "India: The Seed of Destruction," *New York Review of Books*, 27 June 1991, p. 4.

15. Neither this statement nor those above generalizing about developing areas are meant to suggest that matters are substantially different in "developed" countries. But, ambitious as I intend to be in drawing lessons from the Indian case, I am not so foolish as to take on more than the two-thirds of the world already so brazenly embraced.

16. For example, Neera Desai and Maithreyi Krishnaraj, *Women and Society in India* (Delhi: Ajanta Publications, 1987) and the more theoretical Joanna Liddle and Rama Joshi, *Daughters of Independence: Gender, Caste and Class in India* (London: Zed Press, 1986).

17. Among others, Jana Everett, *Women and Social Change in India* (New Delhi: Heritage, 1981).

18. Patricia Caplan, *Class and Gender in India: Women and their Organizations in a South Indian City* (London: Tavistock, 1985).

19. Jennifer Sebstad, *Struggle and Development Among Self Employed Women: A Report on the Self Employed Women's Association, Ahmedabad, India* (Washington, D.C.: AID, 1982).

20. I was also able to talk with, or correspond with, activists in Bangalore and Madras and have updated information through telephone conversations with Indian activists as recently as 1991. Here's the caveat: While, through these interviews and through written sources, I feel that I have acquired enough information to make generalizations about a national movement, there are geographical gaps. I regret especially that I was able to gather very little information on women's movement activities in Bengal, and so I cannot say with certainty that the generalizations I develop here apply completely to this vibrant region of the country. The same must be said of the troubled northeastern state of Assam and its regional neighbors.

Toward Empowerment

PART ONE

Development of the Indian Women's Movement

1

Introduction:
Theoretical Approaches
to Defining the Movement
and Evaluating Its Results

The women's movement emerged in response to a crisis of the Indian state. By the mid-1970s, the government appeared to be corrupt and increasingly inept. Economic development had failed to reach hundreds of millions of Indians who remained mired in poverty and illiteracy, and the state increasingly violated the human rights of its citizens. Anger at political elites and lack of confidence in state institutions, including opposition political parties, led to a blossoming of movement politics. Increasing numbers of people ventured outside of established political channels to pressure the state to protect human rights and expand economic development.

The women's movement was part of this surge. Like other secular, democratic and non-party movements that developed during this period (including those to improve the standing of Dalits [untouchables], tribals, and others among the poor, and movements to protect the environment on which the livelihoods of so many depend), the women's movement has wanted to have an impact not only on the state, but on society as well. The movement wants political rights for women, and it seeks their social and economic empowerment.

By exploring the structural opportunities provided by the crisis of the Indian political system, and examining what domestic and international resources have been available to help the movement develop, the next three chapters will analyze in detail why and how the women's movement emerged. This chapter briefly introduces the structure and goals of the movement, and presents a theoretical approach to answering both a prior question and a subsequent one that is at the heart of this book. First, how does one define a movement and judge whether or not it exists: is there indeed a women's movement in India? Second, how should an analyst go about predicting what a movement will (or will not) be able to accomplish? Some additional questions are necessary to answer the latter question: How is the structure of a movement related to its outcome? And in what arenas do we judge movement results: movement results with relation to what?

The first question is necessary because women who are politically active on behalf of women's causes in India often demur when asked if there is an Indian women's *movement*. The question seems to them to imply a singular, unified entity, perhaps with one guiding ideology and a compact leadership group. Such a phenomenon certainly does not exist. A movement, however—vibrant, energetic, and multi-faceted—does. That its parameters are difficult to pin down and that its tactics and leaders are many and varied make it no less a movement. Indeed, this chapter begins to argue that the decentralized structure of the Indian women's movement and its resulting capacity to engage simultaneously with many levels of government and society marks a strength, not a weakness, in its capacity to build the rights, economic and political power, and status of women.

What Is a Movement?

A movement is a collective effort to seek change. Throughout this book, I will use the term "movement" rather than "social movement" or "political movement" in order to stress that these phenomena often address change both with respect to social life and with respect to the state. Political scientists have generally attended only to the latter aspect. But many women are prevented by social constrictions from significant participation in the economy and in politics. In defining the parameters of a women's movement, then, one must make the connection between the private, or social exercise of power, and its public, or political exercise.

A movement may aim to overthrow the state, to transform it, or just to get something from it. Although it was once thought that movements were symptoms of anomie and irrationality, movements in democracies are now generally seen more prosaically as a means of aggregating and articulating interest in order to affect state policies.[1] Movements, like interest groups, are contenders for influence.

Or, and this makes them no less political, movements may decline to directly confront the state, preferring to try to supplement it with alternative institutions that fulfill needs that the state has not. Such a strategy is not necessarily antithetical to a later confrontation with the state; indeed, for the poor and powerless, the political mobilization and social and economic empowerment that can occur through direct participation in local groups may be a prerequisite to eventual engagement with the state.

Thus in India many organizations within the women's movement have as their goal moving the state to action; it is primarily the government, they believe, that should provide women with equal rights and economic opportunity. But other organizations, instead of or in addition to targeting the government, strive to improve women's lives within the context of movement participation itself. The goals of economic cooperation and development, greater autonomy within the family, and access to participatory, democratic decision making are pursued within the movement's own activities.

Thus in order to evaluate what a movement does, the analyst must not only look at a movement's relationship to the state, but at three potential arenas of action. A movement can target society, particularly with regard to social consciousness or ideology; it acts to influence the state; and it can act on participants within the movement itself.

Fluidity of "Membership" and Structure

A movement is not a mob, but neither is it an interest group. The former is completely anarchic; the latter is characterized by stable bureaucratic organizations and formal interaction with government. A movement is ordinarily somewhere in between.[2]

It is helpful to think of a movement as containing both groups and individuals; it is bigger than the sum of its formal, cardcarrying membership. Within a movement, there may be a number of movement organizations with identifiable leaders and members, as well as unaffiliated individuals who sympathize with the goals of such organizations,[3] and who may intermittently contribute time or money, or be mobilized by those groups for particular political actions: demonstrations, letter writing campaigns, and the like. Thus Indian women activists are mistaken when they think that the decentralized character of their activities constitutes a nonmovement; that quality is, in fact, more typical of movements than not.

A Movement Mobilizes for Action

Movements are not content merely to influence the behavior or thinking of the already converted. Movements are by their nature evangelical; they seek to convert—to *move*—people both to new consciousness and to action.[4] The desire and ability of movement organizations to mobilize new constituents is a key aspect of what distinguishes a movement from an interest group. If they fail to grow, movements may instead become more formally organized interest groups seeking only to protect or further the interests of their existing membership.[5] Movements, on the other hand, seek to persuade, to mobilize, to build.

The next section argues for the importance of belief in defining, generating and building a movement. But however important belief is, it is not all that makes a movement. If, as Mao said, a revolution is not a dinner party, so a movement is not a meditation or, for that matter, a colloquium. A movement agitates and acts: it mobilizes people to attack and transform power relations in their social and political lives.

A Movement Is Characterized by Shared Beliefs

In response to Mancur Olson's suggestion that rational individuals will participate in movements only if they receive some selective, or individual, reward,[6] a number of resource mobilization theorists have argued convincingly for the importance of ideological belief as a factor in movement emergence. For example, in his discussion of the causes of the 1960s U.S. anti-war movement, Perrow maintains that self-interest is an inadequate explanation: the war, he argues "was an issue with youth because it was seen as immoral." Similarly, her study of the U.S. feminist movement brings Carden to conclude that ideological incentives motivate most members, who "enjoy working for a cause in which they believe." In short, people may join a movement not because they have rationally balanced the selective rewards that participation will bring them against the collective rewards they can reap by letting someone else do it; people may join a movement because they feel ideologically committed to changing society and because they will find it hard to live with themselves if they don't.[7]

This is an important point to consider when thinking about what movements can achieve. Ideas are not only a critical resource of movement emergence, but of movement growth and success. The transformation of public consciousness is critical to the dual goals of moving the state and altering society. One of the main tasks of a movement, then, is to develop and disseminate ideas that challenge the status quo and suggest more satisfying alternatives. This need not be a fully developed ideology that comprehensively analyzes society's problems and gives specific, detailed guidelines for action, although this, and the charismatic leadership that sometimes accompanies it, may be the best mobilizers of movements. The belief may instead be a more vague sense that a wrong needs to be righted, and that it can be righted.

Except in highly centralized or authoritarian movements, views on precisely what tactics to utilize toward what specific future will vary widely. Movement organizations and movement members will agree about some things, disagree about others, come together when they agree, diverge when they disagree. As long as the broad goals—such as greater equality for women—remain the same, there is a movement.

What Do Movements Do?

There are limitations to the existing theoretical approaches to answering the question of what movements can accomplish, but there are some useful analytical insights.

Movements Contend Against Others

It is helpful to view movements, as Alberto Melucci does, as *"action systems operating in a systemic field of possibilities and limits."*[8] What a movement can accomplish, in other words, is substantially influenced not only by what resources the movement brings to the battle, but by the strength of those institutions with which it contends. Thus, to the extent a movement's goals include the changing of state policy or action, the analyst must explore why the state is disposed to facilitate or to hinder the movement's achievement of its goals and what resources it can bring to bear to enforce its desires. Similarly, one must examine the strengths of other movements or interest groups that are in alliance or in contention with the movement for influence and power.

In evaluating the possible outcomes of the Indian women's movement, then, one line of questioning has to concern what groups oppose its goals, and what are their relative strengths. Similarly, it is necessary to ask two questions about the state: What incentives does it have and what capacity—economic and political—does it have to respond positively to movement demands?

Movement Structure Helps Determine Outcome

What a movement will be able to accomplish is dependent, too, on the structure of the organizations within it, and the overall structure of the movement itself. A consensus seems to have emerged among theorists on the relative merits of centralized, hierarchical organizations with well-developed divisions of labor as compared to those of organizations characterized by little division of labor.[9] Centralized movement organizations are thought to be more successful in the short run in influencing established institutions of government because they can coordinate the support that exists and can provide the type of technical expertise to which bureaucratic government institutions respond. On the other hand, grassroots mobilization and ideological innovation seem to be better accomplished by smaller organizations that can more precisely fulfill the individual desires of prospective members for such selective incentives as direct participation, consciousness raising activities (such as small group discussions and projects), the learning of new skills, and the development of interpersonal bonds and thus group solidarity. A number of small organizations linked together loosely are better able than one hierarchical organization to embrace a diversity of ideological beliefs and choice of tactics; this characteristic, too, makes them better suited to mobilizing the grass roots.

The insight that different structures give individual organizations different strengths can be applied with equal value to the structures of movements as a whole. Movements come in diverse structural forms—some, like the Indian nationalist movement, centralized with a single organization and authoritative leadership at their core; others, like the U.S. feminist movement that began in the late 1960s, characterized by a large number of organizations (some with identifiable leadership, others more collective in nature) that share related goals. An assessment of how promising is a movement's overall structure therefore requires an examination not only of the *type* of organizations within the movement, but also of the *mix* of organizational structures and how well it corresponds to the goals of the movement. There may be, within a movement, a role for organizations that concentrate on persuading government to institute or implement law (much as the Women's Equity Action League acts in the U.S.), while other groups contribute to the development of ideology and mobilization at the grass roots (as U.S. "radical feminist" organizations have done). Indeed, it can be hypothesized that a friendly alliance among such structurally disparate groups provides a strong model for a movement with broad aims. As will be discussed below, the women's movement in India is characterized by such a structure of alliance; this book's conclusion will revisit the question of how promising this structure is.

The Limitations of Existing Theoretical Approaches

The above contributions aside, theorists of movements have devoted too little attention to the question of what movements can accomplish. Having overcome the prejudice of the collective behavioral school of the 1950s and early 1960s that movements are a social pathology, resource mobilization theorists have gone too far in the direction of seeing movements as merely contenders for influence with regard to state policy. In their efforts to legitimize movements, they have rendered them one dimensional. Whether or not movements have some unique qualities that provide opportunities—personal or political—that other institutions do not is not a question that resource mobilization theorists ask.[10]

"New social movement" theorists do ask if movements have special qualities, and find that they do.[11] Unfortunately, they concern themselves only with advanced capitalist societies characterized by great wealth and highly developed technologies. Specifically they argue that the new social movements, such as European and North American feminist, peace, human rights, and environmental movements, are a response not to class issues, but rather to political systems that are overly hierarchical, centralized, bureaucratized and unresponsive. In the absence of meaningful avenues of participation provided by the state, these movements attempt to create channels for participatory democracy. It is within the context of the movement itself that activists (who are of at least middle-class status, because only they have the time and material resources to support their activities) find the rewards of community, personal autonomy, access to decision making, and growing self-esteem.

Thus, while such movements attempt, in part, to have an impact on state policies, their concern is as much to recapture from the state a space within civil society in which there can be meaningful participation and thus personal and community empowerment. This requires resisting the expanded capacity of the industrialized state to control social and cultural life, and regaining from the state the means of production of "symbolic goods . . . of information and images, of culture itself."[12] By so doing, the movements hope to alter public opinion and public demands, to change the way people perceive their society and their government.

This study of the Indian women's movement will show that some of the impulses and some of the potential that new social movement theorists find in movements in advanced capitalist society exist in movements among women, including the very poorest women (who do indeed have class issues), in one of the world's poorest nations. The assumption is incorrect that movements that value the means of direct democratic participation and access to cultural production as much as the ends of moving the state are products of advanced capitalism. In India, too, the desire for participatory democracy, for individual and group autonomy, for a redefinition of politics to include the production of cultural norms are present. For some parts of the women's movement—what I call the "empowerment wing"—the drive to create them constitutes as important a part of potential movement achievement as winning concessions from the state.

Considering Movement Results Externally and Internally

A movement interacts with the state and with society. Additionally, however, the movement has an environment internal to itself. To fully judge a movement's achievements one therefore must also evaluate its interaction with individual movement participants and groups.

This study refers to those organizations within the women's movement whose central goal is moving the state to protect and enhance the rights and opportunities of women as the "rights wing" of the movement; the exploration of its strengths and weaknesses constitutes a major portion of the analysis that follows. But the state does not exist in a vacuum, and these organizations are keenly aware of that. An analysis of their activities leads in the direction, too, of looking at the interaction of the movement not only with the state but with society.

For while to be sure many policies of the Indian state inhibit the growth of women's equality, participation, and development, and while it has resources that could be put to better use, it is not an all-powerful state. Instead, the state is but one of several institutions, including religion and the family, that are rightly seen by movement participants to construct culture and limit women's access to meaningful decision-making about their own lives. The women's movement thus hopes to transform social consciousness: to name and analyze the problem of women's inferior status and power, and to point the way toward their transformation.

In thinking about what a movement may accomplish, one needs, then, to think about state power, but also about social power and ideology, and about the ways in which they intersect and uphold one another. As the women's movement in India shows, both areas may be targets for movement action. And, this study will suggest further, if women are to experience meaningful change toward equality, both of them *should* be targets.

Additionally, to understand what a movement does, one must ask what happens to people during their participation in the internal environment of the movement. This is particularly so for less empowered people and especially women in the third world, whose opportunities for political participation in traditional political institutions are normally limited, and for whom movement participation is therefore the first, or the most involving, political action in which they have engaged.

This study will show that through the experience of movement participation itself, women can become more empowered personally, familially and socially. They can learn skills and gain self-confidence that are in turn essential to increasing their economic and political power. Thus the resource mobilization theories that look for movement causality and movement results only in the field of play outside the movement miss a major part of the story of what a movement can achieve.

The Interconnectedness of the Goals of
Women's Movements and Their Implications for Democracy

The interplay of the various types of power mentioned above is complex: without economic power, women have a hard time exercising power within their families and communities. When they are plagued by poverty, malnutrition, ill-health and illiteracy, they are destined to be politically and socially negligible. So movements that seek to empower women attempt to make concrete changes in their material lives.

But at the same time, unless women have some autonomy and power within their families and communities, some capacity for direct community participation and decision making, they cannot develop economically and politically. Attacking patriarchal institutions that proscribe women's lives is thus an activity of instrinsic importance to the furtherance of women's status and power. It is a task to which movements, by virtue of their ability to generate and disseminate new ideologies, change consciousness, and provide support to individuals, are better suited than political institutions that operate from above, such as legislatures, bureaucracies and courts.

It is also a political task, with implications for women's ability to make claims on the state. By empowering women economically and socially, movements provide a bridge between institutions of the state and people who heretofore have lacked access to political power or a political voice. The empowerment of women "privately"—within the family in particular—is a prerequisite for their participation in public life. They must have some control over their own lives, some confidence in their own powers, some sense of personal efficacy, some freedom from physical violence, some alleviation of malnutrition and disease if they are to engage in politics.

Thus movements, far from being the anomic enemies of democratic systems depicted by some political theorists,[13] can, in fact, serve to educate, mobilize and empower the disaffected and disempowered for participation in democratic processes at local and national levels. Whereas Samuel Huntington, for example, sees "the highly institutionalized political party" in developing countries as the institution that best functions "to organize participation, to aggregate interests, to serve as the link between social forces and the government,"[14] this writer sees in India a case where parties have increasingly failed to fulfill this function and where movements, including the women's movement, can and have served it.

The Structure of the Indian Women's Movement: An Introduction

Now that movements have been defined, and some of their meanings suggested, it can be said with certainty that there is a women's movement in India.[15] Its structure is highly decentralized. The movement is composed of uncountable organizations in both cities and rural areas; it claims participants who are wealthy, who are middle class, who are poor; who are communist, socialist, or resolutely non-ideological; who are members of parties or who hold political parties in contempt as elitist, opportunist or corrupt.

Although the movement organizations are many, and the web of communications that connects them informal, this study sees two major ideological and organizational tendencies within the movement (although each of them is further subdivided by disagreements over the proper relationship of the movement to the state). One, which is largely urban-based, focuses on issues of rights and equality; the other, with both urban and rural components, emphasizes empowerment and liberation. "Tendencies" or "emphases" are more accurate descriptions than "divisions" or "splits" because while different movement organizations devote their energies to different tasks, the activities are in many repects complementary rather than conflictual, and there are many individuals and groups whose loyalties and actions appear to crosscut the differences in emphasis. Additionally, the two wings of the movement share a desire to transform the consciousness of women and men, first to understand that women in contemporary India occupy an inferior position relative to men economically, socially and politically, and then to realize that this position is unjust, unacceptable, and alterable.

The Rights Wing

Women's rights advocates see women's concerns as issues of human rights within the secular democracy that India's constitution proclaims. Their demand is for equality for women under the law;[16] they see themselves as modernizers and social democrats seeking basic human rights, rather than as "feminists" pressing a radical social agenda.[17] The rhetoric of rights groups refrains from positing a conflict between women and men; it does not even present itself as a challenge to gender roles, fearing that such an attack would mark the movement as overly influenced by the West,[18] and as attacking the family (which, in India, enjoys a place on a high pedestal). They are determined to be in the mainstream of an attempt to modernize India without sacrificing essential Indian culture or values except insofar as those values violate women's rights as human beings and as equal citizens.[19]

Rights groups urge the state to pass and implement laws that give women equality in those family matters subject to legislation (such as inheritance, marriage, divorce and child custody); to act to improve women's health and access to education; to move toward equality in employment; and to pass and implement legislation with regard to rape and dowry that will free women from violence.

The diversity of the roots of different movement organizations has led to differences in their structures, modes of operation, and particularly in their degree of cooperation with political parties and electoral politics.[20] Some of the groups that operate within this wing of the movement were born from opposition political parties and generally act in concert with the politics of those parties. These include the Janata Party's Mahila Dakshata Samiti, the Communist Party of India's National Federation of Indian Women, and the All India Democratic Women's Association and All India Coordinating Committee of Working Women, both of which are affiliated with the Communist Party of India (Marxist). It may seem ironic that those parties rhetorically committed to communism operate, at least in part, within the "rights" wing of the movement. But in India, the CPI and CPM have resolved to work within the parliamentary system; that the women's organizations associated with them share this strategy is therefore not surprising.[21]

Other groups within the rights wing of the women's movement include venerable independent social service agencies, such as the All India Women's Conference, which has historical connections to the Congress Party, and the Young Women's Christian Association. These have a long history of action on behalf of women and, influenced by the broad feminist stirrings that have taken place since the 1975 Emergency, are now becoming increasingly radicalized.

With the exception of the Mahila Dakshata Samiti, which is based in New Delhi and has affiliated groups in only a few states, all of the above organizations are national in scale, have local chapters, and are organized hierarchically with the national leadership based in the capital. They are mobilizational organizations with large memberships. NFIW, for example, claims 800,000 members, while AIDWA claims 115,000 are enrolled in its branches.[22] The YWCA has 67 branches all over India and considerable financial resources. Along with their access to and skill in using media, the ability of these organizations' leaders to mobilize large numbers for agitational purposes confers on them considerable political clout; they have entrée to high government bureaucrats and to elected officials, including the prime minister.

Differences Within the Rights Wing: Party Affiliation Versus Autonomy. The divide in the rights wing comes between those organizations with ties to political parties and those that reject any direct connection to electoral politics and to the parties, which they regard as elitist and opportunist. The latter, "autonomous" groups are generally small, with a strong emphasis on internal participatory democracy. Both in this emphasis and in their efforts to raise consciousness and to empower individual women through personal support, they share much with the "empowerment" wing of the movement described below. Examples include Saheli ("sister") in New Delhi and the Women's Centre in Bombay, both of which provide informal counseling and some material support (including temporary housing) to women faced with a variety of problems, particularly domestic violence, but also health and employment concerns. However, while the internal democracy, counseling, consciousness raising, and support activities mark these autonomous organizations as empowerment groups, they also engage in agitational political activity (sometimes in cooperation with party-affiliated organizations) designed to pressure the government to change laws or implement existing laws.

Such organizations tend to have few members—Saheli, for example, has 25 to 30 active members at any given time—but unlike the mass organizations in which members are mobilized by the leadership for political activities, members of the autonomous organizations tend to be personally active in both policy making and implementation. Since, by definition, the autonomous organizations are small, localized, and unaffiliated with any larger group, it is impossible to get an accurate count of how many exist. However, they do appear to exist in most parts of India; a 1985 national conference of autonomous women's organizations attracted 85 groups from 15 cities and states, while a 1988 conference drew 750 representatives, with 8000 attending its final rally.[23]

Commonalities. The rights wing of the movement is largely urban. Its leaders, and the participants in the collectively-operating autonomous organizations, are generally middle-class, highly educated, and Hindu; while there is also representation from the small Indian Christian and Parsi communities, only a very few are Muslim. The leaders often have prior experience working within the political system, either as members of opposition parties or as intellectual leaders who have contributed to government-sponsored studies or forums. While, measured on a standard scale of left-wing to right-wing politics, they represent a range of ideological beliefs, they have nonetheless been able to adopt common demands for legislation with regard to dowry and dowry deaths, inheritance, police brutality, and other matters upon which the government can act. Organizations spanning the ideological spectrum from the women's wing of the CPM to the YWCA have formed coalitions around such issues and acted in unison to build public opinion and bring pressure to bear on parliament and government bureaucracies to act.

Organizationally, they have their differences. However, they share in common a strategy of trying to move the government. This should not be taken to mean that the rights wing of the movement places unending faith in the capacity of government to provide sufficient redress for women; but activists do recognize that government has resources and powers—to create law, to police the law, and to expend large sums of money—that are unique. They attempt, then, to push the state apparatus for all it is worth, but not necessarily to become a part of it.

Those who operate within opposition parties obviously believe that the strategy of pushing government from within parliamentary structures is the most efficacious; there is no doubt, too, that organizations attached to parties of the left hope to build their parties' strength by mobilizing women voters around women's issues. But as will be discussed in Chapter 2, that strategy offends many other activists, who see the parties—both Congress and parties of the left—as opportunistic and corrupt. The nonparty activists thus do not engage in electoral politics themselves, but instead lobby members of government and build public opinion through agitation and publicity. Still, this does not negate the fact that their goal, too, is government action to bring about and guarantee rights for women.

The Empowerment Wing

The other organizational and ideological segment of the movement, the "empowerment" wing, aims at the personal and community empowerment of poor women in both urban and rural areas. Not infrequently (and this is why the common categorization of the movement as divided along urban/rural lines is incorrect) it is educated, middle-class city and town dwellers who are instrumental in organizing the rural and urban poor; the largest organizations are headed by educated, urbane women with extensive prior experience in politics whose backgrounds are strikingly similar to those of leaders in the rights wing. Their leadership has been the most vital resource in the establishment of empowerment groups; poor, illiterate women do engage in spontaneous protest, but cannot sustain an organization without the help of educated activists.[24]

In the empowerment wing, there is also a notion of rights, but the goal is economic and social rights—the right to a livelihood and to determine one's own future. These require both political empowerment at the local level and access to the tools of economic well-being. The search is for empowerment from below, not the conferring of rights or economic development from above. Typically, the organizations mobilize poor women to seek expanded economic opportunity. In rural areas, this may involve seeking land ownership or improved agricultural wages. In both rural and urban areas, the creation of small cooperatives, sometimes linked together through a parent organization, is a staple of women's organizing.

Economic development is just one aim of such movement organizations. There is also a self-conscious attempt to create organizational forms in which women become empowered psychologically and socially. Participating in decision making and in the implementation of decisions; raising consciousness about the situation of women in the family and community; creating mutual interdependence and group solidarity; developing skills, self-confidence, and assertiveness: All these are seen as integral to the process of empowerment. The small local groups that form the grass roots of these movements foster economic growth, but become more than that. They are support groups that emotionally and intellectually empower, the location of access to local political participation, as well as the aggregators and articulators of political interests vis-à-vis the state.

For, while the empowerment organizations emphasize self-help and the power of the local community, most are not averse to seeking and accepting resources both from international donors (including development agencies such as the Ford Foundation, organizations affiliated with the United Nations, and bilateral aid from friendly governments, including several Scandinavian countries) and from the Indian government to assist in organizing or in implementing the economic development schemes they pursue. However, some of the empowerment organizations, motivated by a socialist disdain for the existing parliamentary system and for international capitalism, do not seek any such outside intervention, which they regard as inherently cooptative. Thus, within those organizations that seek empowerment, a distinction must be drawn between those that view the state as an enemy with which they must inevitably clash, and those that see the state as a potential ally and store of resources.

While the truly rural-based movements tend to be small and localized, some of the urban-based organizations are very large and have expanded into rural areas. For example, the Self Employed Women's Association has over forty thousand members in Ahmedabad and its chapters in several states; the Working Women's Forum has forty thousand women in the city of Madras and in rural areas of Tamil Nadu, Andhra Pradesh, and Karnataka; and the Annapurna Mahila Mandal has some fifteen thousand members in Bombay.[25]

To distinguish between the "rights" and "empowerment" wings of the movement will be helpful as a way of marking differences in priorities but, on the ground, the barrier between the two is a fluid one. The emphases are different but not mutually exclusive, and often a single organization will engage in both types of activities simultaneously. Thus, for example, the women's wing of the CPM, the All India Coordinating Committee of Working Women, not only engages in demonstrations and lobbying aimed at influencing legislation on such "rights" issues as dowry and changes in law regarding Muslim women's right to receive maintenance upon divorce but also organizes working women within the rubric of the CPM sponsored labor union, CITU. Urban "think tanks" such as the Centre for Women's Development Studies in New Delhi or the Research Centre on Women's Studies of SNDT University in Bombay will provide scholarly support for legal arguments made by groups attempting to influence legislation. They will also sponsor study groups—or even entire projects—directed at organizing and empowering poor rural women. By the same token, SEWA and Working Women's Forum, as they work to empower women, continually interact with government agencies to obtain resources, ease police harrassment, or make labor laws more responsive to the needs of the self-employed.[26]

It is the quest for empowerment that most marks movement activity as distinct from politics-as-usual within the electoral system. As the next chapter shows, it is here that the women's movement can be seen to be part of a broader set of Indian non-party movements that eschew electoral politics and focus instead on empowering the grass roots.

Notes

1. This compares the "collective behavior" school of the 1950s and early 1960s with the resource mobilization theory that developed in the wake of the civil rights and anti-war movements in the West. The latter sees movements as a normal part of the pluralist continuum.

2. Jo Freeman, "Introduction" in *Social Movements of the Sixties and Seventies,* ed. Jo Freeman (NY: Longman, 1983) discusses this idea of the continuum.

3. John D. McCarthy and Mayer N. Zald, "Resource Mobilization and Social Movements," *American Journal of Sociology* 82:6 (1977), pp. 1212–1241. They include those individuals who share only sentiment but not action as part of a social movement, while I do not.

4. William Gamson, *The Strategy of Social Protest* 2nd edition (Belmont, CA: Wadsworth Publishing Co., 1990), p. 16 makes this point about the United States. Lloyd I. Rudolph and Susanne Hoeber Rudolph, *In Pursuit of Lakshmi: The Political Economy of the Indian State* (Chicago: Univ. of Chicago Press, 1987), p. 253 make the same point about India, in which they contrast the bureaucratized character of "formally organized interests" to the less bureaucratized, more mobilizational and consciousness-raising style of the "demand group."

5. This is analogous to Weber's description of the routinization of charismatic leadership. Just as charismatic movement may evolve into staid bureaucracies, so too a movement may come to be dominated by a single organization or a very few such organizations as others are absorbed or fade away. This may then cease to be a movement and become an interest group. For example, consider the transformation of the socialist labor movement in the United States into a handful of large unions with close connections to government. See Theodore Lowi, *The Politics of Disorder* (New York: Basic Books, 1971), chap. 1.

6. Mancur Olson, *The Logic of Collective Action* (NY: Schocken, 1971).

7. Charles Perrow, "The Sixties Observed" in *The Dynamics of Social Movements,* ed. Zald and McCarthy (Cambridge, MA: Winthrop, 1979); Maren Lockwood Carden "The Proliferation of a Social Movement: Ideology and Individual Incentives in the Contemporary Feminist Movement" in *Research in Social Movements, Conflicts and Change* 1 (1978), pp. 178-196. See also Bruce Fireman and Willam A. Gamson, "Utilitarian Logic in the Resource Mobilization Perspective" in *The Dynamics of Social Movements; Gamson, The Strategy of Social Protest; Charles Tilly, From Mobilization to Revolution* (Reading, MA: Addison-Wesley, 1978); and Bert

Useem, "Solidarity Model, Breakdown Model and the Boston Anti-Busing Movement," *American Sociological Review* 45 (1980), pp. 357–369.

8. Alberto Melucci, "The Symbolic Challenge of Contemporary Movements," *Social Research* 52 (1985), p. 792. See also Mayer N. Zald and Roberta Ash, "Social Movement Organizations: Growth, Decay and Change," *Social Forces* 44 (1966), pp. 327–340.

9. See Jo Freeman, "A Model for Analyzing the Strategic Options of Social Movement Organizations," in *Social Movements of the Sixties and Seventies*, p. 204; Carden, "The Proliferation of a Social Movement"; Paolo R. Domati, "Organization Between Movement and Institution," *Social Science Information* 23:4/5 (1984), pp. 837–859; and J. Craig Jenkins, "Resource Mobilization Theory and the Study of Social Movements," *Annual Review of Sociology* 9 (1983), pp. 527–553.

10. An exception is Maren Lockwood Carden, "The Proliferation of a Social Movement," who, not coincidentally, analyzes a women's movement. Her discussion of selective and ideological incentives to participation in the U.S. feminist movement helped me to think about the empowerment that comes to women (as a "selective incentive") from their participation in the Indian women's movement.

11. See Alberto Melucci, "The New Social Movements: A Theoretical Approach," *Social Science Information* 19 (1980); Melucci, "An End to Social Movements?" *Social Science Information*, 23 (1984), pp. 819–835; and an edition of *Social Research* 52:4 (1985) with representative articles on new social movements by Melucci, Jean Cohen, Alain Touraine, Claus Offe and Klaus Eder. Two useful survey articles on movement theory are Sidney Tarrow, "National Politics and Collective Action," in the *Annual Review of Sociology*, 14 (1988), pp. 421–440, and Doug McAdam, John D. McCarthy, and Mayer N. Zald, "Social Movements," in *Handbook of Sociology*, ed. Neil J. Smelser (Beverly Hills: Sage, 1988), pp. 695–737.

12. Alain Touraine, "An Introduction to the Study of Social Movements," *Social Research* 52 (1985), p. 774.

13. For example, Neil Smelser, *The Theory of Collective Behavior* (NY: Free Press, 1962) and Samuel Huntington, *Political Order in Changing Societies* (New Haven: Yale Univ. Press, 1968).

14. Huntington, p. 91.

15. Parts of this discussion have appeared in Leslie J. Calman, "Women and Movement Politics in India," *Asian Survey* 29:10 (October 1989), pp. 942–946. © by The Regents of the University of California, reprinted by permission of the Regents.

16. Although in a polity subdivided under different *religious* laws, that poses the question of equality of which women to which men. This topic will be discussed fully in Chapter 6.

17. In the wake of growing communalism in India throughout the 1980s and into the 1990s, from the tragic violence in Punjab and Kashmir, the conflict over the Babri Masjid in Uttar Pradesh, and the increasing popularity of the Bharatiya Janata Party, with its message of Hindu supremacy, women's rights activists increasingly see their struggle as one to preserve the democratic secular soul of the Indian nation. Interview, Vina Mazumdar, New York City, 9 September 1991.

18. This is a problem common to women's movements throughout the developing world. In Kenya, for example, any use of western feminist language "is easily

dismissed as yet another imperialist tool in the oppression of Third World people." Patricia Stamp, "Burying Otieno: The Politics of Gender and Ethnicity in Kenya," *Signs* 16:4 (1991), p. 827.

19. They have been aided in their efforts by the fact that there is an indigenous Indian tradition, developed as part of the independence movement, of struggling for women's equality. Mahatma Gandhi consistently advocated women's partici-pation in the movement, and when India did achieve its independence it was axi-omatic that all women would receive the vote. For an interesting analysis of the im-pact of Gandhi's advocacy of women's participation, see Madhu Kishwar, "Gandhi on Women," *Economic and Political Weekly* 20:40–41 (1985), pp. 1691–1702 and 1753–1758.

20. As will be discussed in Chapter 2, these differences over the merits of party affiliation are typical of a number of Indian movements.

21. Furthermore, as Amrita Basu notes, although "Communist Party women's organizations regard themselves as the most authentic representatives of women's interests and have been extremely critical of the reformist character of the [pro-Congress] All India Women's Conference. . . there is little to differentiate Communist from other women's organizations." Basu, "Two Faces of Protest: Al-ternative Forms of Women's Mobilization in West Bengal and Maharashtra," in *The Extended Family*, ed. Gail Minault (Columbia Mo: South Asia Books, 1981), p. 224.

22. Interviews with Vimla Farooqui, General Secretary, NFIW, New Delhi, 19 June 1986 and with Vimal Ranadive, Secretary, AICCWW, and Vice President, AIDWA, New Delhi, 18 June 1986.

23. *Report: National Conference: Perspectives for the Autonomous Women's Move-ment in India* (Bombay, 1985), and Mary Fainsod Katzenstein, "Organizing Against Violence: Strategies of the Indian Women's Movement," *Pacific Affairs* 62:1 (1989), p. 57.

24. This is hardly unique to India. In the U.S. civil rights movement of the 1960s, for example, the college-educated Ella Baker was central to the sustained organiza-tion of poor, rural, southern black women. Conversation with Prof. Rosalind Rosenberg, New York, 15 September 1991.

25. *Shramshakti: Report of the National Commission on Self Employed Women and Women in the Informal Sector* (New Delhi: Gov't of India, 1988).

26. Ela Bhatt, "Toward Empowerment," *World Development* 17:7 (1989), pp. 1059–1065.

2

Why the Women's Movement Emerged: The Context of Indian Politics

What was it about Indian politics that caused the women's movement to emerge? This chapter analyzes the development of structural strains in the Indian polity that generated the growth and deepening of grievance and enhanced citizens' willingness to act politically through movement participation.[1] It then points to special qualities of movements that distinguish them from other political institutions; it is these qualities that in part account for the growth of movements as a response to crisis in India.

In situating the women's movement within the context of Indian politics, I suggest two meanings of movements in democratic political systems. First, a growth in movements and movement participation marks a belief that existing political institutions cannot produce desired remedies. In polities characterized by political repression, movements provide one of the few avenues of political participation.[2] When movements appear in democracies, it is a sign that political channels that should provide meaningful opportunities for participation, such as electoral politics, parties, and interest groups, are inaccessible to movement participants or are ineffective. The dramatic growth since the 1970s in the number and type of political movements in India—including the women's movement, subnationalist movements, caste movements, poor peasant movements, middle peasant movements, tribal movements and others[3]—indicates a growing failure of state institutions to incorporate and expand grass-roots participation and respond positively to demand.

A second meaning of movement emergence is that participants believe that the state is not the only appropriate arena in which to resolve their grievances. Because movements can target and alter social consciousness, and because they can provide within themselves a new supportive community that can itself transform economic, social and political aspects of people's lives, movements provide possible venues for problem resolution apart from state influence or control.

In India, the women's movement has been part of an explosion in the number of non-party affiliated, ideologically left-of-center movement organizations, known variously in India as "non-party formations," "non-governmental organizations," and "action groups."[4] Their goals include the types highlighted by new social movement theorists: decentralized political decision making, women's rights, civil liberties, the achievement of economic power at the grass roots, the right to a safe environment, to education and health care, and a growth in personal and small group autonomy. At the heart of all these movements is a concern with empowering those who lack power to make decisions affecting their own lives. By and large, the movement organizations have focused on the economically deprived, but powerlessness and underprivilege are also associated with non-Hindu ethnic minorities, including Muslims and the scheduled tribes; with the lower castes (thus the movements seeking Dalit rights and development) and with the female sex (thus prompting the women's movement).[5]

While seeking rights suggests the need to push for state action—either to insure rights or to refrain from violating them—the movement itself can provide the space in which to achieve some of the goals mentioned above. A movement can create access to decision making, heightened autonomy, and some economic development within the context of the movement itself. It can transform consciousness about self-worth and heighten self-confidence.

While different from the goal of influencing the state, the search for empowerment is not antithetical to it. Indeed the empowerment that develops within movements can transform the politically powerless into groups capable of engagement with the state. One of the factors motivating the formation and growth of movements is a belief that movements can perform this function better than political parties, which are normally thought to be appropriate aggregators of interest and mobilizers of democratic participation. In addition to the crisis of the Indian state, then, this chapter explores the choice increasing numbers of activists make to participate in movement rather than party politics.

The Developing Structural Crisis:
Indira Gandhi's India

By the mid-1970s it had become evident that the state was in crisis. It had failed to integrate large sections of the Indian population into the political process and the benefits of economic development, and it seemed unlikely to do so in the near future. Incumbent governments at the national level and in many states appeared corrupt and intent on destroying democratic liberties. They seemed incapable of promulgating the political and economic changes necessary not only for economic growth but, at least as importantly, for distribution of economic means and assets to the hundreds of millions living in abject poverty. In the absence of effective government, increasing state coercion threatened to undermine the democratic basis of the Indian political system completely. It was this destruction of civil liberties and the realization that the Congress government led by Indira Gandhi (and in the eyes of some, the very parliamentary system from which it arose) was incapable of moving toward overcoming poverty that set the stage for the rapid growth of movements of the left. The following account explains how Indian politics came to such a juncture.

Indira Gandhi Consolidates Power

The story of Indira Gandhi's prime ministership from her entry into office up through the end of emergency rule is one of increasing centralization of party and governmental power.[6] Despite her overwhelming personal popularity and unprecedented power, however, her government was unable to deliver on promises she made to ameliorate poverty among India's poorest citizens. This incapacity of government was not in itself new, but was coupled with a grasping for power that led to the weakening of the Congress organization, the imposition of central government control over state governments, the diminishment of democratic decision making within party and government, increasing coercion and a widespread loss of civil liberties.

Indira Gandhi initially came to power in 1966, following the sudden death of Prime Minister Lal Bahadur Shastri. At that time considerable party power rested in the state organizations of Congress, the party that had controlled the Indian government since independence. Gandhi was chosen by state party "bosses" (known collectively as "the Syndicate") who believed that the selection of Nehru's daughter would please the electorate, and that they could easily control her. Their intention was for the nexus of power in national politics to continue to move away from the center and toward the states. Gandhi was soon to surprise them.

The results of the 1967 parliamentary elections reflected a startling breakdown in Congress party strength: Congress managed to hold on to power at the center only by a very slim margin. Amid a growing anger over rising prices and ineffectual government, Congress failed to achieve majorities in eight states. Congress dominance was replaced by a mosaic of regionally based parties, some of them to the left of Congress, some of them to the right. Unstable coalition governments formed in a number of states, and many of them quickly came unglued.

In the face of this challenge to Congress unity and power, Indira Gandhi chose not to act as a conciliator, but, instead, began to consolidate her own power within both party and government. Moving away from the politics of consensus building, she sought to centralize what had been a federal party and particularly to reestablish the dominance of the prime minister within the party.

Gandhi began to seek new sources of electoral support outside of party channels (which were, to be sure, already corroding) by adopting a more populist economic stance. She urged the effective implementation of land reforms, curbs on industrial monopolies, and ceilings on urban income and property. In an action that garnered widespread popular support, she nationalized fourteen of India's largest banks. The portrayal of Indira as the champion of the poor against the vested interests had begun in earnest.

In 1971, seeking a stronger mandate, Gandhi dissolved the lower house of parliament (Lok Sabha) and called for new elections. The newly constituted Congress(I) (the "I" stands for Indira) won an overwhelming victory, capturing 352 of the 518 seats in the Lok Sabha. Adding to that number her allies in two political parties, the CPI and the DMK, Indira Gandhi had control of two-thirds of the parliament. This victory was further enhanced by Congress domination of the state elections held in 1972. Both outcomes were the result of populist appeals made directly to disadvantaged voters, including members of scheduled castes and tribes who had been ill-served by local party officials, and Muslims, who faced continuing discrimination. Armed with her motto "Garibi Hatao" (abolish poverty) and her personal popularity, Gandhi was able to bypass the state and local party organizations ordinarily relied upon to get out the vote.

She appeared not only to have a mandate for change that would benefit India's poor, but the political power with which to implement it. There was a widespread expectation that Gandhi's government would outperform its predecessors and make significant progress in increasing employment and agricultural production, in reducing labor strife, and in reducing disparities between rich and poor. However, the appearance of strength masked an emerging institutional crisis that was to limit Gandhi's ability to implement her populist program.

The Decline of Congress and the Emerging Crisis

Gandhi set about centralizing power by reconstructing a Congress leadership that would owe personal loyalty to her. She selected as central cabinet ministers and state chief ministers people with no personal bases of support in the party, so that their continued tenure in office was entirely subject to her whim. These outsiders were resented, and within the states, dissident factions emerged to challenge Gandhi's hand-picked "leaders." State politics soon become chaotic: within eighteen months, six newly elected chief ministers had been ousted by dissident Congress factions and President's Rule (rule from the center) had been imposed on four other states.

What Gandhi had succeeded in doing was creating a government and party that lacked institutional connection to the people and thus had little ability to lead or even manage. The organizational ties linking the localities through the states to the center had been severed; incumbent politicians at central and state levels had support from above, but not from below.[7] With the Congress organization greatly weakened, with political energies being expended in constant factional disputes, the government's ability to implement its programs was greatly attenuated.[8] Whatever progressive legislation might be passed at the center—for example, concerning land ceilings, land redistribution, or measures against hoarding or smuggling—implementation occurs at the level of the state and localities; Gandhi might have enjoyed dominance in party and government, but party and government *institutions* capable of *implementing* her wishes did not exist.

As important a problem for a government that had made populist promises was that the lack of a strong party structure left the government with no institutional means of organizing the popular support from below necessary to implement populist programs that were unpopular with local vested interests.[9] The government had no means of mobilizing the poor; Indira Gandhi controlled state governments that, in turn, controlled or influenced almost no one. Nor did she command a party structure that could mobilize and sustain support at the grass roots.

In contrast to the raised expectations generated by Gandhi's victory, the early seventies brought a period of grave economic crisis. Droughts in 1972 and 1973 compounded the economic drain imposed by the 1971 Bangladesh War, and brought about a sharp drop in food production and scattered famine. OPEC's increased oil prices helped to spur severe inflation, an industrial recession, growing unemployment, and a slowed economic growth rate. These conditions, in turn, sparked a rapid increase in industrial strikes: in 1974, labor strikes cost industry more than 31 million days of labor.[10]

Nor were conditions any better in the agricultural sector. Government studies revealed that one-third of all agricultural laborers experienced chronic underemployment, and that the number of landless workers was on the rise.[11] Gains from government-sponsored development projects were devolving largely not to the poor but, instead, to the dominant landowning castes. Indeed, India was dividing ever more into haves and have-nots.[12]

A political crisis was developing. The central government was unable to implement programs of economic development and distribution, and the state governments were apparently too preoccupied with their internal political battles to be effective; corruption, influence peddling and power grabbing seemed to dominate the minds of politicians.

The urban middle and lower-middle classes—including, but not limited to university students—lost patience with the evident mismanagement and growing corruption in government (corruption that was as close to Indira Gandhi as the accusations leveled against her son Sanjay for influence peddling) and took to the streets. The nation was increasingly besieged by strikes and demonstrations. The growing repression exercised by the government helped to harden the line developing between dissenters and government: Gandhi perceived attacks on corruption in state governments to be attacks on herself. Since she often stood behind such governments, they increasingly were.[13]

Gradually, consensus about the legitimacy of government at the state and national levels began to break down. Some seemed to see the corruption and ineptitude as characteristic of a particular group of individuals; others, though, seemed doubtful about the efficacy of parliamentary government itself.

The Crisis Erupts

The situation became gravest in Gujarat and then, soon after, in Bihar. Once joined by the venerated independence leader Jayaprakash Narayan, what began as student demonstrations against two state governments became transformed into a movement with national impact. Under "J.P.'s" leadership, the target of the movement became Indira Gandhi's "tyrannical rule"[14] and the goal, at least for some participants, what J.P. called "total revolution." The movement was symptomatic of a deepening legitimacy crisis not only for the incumbents in New Delhi, but for the structures of government.

In a survey conducted by the Centre for Regional Development Studies in Surat, Gujarat's second largest city, just prior to the outbreak of widespread demonstrations there in January 1974, 90 percent of the respondents felt that government officials paid no attention to the problems facing the average citizen; 70 percent felt that the overall condition of the average citizen had deteriorated during the past twenty years; and 84 percent, evincing a growing despair about the capacity of government, predicted that their children would face greater economic hardships than they had.

This disillusionment with the efficacy of government was coupled with doubts about its legitimacy: 40 percent of the respondents in the Surat survey said they had lost faith in the system of elections; they believed that only those with influence and money could run for office and that, once elected, politicians worked only in their own interest.[15] Events in Gujarat and Bihar were soon to demonstrate that large numbers of urban citizens, particularly among the middle class, were prepared to go outside the parliamentary system to seek redress.[16]

In Gujarat, middle-class town and city residents participated in protests ranging from silent marches, relay fasts, and strikes to stone throwing, looting, and destroying government property. The indiscriminate use of violence by the police in middle-class neighborhoods contributed to people's willingness to engage in extralegal behavior.[17] A variety of middle-class organizations—unions of white-collar employees, teachers' unions, lawyers, doctors, *sarvodaya* workers, and women's groups—joined in the agitations. Several groups tried to claim a leadership role. But the anti-government agitations appeared to be erupting spontaneously and simultaneously among the middle class so that, in the words of one observer, "it would be difficult to say who led whom."[18]

The movement signified nothing so benign as discontent with particular policies, but rather a breakdown in the consensus that government was legitimate, and an expanded willingness to engage in extra-legal, including violent, political behavior. Widespread contempt for political institutions and processes, and particularly for corrupt politicians, rather than adherence to any political ideology, seemed to motivate most movement participants.

The Gujarat movement, lacking an enduring organizational structure, ended in March 1974 after achieving the dissolution of the state Assembly. Vehement expressions of public discontent with government, and demands for improved economic conditions, were continued, however, on two new fronts: a nationwide railway strike and the Bihar movement led by J.P. Narayan.

The Crisis Builds

The "J.P. movement" erupted days later. It was a less spontaneous outburst than the Gujarat movement had been and from the outset was more radical and more politicized; in Bihar, the target was a system of government thought to be corrupt and obstructionist, rather than the corruption of one Chief Minister.[19]

That the state had failed in Bihar was evident in two respects. Bihar was (and remains) one of India's poorest states, with two-thirds of the population subsisting below the poverty line; most experience malnourishment, chronic indebtedness, illiteracy and poor health.[20] While the pervasiveness and depth of poverty was thus extreme in Bihar, poverty *per se* has not been a sufficient motivator for political action in India. What did push Biharis, though, was a feeling that government was not capable of

and, worse, not truly in pursuit of, progressive changes. Prices and shortages of essential commodities continually increased during the late 1960s
and early 1970s. But government officials, far from coming to grips with
the state's problems, were, in the words of one observer, preoccupied with
"making money, enjoying official privileges and distributing jobs and patronage among relations, friends and hangers-on."[21]

The Bihar movement began with student agitations for the resignation
of the Congress ministry and the dissolution of the Assembly. A "Gujarat
style" agitation had been planned for several months by an alliance of the
student wings of the Jana Sangh and the Samyukta Socialist parties, and
they attracted a wide base of support ranging from the conservative Jana
Sangh to the Communist Party of India (Marxist). The agitations and the
police response were both violent, with looting and shootings by the police widespread.[22]

The student leaders quickly appealed to the elderly J.P. Narayan to lead
their cause. It was a smart move. J.P. had great moral standing throughout
India, a result of his long service to rural communities through the Sarvodaya ("the welfare of all") movement, much of it in his native Bihar; his
reputation as a nationalist leader; and his early retirement from the party
politics in which he had once held considerable influence. Over the years,
his ideology had evolved to become a uniquely Indian amalgam of socialist and democratic doctrines, strongly echoing the ideas of Mahatma
Gandhi.

Narayan's rejection of politics-as-usual and his advocacy of power to
the people closely fit the mood of the times. He wanted to build democracy and socialism from the ground up; his goal was a democracy without
parties, in which political and economic decisions would be in the hands
of the community. Parliamentary politics, he believed, left the people with
too little power. His insistence upon non-violent tactics, his own life of
service to the poor, and his unquestioned personal integrity conferred
upon the movement a moral legitimacy that it otherwise would have
lacked.

J.P. quickly radicalized the movement, expanding its scope to include
not only the government of Bihar, but the government of Indira Gandhi
and the system of parliamentary government itself. The Bihar struggle, he
said, would replace *raj niti* (state politics) with *lok niti* (people's politics).[23]
J.P. made it a condition of his leadership that the movement be affiliated
with no political party; the students were to put the objectives of the
movement ahead of party ambitions or programs.[24]

Within weeks, the movement began to build a decentralized form of organization, with "students' struggle committees" and "people's struggle
committees" being formed in the universities, the districts, and the villages. From these, volunteers were expected to mobilize all sections of the

population, but particularly members of backward castes and classes and religious minorities. Work on local issues was to go hand in hand with raising public consciousness and organizing demonstrations.[25] These activities were to culminate in the establishment of "people's governments" that would "carry on the day-to-day affairs of the people," adjudicate disputes, distribute commodities, teach sanitation and eliminate dowry and other social evils.[26]

The energy and idealism of the students, the growing anger of the urban middle class toward corrupt and ineffective government, and J.P.'s own strength among the rural poor provided him with a solid base of support. Massive demonstrations demanding the removal of the state ministry followed one another in close succession from March through November. These included a three-day "Bihar Bandh" in March; a "Paralyse the Government" agitation in April, which erupted into rioting and police shooting that left eight people dead; and, in June, a march of a half-million people that presented millions of signatures to the state government, calling for the resignation of the ministry.

At the June demonstration J.P. declared the goal of the movement to be total revolution. As he defined it, total revolution relied on non-violent means to achieve a decentralized political and economic structure. "Partyless democracy" and self-governing "communitarian" villages were to result from the intensive organization of people at the grass roots. The economic program included land distribution; the development of "appropriate technologies" for agriculture; and an emphasis on small industries based in rural areas. An increase in the number of rural schools, the elimination of dowry, and the eradication of caste were all part of the desired social transformations.[27]

But while total revolution may have been the goal, more immediate political considerations continued to dominate day-to-day activities. Despite the movement's success in paralyzing the state government, Indira Gandhi dug in her heels and refused to allow the resignation of the Bihar ministry. As the movement began to capture the national imagination, and as large-scale demonstrations against government offices continued steadily, the government responded with growing force. When police gunfire proved ineffective, the central government posted 40,000 security forces to Bihar. By August, "Bihar was like an armed camp, with police and military guarding all major government and educational institutions at a reported cost of Rs. 100,000 a day."[28]

As the J.P. movement grew, the central government confronted yet another challenge. Under the leadership of George Fernandes of the Socialist party, the left opposition parties had demonstrated unprecedented cooperation in forming a single committee—the National Coordination Committee for Railwaymen's Struggle—to lead a railway strike of some 1.7

million railway workers. A week before the scheduled strike deadline, with negotiations at an impasse, the central government invoked coercive powers available to it under the Emergency Proclamation still in force since the Bangladesh war of 1971. The strike was declared illegal, and the government arrested the leaders of the National Coordination Committee and 600 railway workers. Nonetheless, the strike proceeded. Harsher steps followed: the arrest of twenty thousand workers brought an end to the strike less than three weeks after it had begun. These events contributed to the growing polarization of politics; Congress again condemned the "fascist" extra-parliamentary tactics of the opposition, who in turn were increasingly persuaded of the government's abuse of power.[29]

In Bihar, despite the influx of Central Reserve Police, massive demonstrations continued. During a three day *bandh* in October seventeen people were killed by police gunfire and hundreds injured. A march followed in November, in which J.P. and other nonviolent demonstrators were struck with heavy wooden sticks by the police.[30]

A nationwide outcry ensued, and the movement appeared to be gaining adherents in many parts of the country. In Bihar, however, with the backing they enjoyed from the central government, ministers and legislators stood firm. Gandhi put forward a challenge to J.P. to wait until the next general elections, scheduled for March 1976, to determine the peoples' wishes. J.P., stymied in his immediate goals in Bihar, but developing an all-India following, agreed.

At this juncture the strategy of the movement shifted dramatically toward electoral politics. J.P., the leader who had long disavowed any interest in parliamentary politics, became the head of an alliance of political parties whose aim was to remove Indira Gandhi from office and replace Congress ministries in the states. The call for total revolution was not abandoned, but became part of a continuum of actions, the most pressing of which was now to win government office.

J.P. answered Indira Gandhi's criticism that he was intent on subverting parliamentary democracy by arguing that democracy would work better if there was a consolidation of the fragmented opposition.[31] As was becoming apparent, this was a task for which he was remarkably gifted: Representatives from the Bharatiya Lok Dal, Jana Sangh, Socialist, Congress(O) and Akali Dal parties and leaders of the Sarvodaya movement came together in a National Coordination Committee whose first goal was to transform what had been a regional movement into a coordinated nationwide effort to capture parliament.[32]

In addition to unifying the opposition, Narayan's success threatened to split the Congress party and destroy Indira Gandhi's base of support. Although the pro-CPI faction within Congress remained firmly behind Gandhi, the socialist wing was very sympathetic to Narayan, and many centrist Congress supporters, like many of India's urban intellectuals and students, were moved by his Gandhian rhetoric and morality.[33]

Whatever their ideology, members of Congress were fearful of the impact Narayan's movement would have at the polls, a fear that was soon realized in the Gujarat elections. After a year of President's rule in that state, Indira Gandhi's old Congress rival Morarji Desai staged a "fast unto death" in April 1975 to force Gandhi to call elections. He received warm support for his effort from Narayan. Gandhi, apparently fearful of the political repercussions should the elderly Morarji die in his quest for democratic elections, yielded. A non-Communist opposition alliance was quickly organized. This newly named Janata (people's) front charged Congress, the government of Gujarat, and Gandhi herself with corruption. With her prestige and her party's rule on the line, Gandhi fought back with extensive campaigning throughout the state, only to meet with a devastating defeat: on June 10, Janata won a clear majority and formed the government in Gujarat.[34]

The Emergency and Its Causes

As if this was not trouble enough, two days later, Gandhi received a stunning personal blow. The Allahabad High Court found her guilty of corrupt election practices in a case that had been brought against her after the general elections in 1971. This conviction carried the automatic penalty of invalidating her election; beyond that, she was prohibited from holding elective office for the next six years.

Although the Allahabad Court granted Gandhi a stay of twenty days in which to appeal, the non-Communist opposition parties and a number of the national newspapers called for her immediate resignation. So, too, did some members of the Congress parliamentary party. This, and factional disputes within Congress over a possible temporary successor, seemed likely to split the party.[35]

On June 24, Gandhi's request to the Supreme Court for a complete stay of the Allahabad decision was denied, but the "vacation judge," Krishna Iyer, granted her a conditional stay until the full Court could convene to consider her appeal. He ruled that in the interim she could remain in office as prime minister, but could not participate in parliamentary proceedings.

The next evening, Jayaprakash Narayan, Morarji Desai and other opposition leaders led a massive demonstration in New Delhi calling for Gandhi's resignation and denouncing her move toward, in J.P.'s words, "dictatorship and fascism." Not for the first time, he called upon the police and the army to uphold the constitution rather than obey "illegal and immoral" orders.[36]

Early in the morning of June 26, Indira Gandhi lashed out at these legal and political challenges to her rule. Citing internal threats to the nation's security, the Government of India, acting on a decision Gandhi had reached as early as June 22, issued a Proclamation of Emergency under Article 352 of the Constitution. 676 leaders of the opposition, including J.P., Morarji Desai, and Raj Narain, the man who had brought the corruption charges against Gandhi, were arrested just before the issuance of the proclamation. At eight o'clock that morning, Indira Gandhi spoke to the nation, naming as reasons for the emergency the "deep and widespread conspiracy which has been brewing" since the introduction of "certain progressive measures of benefit to the common man and woman"; the incitement by "certain persons" of the police and armed forces to mutiny; and threats to the normal functioning of the government and the economy.[37]

During the next 21 months, over 110,000 people were arrested and detained without trial and without being informed of the charges against them. There was no judicial review of the arrests. Incidents of torture and murder in the jails were rumored and later, during post-emergency investigations, often confirmed. Freedom of the press was abrogated, and a number of political organizations were banned. Parliament passed the 42nd Amendment allowing the government to limit civil rights if they were seen to interfere with the pursuit of economic or social progress. The same amendment denied the Supreme Court the power of judicial review over subsequent amendments affecting the basic structure of the constitution, expanded the parliamentary and state assembly sessions to six years from five, and limited presidential actions to those approved by the prime minister and Cabinet.[38] The 42nd Amendment was a design for prime ministerial dictatorship.

Plainly, Gandhi perceived her own rule and the success of her populist goals to be deeply threatened by demagogues. It was these lawless people, she argued, who created the crisis that necessitated the emergency. A more accurate interpretation, however, is that the crisis was created by the incapacity of government and party institutions. The urban middle-class, in particular, had become disillusioned with the growing corruption, mismanagement and instability in both government and party politics.

Of all institutions, the Congress party in particular had lost much of its patina of legitimacy and reliability. Congress once had been an umbrella sheltering diverse regional and ideological factions. Differences were fought out within the party, and, amidst the give and take, weaker groups, by aligning with one or the other of the stronger interests, could exert some (from time to time considerable) influence. The party was able to balance many interests, and thus, when it governed, it could call upon a wide range of regional, economic, ethnic and ideological loyalties.

In addition to building consensus, Congress had served other critical functions: It provided a channel for communication and political socialization. It brought huge numbers of citizens into political participation, connecting those in the villages to the center through vertical linkages dependent on a variety of traditional and modern incentives: patronage, caste or other traditional loyalties, or bargaining.[39]

The personalization of politics within the Congress party had wiped out many of these linkages. Vertical linkages were severed as, under Indira Gandhi, candidates were selected for party slates and ministers were appointed not on the basis of their ability to link constituencies at the bottom to the state or central government, but rather on the basis of their loyalty to the top. The result was the destruction of the key means of interest aggregation and articulation, as communications from the bottom had no way to travel upward; a concomitant loss of administrative ability, as party and government bureaucracy increasingly lost touch with the villages; and a decline in the ability of Congress, now without strong influence in the villages, to rally support among the rural poor for any of the programs of agrarian reform to which Gandhi claimed commitment.[40]

On the level of horizontal linkages, too, the deinstitutionalization of politics under Indira Gandhi was disastrous. A country as diverse as India, with so many distinct regional, ethnic, class and caste interests, requires a political process that allows for bargaining and negotiating among different interests.[41] Gandhi's centralization of power and the weakening of state leadership left little room for consensus building and conflict resolution. Conflicts were then fought out not within Congress prior to the formation of strong state governments, but after the formation of weak governments enjoying little support. The result was political instability and incapacity as the energies of many state governments were expended more in fighting off factional and inter-party challenges to their incumbency than they were in governing.

While criticism of Gandhi's centralization and personalization of power was widely expressed by Indian political analysts, the criticisms apparently carried little weight with her. During the period of emergency rule, these trends were continued and strengthened. The personalization of politics reached new heights with the ascendance of Gandhi's son, Sanjay, to a position of tremendous influence within Congress. Conflicts were resolved through repression rather than reconciliation. The increased use of the police and paramilitary forces, the expanded use of surveillance against Indian citizens,[42] and the arrests of political opponents were Gandhi's answers to the crisis of governmental and party incapacity.

The Emergency Ends

In January 1977 Gandhi made a surprise announcement: she relaxed the rules of the emergency and called for a parliamentary election to be held in March. It seems that she sought to legitimize the emergency and the 42nd Amendment through electoral victory. Gandhi was not insensitive to India's reputation, and her own, within the world community, and she had been battered in the Western press for her destruction of Indian democracy. An election would also provide her son Sanjay with the opportunity to build and formalize his power within the Congress, for despite his enormous influence during the emergency, he held no government post. Gandhi may also have called for the election in order to deflect growing opposition within Congress itself to her increasing centralization of power.[43]

And Gandhi called for an election because she expected to win. With the press censored, Congress' channels of communication withered, and opposition politicians silenced, she had no accurate reading of the mood of the nation. She had no idea of the deep anger created by the censorship, the jailings, the police repression, the assault on civil liberties, the destruction of slums (and the displacement of slum residents) in the name of "beautification," and, most importantly, the forced sterilizations of millions in a misguided attempt at population control.

Congress lost the 1977 election to an opposition that for once, motivated by a passionate desire to topple Indira Gandhi from power, put aside its differences during a national election. Merging under the name of Janata, the Congress(O), Jana Sangh, Bharatiya Lok Dal and Socialist parties (and their ally, the untouchable leader Jagjivan Ram and his Congress for Democracy) made the restoration of Indian democracy the central issue of the campaign. While Congress trusted that illiterate peasants were uninterested in civil liberties and that the two good harvests just past would bring in the rural votes for Gandhi, Janata pressed the issue of freedom. "The choice before the electorate," Janata's manifesto declared, "is a choice between freedom and slavery; between democracy and dictatorship."[44]

Janata's victory was massive. The Janata/Congress for Democracy alliance won 298 of the 542 parliamentary seats, a clear majority. Along with other allies, they controlled 330 seats. Congress controlled only 154, most of them from the southern region of the country which had been little affected by the most repressive aspects of the emergency. Indira Gandhi failed to win a seat in Parliament, and so did Sanjay, her chosen political heir. Her assault on liberty had been found unacceptable.

With the ending of the emergency, there was an explosion of new movements dedicated to the attainment of human rights and socioeconomic progress. The bubbling up of activity seemed to one observer "like a soda bottle opening—right across the country."[45] There was a widespread sense that democracy could no longer be taken for granted, that if there was to be a renewal and then a deepening of freedom and democracy, people would have to become involved.

During the period of Janata rule, from 1977 to 1979, some activists chose to work within the parliamentary structure. For example, the People's Union for Civil Liberties (PUCL), started quietly during the emergency, became nearly moribund during Janata rule as many of its members worked within the government.[46] But after three years of Janata factionalism and mismanagement, Gandhi regained power in 1980. The need for movement activity outside of government and party channels therefore became even more apparent. Nothing had changed within Congress, and the opposition parties had failed to rule effectively. For many, it was the final blow to their hopes for change through parliamentary channels alone.

The Search for Alternatives:
The Growth of Movements

Movement politics became an alternative to party politics. The growth in the number and size of non-party organizations seeking rights and empowerment for the powerless developed from the belief that existing state structures—bureaucracy, parliamentary bodies at state and national levels, national and state executives, the Planning Commission and opposition political parties—could create neither meaningful economic development nor more political power for the poor and those who, like women, exercised less political influence than their numbers would seem to warrant. This discontent with government and with opposition political parties, discussed in the sections that follow, led activists away from institutional politics as they searched for other ways to empower the powerless.

Critique of Government Capacity
for Economic and Political Development
and the Desire to Create Alternative Forms

Thirty years after independence, India had made progress in combatting poverty and increasing access to political power, but, in the eyes of many Indian citizens, not nearly enough. Poverty still appeared to be intractable. The community development schemes of the 1950s and the green revolution of the 1960s had failed to close the gap between rich and poor. India's cities were becoming a refuge of last resort for the rural poor at a rate that far outstripped the capacity of urban governments to provide jobs, housing, sanitation or transportation.[47] Except in government rhetoric, the poor were being left farther and farther behind.

The generation that came of age towards the end of the nationalist struggle put its trust in parliamentary procedures and specifically in the Congress party. But the generation coming of age thirty years later had not been part of the independence struggle and did not share the same loyalties with equal certitude. Trust in the Indian state was replaced by impatience and skepticism. As the "revolution of rising expectations" began to give way to what Robert Hardgrave calls a "revolution of rising frustrations,"[48] movement organizers, often middle-class, urban and educated, worked to aggregate and articulate the demands of women, of the rural and urban poor, and of the scheduled castes and tribes, to bring pressure to bear on the state from outside the party structures.

The deep despair with party politics continues to exist throughout the rights and empowerment movements. Movement activists view politicians with a great deal of cynicism; like many other Indians, they are prepared to believe the worst about them. One prominent women's activist counts herself among the disillusioned, claiming that no self-respecting person would wish to be involved in electoral politics, since it has become, in her words, the province of "hoodlums."[49] Another activist explains that the women's movement does not put much effort into gaining elective office for women because legislators are generally "draftees" selected by party elites, who come "without support from the people and without good ideas. They're totally dependent on [those] above." Thus, most women legislators have no more positive impact than their male colleagues.[50]

For most activists, the critique is much deeper than that of particular politicians or parties; it is a critique of the model of development that has been pursued by the Indian state. "Development" has meant not a decrease, but an increase in the gap between rich and poor, and between those with social and political power and those without. Those concerned with empowerment recognize that efforts to have an impact on government policy can bear only limited fruit since the government does not control the means of social transformation; resources and authority are predominantly in the hands of dominant elites. Thus, action within or aimed at government cannot be enough; movement organizations must also aim to challenge the structure of the economy and the "sociocultural" barriers[51] that prevent the poor and powerless from taking purposeful action.

However, although government is neither the entire problem nor the entire solution, organizers and "activist theorists" of the nonparty movements do accuse the political system of not providing opportunities for genuine participation as opposed to "rituals of plebiscitary democracy."[52]

Elections, they argue, only result in the replacement of one block of elites with another, each "equally antagonistic to the peoples' interests." As any investment the poor might make in electoral politics yields little in the way of concrete returns, participation becomes ever more demoralizing.[53] Neither the opposition parties discussed below, nor the Congress party, particularly following the de-institutionalization that took place under Gandhi, are seen as offering any room for the genuine involvement of most people in meaningful political decisions crucial to their own existence.[54]

In addition, then, to the goal of mobilizing outside pressure to move the state, the agenda of the non-party organizations is like that of the "new social movements" in more economically advanced countries: They want to create alternative political spaces in which the powerless can learn to organize and act politically, and in which they can exercise self-determination immediately. In terms of building the self-esteem of the participants, the practice of independent decision making within the groups is intended as an end in itself. Indeed, at the core of these movements is the effort to build empowerment through the creation of consciousness and the reconceptualization of politics as something deeper than the exercise of influencing state power.

Critique of Left Parties

As discussed in Chapter 1, some women's groups do work with, or are part of, political parties. However, members of autonomous organizations go so far as to lay the blame for the crisis in politics and in development not only on the government, but on what they see as the failure of "organized political parties, trade unions and other traditional forms of opposition to the ruling elite."[55] The growth of non-party movements thus results in part from widespread dismay with "the continuous limitation and failures of Left parties":[56] the Communist Party of India (CPI), the Communist Party of India Marxist (CPM), the Communist Party of India Marxist-Leninist (CPML) and with Janata, the inheritor of the socialist party mantle. Criticisms of the left parties include charges of opportunism: that parties organize the poor primarily in order to generate electoral support for their own bids for office. In addition, activists reject the left parties' hierarchical style; criticisms of the "bureaucratic" and "vanguardist" structures and principles of the political parties are common.[57]

At the heart of these tensions are differing views of what constitutes genuine progressive change and how best to achieve it. Both the CPI and the CPM seek elective office, a strategy that from the perspective of the non-party movements is too narrow and too elitist. The parties, they believe, seek to mobilize votes, not to transform consciousness. Such a transformation, movement participants argue, is a prerequisite for lasting

change. For example, one activist in an autonomous women's organization, the Forum Against the Oppression of Women, has found the left parties' attitudes towards women to be "instrumentalist." While acknowleg-
ing, she said, that violence against women is a problem, the left parties
maintain it is primarily a law and order issue. Once a communist party is
elected, they argue, the problem will be solved.[58] Activists of the women's
and other non-party movements feel instead that creating real social
change is much more complicated and difficult. Change must come from
below, not be instituted from above by those who believe their party line
is scientific and thus infallible.

From the time of its founding in 1928, the CPI was closely associated
with Moscow. Nevertheless, it took a benign view of parliamentary democracy and capitalism in India, viewing "the bourgeois democratic
state" as "a historic advance." The CPI believed that it must assist the
bourgeoisie to complete the capitalist stage of development. Its self-
assigned task was to organize the working class, so that the party could
first share power with the bourgeoisie and then lead the bourgeois-
working class alliance. To this end, the CPI pursued two complementary
strategies: the organizing of trade unions and the pursuit of electoral alliances with what it believed to be progressive elements of the nationalist
bourgeoisie, or, most particularly, Congress. At the time of the Congress
split in 1969, the CPI allied itself with Indira Gandhi; it remained loyal to
her throughout the emergency.[59] To those who, like most activists in the
non-party movement sector, found the rule of Congress and Indira
Gandhi during the 1970s to be wanting, CPI strategy appears to be part of
the problem rather than the solution.

The CPM, which split from the CPI in 1964, seeks to replace the present
"anti-democratic and anti-popular government" with one composed of
"democratic, anti-feudal and anti-capitalist forces." While the CPM does
not believe that parliamentary politics can create revolutionary change, it
nonetheless considers the pursuit of office at state and national levels to
be a worthy tactic: communist governments can help to solve local problems, "bring greater morale to the democratic masses," and "intensify the
struggle" between progressive and reactionary forces within the ruling
Congress party. As a step towards these goals, the CPM organizes "mass
struggles" among trade unionists and peasant groups. The mobilization
of the peasantry is a priority, a fact which distinguishes CPM strategy
from the proletariat-centered strategy of the CPI. But unlike the CPML,
which hoped to generate peasant-based revolution, and which was
crushed in Bengal in 1967 by a CPM-led state government, the rural
mobilizations sponsored by the CPM are conducted so as to enhance the
party's electoral performance. How well this serves the peasants is a question answered with skepticism by many non-party movement critics.[60]

Neither party has met with much electoral success on the level of national politics.[61] The CPI has not had much influence in state elections either; only in Bihar does it enjoy concentrated support. The CPM, though, has several times been able to govern in West Bengal, Tripura and Kerala. However, the communist movement has been unable to expand beyond these regional bases, and it has lost support in Andhra Pradesh and the Punjab. In the judgment of one scholar, "Communism in India is stagnant, and there is no state where support for either the CPM or CPI is growing."[62]

Their inability to move forward at the polls and to claim the loyalty of much of the organized working class does not inspire confidence in those not already converted to the communist cause. Still, it is not their electoral weakness that earns them the distrust of those in the autonomous movements. More fundamental are questions about means and ends, about how a movement should proceed and what it should achieve.

Movement activists are particularly critical of the hierarchical structure of the communist parties, and of any suggestion of the party as "vanguard." These result, they assert, in a lack of flexibility, and an unwillingness to learn from the masses. They accuse party members of having an "egotistical attitude with respect to their own fallibility"[63] and reject the communists' alleged "objectivity." Movement activists believe the parties rely too heavily on the Marxist canon, isolate themselves from the knowledge that might flow from below, and thus separate theory from practice.[64]

The disagreement is about means rather than ends, for most groups who seek to empower the poor and powerless hold to a vague socialist notion of a classless society.[65] But the non-party movement participants favor a non-hierarchical, collective style of work. They value the encounter between middle-class activist/intellectuals and the poor, and the learning that comes to each from this interaction.[66] Rather than approaching those they hope to organize with a detailed blue-print of an anticipated revolutionary outcome, non-party movement activists believe instead "that the awakened people will mould the socio-economic system according to their needs and it is not necessary to insist on loyalty to everything that goes under the Marxist label."[67]

Another difference between the communist parties and the nonparty activists is that the latter have rejected any insistence that class is the sole determinant of revolutionary preparedness. Their writings repeatedly take the communist parties to task for their adherence to ideological doctrines "evolved in a different cultural context and historical condition."[68] Whereas the parties focus most attention on organizing labor, the nonparty movements target "groups and strata considered unorganisable for social transformation . . . in conventional Marxist theory."[69] Their reason for this is twofold. First, theorists involved with the new movements see the poor as hampered not only by a lack of wealth, but by a culture that separates them from the "world of development."[70] Thus revolutionary strategy must include a fight for social and cultural uplift, for the conferring of a sense of empowerment and confidence on those who have been vulnerable because of their gender, caste, or ethnicity. Furthermore, the poor and powerless are divided by a myriad of cultural, ethnic, caste and gender differences; these separations, theorists of the non-party sector believe, make class organization impossible. Thus, organizing within groups hampered by their "socio-cultural" position—tribals, backward castes, dalits and women—is a necessary precursor to class-based organizing.

They reject, too, the idea that the capture of the state is a prerequisite for societal change. The non-party movements believe the reverse is true. In fact, they argue for a "redefinition of politics"[71] that moves beyond the question of who controls the state to the issue of how the process of social transformation will occur. It is in the *process* of transformation, in which democratic decision making and collective action are the desired means, that the non-party movements feel that empowerment will first be realized. Thus it is not Lenin and Mao who are frequently cited by non-party movement theorists, but rather Paulo Freire and Saul Alinsky on the importance of community organizing and "conscientization."[72]

Indeed, at the core of these movements is the effort to build empowerment through the creation of consciousness and the reconceptualization of politics as something deeper than the exercise of capturing state power. The most important step, virtually all non-party movement theorists agree, is to "awaken critical consciousness among the poor."[73] From this, the capture of state power might logically seem to be a possibility, but that is not what is emphasized by the non-party groups. When the state is engaged, it is generally addressed on local issues, or issues of enforcement—such as a demand that the minimum wages act or land ceiling laws be implemented—but the purpose of such actions seems always to be twofold. To move the state to action is half the agenda; the other is to build political awareness and a sense of political empowerment among those not accustomed to demanding their rights or exercising power.[74]

The dismay that participants in non-party movements feel, then, with regard to the left opposition parties, derives from profound differences over the desirable relationship between means and ends. Theirs is a fundamentally different approach to how political change, even revolutionary change, is to occur. While to the communist parties the capture of state power is a necessary prerequisite to social transformation, the non-party movements adopt the position that social transformation must occur "from the bottom up through organizations of the people."[75] A revolution is seen not as a seizure of power, but as a transformation in people's ability to exercise power over their own lives.

Thus, the agenda of the non-party movements is twofold. They seek to counter a culture of despair and hopelessness with one charged with purposefulness, self-esteem, self-reliance, and power. This is seen as a necessary precondition for the meaningful participation of the poor or powerless in their own liberation. But most non-party organizations pursue this strategy, too, in order to have an impact on the government and those private citizens with economic power. The non-party movements aggregate and articulate interests; they increase the bargaining power of the less powerful.

Notes

1. This is not to imply that structural dislocations *alone* produce movements. System crisis provides opportunity; whether or not individuals and groups are able to come together to form a collective response depends as well on the resources available to them. See Theda Skocpol, *States and Social Revolutions* (NY: Cambridge Univ. Press, 1979) and Charles Tilly, *From Mobilization to Revolution* (Reading, MA: Addison-Wesley, 1978).

2. This is true, for instance, of movements for women's rights in a number of military-ruled Latin American countries. Ironically, because their organized activities are not always perceived by the state to be political, women have sometimes had more space in which to organize than men, particularly when they organize as mothers seeking to protect their families. See Jo Fisher, *Mothers of the Disappeared* (Boston: South End Press, 1989); and Patricia M. Chuchryk, "Subversive Mothers: The Women's Opposition to the Military Regime in Chile," in *Women, the State and Development*, ed. Sue Ellen Charlton, Jana Everett and Kathleen Staudt (Albany: SUNY Press, 1989).

3. Ghanshyam Shah, "Grass-Roots Mobilization in Indian Politics" in *India's Democracy: An Analysis of Changing State-Society Relations*, ed. Atul Kohli (Princeton: Princeton Univ. Press, 1988).

4. Rajni Kothari, "Party and State in Our Times: The Rise of Non-Party Political Formations," *Alternatives* 9 (1984), pp. 541–564; and Harsh Sethi, "Groups in a New Politics of Transformation," *Economic and Political Weekly*, 18 Feb. 1984, p. 305.

5. There has also been a growth in the number and power of right-wing movements that seek to protect the rights and privileges of middle-class Hindus against lower castes, lower classes, and ethnic minorities, particularly Muslims. Because my subject is the women's movement, however, I will focus on those secular, social-democratic movements that spring from similar impulses and share broadly similar goals.

6. Information for this section and the next is derived from several sources: Stanley A. Kochanek, "Mrs. Gandhi's Pyramid: The New Congress," in *Indira Gandhi's India: A Political System Reappraised*, ed. Henry C. Hart (Boulder, CO: Westview, 1976); Myron Weiner, "The 1971 Elections and the Indian Party System," *Asian Survey*, Dec. 1971; Robert L. Hardgrave, Jr. and Stanley A. Kochanek, *India: Government*

and Politics in a Developing Nation (NY: Harcourt Brace Jovanovich, 1986), pp. 204–210; and Francine Frankel, *India's Political Economy 1947-1977* (Princeton: Princeton Univ. Press, 1978). See also Henry Hart, "Political Leadership in India: Dimensions and Limits," and James Manor, "Parties and the Party System," both in *India's Democracy*, ed. Atul Kohli.

7. Rajni Kothari, "End of an Era," *Seminar* no. 197 (1976), p. 24.

8. Kochanek writes, "Inept chief ministers had to spend all their time trying to stay in power and were unable to cope with the problems generated by . . . economic crisis, food shortages, and uncontrolled inflation." pp. 111–112.

9. Frankel, p. 491.

10. Myron Weiner, *India at the Polls: The Parliamentary Elections of 1977* (Washington, D.C.: American Enterprise Institute, 1978), p. 3; and Frankel, pp. 510 and 514.

11. Frankel, p. 494, citing data from the 1961 and 1971 censuses, and a 1972/73 study of the Ministry of Agriculture, Department of Community Development. See also D.N. Dhanagare, "Agrarian Reforms and Rural Development in India," *Research in Social Movements, Conflicts and Change*, 7 (1984), p. 185.

12. Frankel, pp. 510–511. Dhanagare, p. 196 cites a number of studies published between 1969 and 1976 which conclude that the green revolution—the introduction of high yielding varieties of crops requiring considerable fertilizer and irrigation—has led to an increased concentration of land in the hands of a few, and an increase in rural poverty. "The rich," Dhanagare writes, "have become richer and the poor poorer not only in relative terms but also in absolute terms."

13. Hardgrave and Kochanek, p. 210.

14. Narayan, "Total Revolution: Its Future," in *Towards Total Revolution*, vol. 4, p. 180.

15. All survey data is reported in Ghanshyam Shah, "The Upsurge in Gujarat,"*Economic and Political Weekly* 9:32–34 (1974), pp. 1431–1432.

16. The Centre for Regional Development Studies survey anticipated this with its finding that 67 percent of Surat respondents believed that direct action tactics were "legitimate and necessary" tools with which to pursue economic goals. Shah, p. 1440.

17. Shah, p. 1443.

18. Shah, p. 1444. The self-proclaimed leaders included the Jana Sangh (a conservative party), the Congress(O), several trade unions and the major organized student association, the Navnirman Yuvak Samiti. Shah offers as examples of the widespread mood of defiance processions to police stations in Ahmedabad and Baroda undertaken by "more than 200 middle-aged women of middle class families" to demand the release of arrested students. The women told the police that for every boy the police might kill, "Each of us will produce one hundred sons in their places" (p. 1445).

19. John Wood, "Extra-Parliamentary Opposition in India," *Pacific Affairs*, Fall 1975, p. 319.

20. Frankel, p. 531; Ajit Bhattacharjea, *Jayaprakash Narayan: A Political Biography* (Delhi: Vikas, 1975), p. 13; and Narayan, "A Manifesto for Bihar" in *Towards Total Revolution*, vol. 4, pp. 170–178.

21. Ajit Bhattacharjea, "Despair and Hope in Bihar," *Times of India*, 17 Sep. 1973. Quoted by Frankel, p. 531. Even if one did not perceive Bihar's politicians as quite that venal, it would be hard to escape the conclusion that retaining or achieving office, rather than governing, occupied much of their time: from 1967 to 1971 Bihar had eight governments (six by non-Congress and two by Congress-led coalitions) and two periods of President's Rule. In many eyes, the problem with Bihar's government was not just that it was corrupt, but that, in J.P.'s words, it was "inefficiently corrupt." Narayan, "A Manifesto for Bihar," in *Towards Total Revolution*, vol. 4, p. 177.

22. Wood, p. 320, Frankel, p. 528.

23. Although "people's politics" is the usual translation, "niti" also denotes "morality" or "ethics."

24. Wood, p. 321. J.P. estimated that the student movement was largely a "non-party affair" with 80 to 90 percent of those involved having no party attachments. Much of the student leadership, he acknowledged, did, however, have attachments to one of four parties: Jana Sangh, Socialist Party, BLD, and Congress (O). Jayaprakash Narayan, *Prison Diary* (Bombay: Popular Prakashan, 1977), pp. 56–57.

25. Wood, p. 321 and Frankel, p. 533. See also Narayan, "Total Revolution: Its Future" in *Towards Total Revolution*, vol. 4.

26. *Everyman's Weekly*, 18 May 1975, cited in Frankel, p. 533.

27. Narayan, *Prison Diary*, pp. 61–64; "Why Total Revolution," pp. 115–117, "Total Revolution: Its Concept," pp. 152–163 and "Total Revolution: Some Clarifications," pp. 198–205, all in *Towards Total Revolution*, vol. 4.

28. Wood, p. 322 and Frankel, pp. 533–534.

29. Frankel, pp. 528–530.

30. Wood, p. 323. The police shootings in October followed violence among the protesters, which was in turn blamed on police provocation.

31. Narayan, "The Revolt Against the System," in *Towards Total Revolution*, p. 125.

32. Frankel, p. 535.

33. Kochanek, pp. 113–114.

34. The alliance included the Jan Sangh, Congress(O), Bharatiya Lok Dal and Socialist parties. Hardgrave and Kochanek, p. 212; Frankel, pp. 538–540.

35. Frankel, p. 541.

36. Hardgrave and Kochanek, p. 213.

37. Ibid. p. 214.

38. Ibid. p. 216.

39. Ibid. pp. 198–99.

40. Frankel, p. 547.

41. Kochanek, p. 118.

42. Hardgrave and Kochanek, pp. 218–219.

43. Weiner, *India at the Polls*, pp. 8–12.

44. Cited in Weiner, *India at the Polls*, p. 17.

45. Interview, Vina Mazumdar, New Delhi, 23 June 1986. One should note that Indian soda is very fizzy indeed.

46. For the story of the PUCL, see Barnett R. Rubin, "The Civil Liberties Movement in India: New Approaches to State and Social Change," *Asian Survey* 27:3 (1987), pp. 370–392.

47. See D.N. Dhanagare, "Agrarian Reforms and Rural Development in India: Some Observations"; and "Urban Decay: A Mega Collapse," *India Today*, 31 Jan. 1988, pp. 60–67.

48. Hardgrave and Kochanek, p. 23.

49. Interview, Madhu Kishwar, editor of *Manushi*, New Delhi, 5 June 1986.

50. Interview, Vina Mazumdar, Director of the Center for Women's Development Studies, New Delhi, 23 June 1986.

51. D.L. Sheth, "Grass-Roots Initiatives in India," *EPW* 11 Feb. 1984, p. 260. See also Kothari, "Party and State in Our Times," pp. 543–544; and Dhanagare, p. 196.

52. Kothari, "Party and State in Our Times," p. 543.

53. See Pendse, Roy, and Sethi, pp. 8–9.

54. Sethi, "Groups in a New Politics of Transformation," p. 314. See also "Lokayan: A Six Year Report," *Lokayan* 3:6 (1985), p. 7.

55. Rajni Kothari, "Party and State in Our Times," p. 548.

56. Harsh Sethi, "Groups in a New Politics of Transformation," p. 308.

57. See, for example, A. Pendse, A.K. Roy and H. Sethi, "People's Participation: A Look at Non-Party Political Formations in India." (New Delhi: Lokayan paper, n.d.), p. 16.

58. Interview, Vibhuti Patel, Bombay, 5 July 1986.

59. Bhabani Sen Gupta, *CPI-M: Promises, Prospects, Problems* (New Delhi: Young Asia, 1979), pp. 35–36.

60. See, for example, the report of a discussion entitled "On Threats to the Non-Party Political Process," held among movement activists and scholars in 1985. *Lokayan* 3:2 (1985), pp. 37–49. For a sympathetic appraisal of the CPM, see Sen Gupta, pp. 39–40 and 55.

61. The highest percentage of votes in Lok Sabha elections the CPI has received is 9.9 in 1962, before the party split in two; its percentage of the all-India vote has been (with the exception of a tiny upturn in 1984) steadily declining ever since. In 1967, the CPI received 5.0 percent of the total vote; in 1971, 4.7 percent; in 1977 (when it supported Gandhi in the first post-emergency election), 2.8 percent; in 1980, 2.6 percent; and in 1984, 2.7 percent. The CPM has done slightly better: in its first contested Lok Sabha election in 1967, CPM candidates received 4.4 percent of the vote. In 1971 they polled 5.1 percent; in 1977 (when it allied with Janata), 4.3 percent; in 1980, 6.1 percent; and in 1984, 5.7 percent. *Elections in India: Data Handbook on Lok Sabha Elections, 2nd ed, 1952–1985*, ed. V.B. Singh and Shankar Bose (Beverly Hills: Sage, 1986). Taken together, the two communist parties have never equaled the 9.9 percent received by the undivided party in 1962.

62. Robert Hardgrave, *India Under Pressure* (Boulder, CO: Westview, 1984), pp. 100–101.

63. Sethi, "Groups in a New Politics," p. 305.

64. These points were made by Corinne Kumar d'Souza, one of the founding members of Vimochna, a women's group in Bangalore. Interview, July 25, 1986, New Delhi. See also Sethi, p. 308.

65. Sharad Kulkarni, "Social Mobilisation Groups—A Review" (New Delhi: Lokayan paper, n.d.), p. 2.

66. See discussion in G.V.S. de Silva, et al., *Bhoomi Sena: A Struggle for People's Power* (Bombay: National Institute of Bank Management, 1978), chapter 6.

67. Kulkarni, "Social Mobilization Groups," p. 2.

68. Kothari, "Party and State in Our Times," p. 549. Corrinne Kumar d'Souza suggests that a rejection of the Eurocentrism of the Marxist paradigms embraced by India's communist parties was one of the central reasons why her colleauges in the Center for Informal Education and Development Studies dropped out of either the CPM or the CPML and subsequently formed SIEDS and Vimochna. Interview, July 25, 1986.

69. Sethi, "Groups in a New Politics of Transformation," p. 309.

70. D. L. Sheth, "Grass-roots Initiatives in India," p. 260.

71. Harsh Sethi, "Some Dilemmas Facing Non-Party Political Groups," *Lokayan* 2:2 (1984), p. 20.

72. For example, see a description of the organizing methods of one non-party group, Bhoomi Sena, in de Silva, et al., ch. 6. See also Sethi, "Groups in a New Politics of Transformation," p. 310.

73. Kulkarni, "Social Mobilization Groups" p. 1.

74. See Sanjit Roy, "Confessions of a Non-Aligned Activist," *Seminar* no. 291 (1983), p. 24; and Calman, *Protest in Democratic India* (Boulder, CO: Westview, 1985), Part II.

75. D.L. Sheth, "Grass-Roots Stirrings and the Future of Politics," *Alternatives* 9 (1983), p. 3.

3

Discovering the Status of Women in India: Grievances Surface and Action Begins

The existence of grievance, or, put differently, a sense of injustice, while not alone enough to spark a movement, is a critical prerequisite to movement emergence. The belief that something is wrong, and that individuals acting alone or collectively must do something, must at minimum go on record in protest, prompt movements to begin. This chapter explains the development and politicization of grievance about the social, economic and political status of Indian women.

The Anti-Price-Rise Movement

The government crisis of the early 1970s that provoked the anti-government movements in Gujarat and Bihar prompted a gendered response in parts of India afflicted by a declining standard of living. The Anti-Price-Rise Movement movement originated in Bombay to protest economic problems with particular resonance for women: scarcities and sharply rising prices of consumer goods, including food and clothing. The Anti-Price-Rise movement drew attention to the possibilities for organization and coalition-building among women, and mobilized many women for the first time around issues presented as gender specific.

Movement activity was directed against government, wholesale traders, and black marketeers, all of whom were held responsible for contributing to the economic decline. The problem was felt especially keenly in Maharashtra, because of several years of drought in that state, but movement protest soon spread to urban areas outside the state, including New Delhi.

Demanding price-cuts, unadulterated foodgrains and increased rations at government stores, women took to the streets in the tens of thousands, *gheraoe*d numerous public officials and important businessmen, and utilized agitational tactics of particular symbolic importance to women: one march consisted of a thousand women carrying small stoves to represent their lack of food; another featured women loudly banging spoons on *thalis* (the steel plates on which meals are served); and a third had as many as 20,000 women marching through the streets of Bombay shaking their wooden rolling pins, which became the symbol of the movement.[1]

The movement was made possible by the existence of leadership and women's organizations already in place; these organizations were not the autonomous ones that were to spring up in the late 1970s and early 1980s, but rather were associated with political parties. Bombay not only had women's organizations attached to each of the two national communist parties, it also had a strong organization of socialist women, the Samajwadi Mahila Sabha (Socialist Women's Group).[2] Together, these three groups led the series of demonstrations that constituted the movement.

The coalition was initiated by the CPI-associated women's group, the National Federation of Indian Women. At the September 1972 meeting of the Bombay unit of NFIW, its president, Aruna Asaf Ali, called for a united fight against the rising prices of daily necessities.[3] A meeting held soon afterward resulted in the formation of the Joint Action Committee of Women for the Resistance of Price Rise. For most of the next three years, the committee was led by a Socialist, Mrinal Gore, and included other women from the Samajwadi Mahila Sabha, most prominently Pramila Dandavate and Mangala Parikh; as well as CPI women from Shramik Mahila Sang (Toiling Women's Group, the local branch of the NFIW), including Manju Gandhi, Sushila Gokhale and Prema Purao; and CPM women of Maharashtra's Shramik Mahila Sabha (Toiling Women's Organization), most prominently Ahilya Rangnekar.[4]

The Anti-Price-Rise movement focused on an issue that in many times and places (including the French and Russian revolutions) has politicized women: the demand for adequate, affordable food on the family table. It was an issue of deep concern around which thousands could be readily mobilized. The movement was a response, expressed in feminine terms, to the structural crises facing the nation.

Whether the movement could have broadened its concerns and developed into a sustained movement attentive to other issues important to women is unclear, because Indira Gandhi's 1975 declaration of emergency was followed by the imprisonment of most of the movement's leaders. In fact, the coalition that led the movement had begun to fall apart just prior to this. While the Socialist and CPM women were supportive of the concurrent anti-Congress movements taking place in Gujarat and Bihar, the CPI women, in keeping with CPI policy, were not. The leaders of the Shramik Mahila Sangh withdrew from the movement as Gandhi's hold on power became increasingly tenuous and the CPI called for support for the Congress government.[5] This action, which betrayed a loyalty to heeding the party line, even at the expense of continuing agitational activity that privileged the needs of women, was one that contributed to the distrust of party-related women's organizations by those beginning to turn to autonomous groups.

Nonetheless, despite its limitations, the Anti-Price-Rise movement was politicizing; it raised the consciousness of many women, and many women leaders, about women's issues and the possibilities for further organizing. At the end of the emergency, Chapter 4 will show, many of these leaders re-emerged at the head of new movement organizations, or became active in parliamentary politics on behalf of women.

The Report of the Committee on the Status of Women

Not all the events that helped to promote new consciousness about women's problems and thus, eventually, movement activity, were products of internal change or activity: many activities to enhance women's status in India have been prompted, ideologically and materially, by international feminism. One critical event in the emergence of the movement was the direct result of such international influence.

In 1967 the United Nations General Assembly adopted the Declaration on the Elimination of Discrimination Against Women. It followed up the Declaration with repeated requests to member states to submit reports on the status of women in their countries. In response, the Government of India constituted the Committee on the Status of Women (CSWI) in September 1971.[6]

The release in May 1975, just prior to the emergency, of the Committee's report, *Towards Equality*,[7] created an effect similar to that experienced in the United States in 1961 with the creation of the President's Commission on the Status of Women. Just as in the U.S., the President's Commission had created a "climate of expectations"[8] that something must be done to help women achieve full equality in American society; so, in India, *Towards Equality* sparked immediate demands for government action. The data it compiled on women's inferior position in religious and family life, in health care and in law, and with regard to economic, educational and political opportunity served as a jolt to the consciousness of many educated and politicized Indians, both women and men, and helped spur their activism in a new direction.

Much of the document is a call for vigorous governmental action to improve the status of women. Significantly, the authors of the report located their advocacy of equality for women not only within the moral scheme of "social justice" but squarely within the developmental needs of the nation as a whole. Women's equality, they argued, is "a basic precondition for [the] social, economic and political development of the nation" (p. 8) and thus should be a governmental priority.

In addition, they argued that their suggestions for the uplift of women are consistent with the goals of the nation as articulated in the constitution. The Indian constitution, they reminded readers, is more than a prescription of rights; it is a "'social' document embodying the objectives of a social revolution" to be attained "by making deliberate departures . . . from the inherited political and social systems" (p. 3). The report praises the constitutional protections for women that were instituted at independence. Article 14 guarantees equality before the law for all citizens, while Article 15 prohibits discrimination on the grounds of sex. Additionally, the Directive Principles section of the constitution, which articulates state goals and acts as a guideline to policy, guarantees to both women and men a right to an adequate livelihood, to equal pay for equal work, and protection of the health of all workers, including, for women, maternity leave. In short, the constitutional imperative is for nondiscrimination in both civil rights and economic opportunity. Of course, in the early seventies, as today, these goals were far from being met.

But even as *Towards Equality* argues that the government should be vigorously pursuing measures to improve the status of women, the CSWI also recognized that the state is not the sole agent of social change, and that the government bears sole responsibility neither for the inferior position of women nor for its remedy. Law, the committee acknowledges, is often in advance of social norms; government actions to reform law can have only limited impact because of "the normative and structural unpreparedness of the society to accept their goals and means." "Religion, family and kinship roles, and cultural norms delimiting the spheres of women's activities obstruct their full and equal participation in the life of the soceity and achievement of their full potential" (p. 37).

Since the government alone cannot alter cultural patterns and social structures that uphold women's inferior position in the family and in the economy, the CSWI, in addition to detailing actions that government should take, called specifically for movement activity. The report urges "community organisations, particularly women's organisations" to "mobilise public opinion and strengthen social efforts against oppressive institutions like polygamy [and] dowry" and to "mount a campaign for the dissemination of information about the legal rights of women to increase their awareness" (p. 101). The uplift of women must be the joint task of an educated and committed government, and a social movement that would enlighten and inspire.

Thus, while some within the women's movement concentrate their political efforts on moving government to pass and implement inproved legislation and others focus their attention on empowering women at the grass roots, the two are not contradictory. In *Towards Equality,* the first document of the contemporary movement, there is certainly faith in parliamentary procedures; but there is also a recognition that the transformation of cultural norms and the empowerment of women at the grass roots is critical to the mobilization of interests necessary to move government, and to be ready to receive governmental assistance when it is offered.

Towards Equality constituted an important ideological first step in mobilizing educated activists. Today, movement activists frequently cite the report as a critical factor in raising their consciousness and motivating them to act.[9] The bulk of the 480-page report is devoted to documenting women's inferior position in society and analyzing its causes; in its scale and comprehensiveness, it is a moving, often depressing indictment of a socio-economic and political system that pervasively discriminates against women.

However, as the report was published just prior to the emergency, its recommendations languished. Along with other concerns about human rights, this was one of the frustrations that burst forth at the emergency's close.[10]

The Status of Women in India

Drawing on *Towards Equality* and other studies, governmental and private, this section briefly expores the status of women in India during the 1970s and 1980s. This survey will provide a sense of what grievances have sparked, and continue to inspire, movement activity.

Demographic Survey

The substantive portion of the report opens with a brutal fact: from 1901 on, each census has recorded a decline in the ratio of females to males in the population. In 1901, for every 1000 males in India there were 972 females; by 1971, there were only 930 females for every 1000 males (p. 9). In contrast, most other countries, both in the "developed" and "less developed" worlds, have a higher percentage of women than men in their population.[11]

The Committee also reported that while life expectancy for all Indians had increased dramatically over the previous fifty years, the *gap* in the number of years of life expectancy at birth had *widened* between women and men in the years since 1921, from a difference favoring men of 0.3 years to a difference of 1.5 years. These patterns together suggest that the "neglect of women in India is a persistent phenomenon" (p. 11). The CSWI deplored the lack of reliable information on the causes of these disparities, but suggested among its hypotheses the marked preference for sons and consequent neglect of female infants; the general neglect of women at all ages; and the adverse impact of frequent and excessive childbearing on the health of women (p. 11). In 1985, a document produced by the Indian government to mark the close of the international decade of women made a more succinct analysis: "The problem of overwork for underfed women," it said, "seems to be responsible for female mortality."[12]

Towards Equality's demographic survey also reported that despite the Child Marriage Restraint Act which designated fifteen years as the minimum legal age for marriage, the marriage of young girls was still common.[13] The 1961 census revealed that in more than one-third of the districts in India, the average female age at marriage was below fifteen (p. 23). In 1971, in rural India, 13.6% of the girls in the age group 10–14 were married and 0.1% widowed; in urban India 3.9% of the girls in this age group were married (p. 25). The CSWI expressed regret that there were no data about marital status for girls aged nine and below, since, in the Committee's travels, members had come across a number of married girls in that age group (pp. 25, 82). As recently as 1986, the Health Minister of Uttar Pradesh found that the state contained villages in which all girls over the age of 8 were married; the girls' parents explained that the dowry expected at the marriage of an eight year old was only five hundred rupees, as compared to the fifteen to twenty thousand rupees expected after puberty.[14]

The CSWI found that family planning is practiced by only fifteen percent of couples in the reproductive age group, and that the level of education and fertility are inversely related; this finding provided one argument for the need to educate women (pp. 29-30).

That need was made further apparent in the 1971 census, which recorded that while the urban female literacy rate is 42.3%, in rural India the female literacy rate was only 13.2%; the nationwide total of 18.7% female literacy compared to the nationwide total of 39.5% literacy for males. Even these figures are wildly exaggerated: among those females counted in the census as literate, 40.3% had less than a primary school education. Only 7.8% had completed a secondary education and 1.4% had graduated from a higher educational institution (pp. 30–31). Thus, the Committtee was quick to point out, the women in India who hold high positions in government and intellectual life constitute a small, elite group and do not reflect the position of the enormous majority (p. 31). By the 1981 census, the percentage of females who were literate had increased to a nationwide total of 24.8% (48% urban literacy and 18% rural). However, the *rate* at which women's literacy increased *slowed* between 1971 and 1981, as compared to the rate during the previous two decades.[15]

Sociocultural Contributors to Women's Status

The Committee understood that social structures are critical determinants of women's troubled status. Acknowledging that many structures of inequality such as caste, community, class, and geographic setting create different problems for women of different spheres (p. 3), the Committee began by considering the impact of religion.

⟶Religion in India is pertinent not only to the cultural valuation of women, but to their legal position. In India, religion is also law. In most matters pertaining to family life—marriage, divorce, inheritance, guardianship of children—religious law is recognized by the state. Modern India continues the practice adopted by the British of letting Hindu law govern the Hindu community and Muslim law the Muslim community; the state also recognizes Christian, Parsi and Jewish law. The CSWI lamented this tradition. The British policy of general non-interference in personal law had the effect, the CSWI argued, not only of encouraging the dangerous feeling of separation that exists between India's two largest communities, the Hindus and the Muslims, but also of preventing the evolution of personal law. Even as society underwent enormous socio-economic changes during the two hundred years of British rule in India, personal law stagnated (p. 102). Despite the constitutional guarantee in Article 14 of the equality of the sexes before the law, *Towards Equality* finds that some aspects of every religious community's law—laws that are still recognized by the courts today—discriminate against women.

The CSWI's argument for a uniform civil code that would eliminate all such gender discrimination in personal law and would end, too, the discriminatory practice of citizens of the same country being governed by entirely different sets of laws has proved to be one of its most important and certainly most controversial recommendations. The CSWI placed its opinion squarely within the logic of "secularism, science and modernisation," stating that the continuance of various personal laws that accept discrimination between men and women not only violates the Fundamental Rights section of the constitution but is also "against the spirit of national integration and secularism."

As Chapter 6 will discuss, the movement in the 1980s has shown ambivalence about the feasibility of a uniform civil code in light of increased communal tensions in India. To many Indian citizens a call for a uniform civil code appears to be a call for the extension of Hindu law to all, and thus even those feminists who hope for a uniform civil code have tended to back down from their demands, preferring to wait rather than give the appearance of abetting Hindu chauvinism or fanning the flames of communal discord.

Of course, no one in the women's movement today would suggest that the Hindu code, and many Hindu social customs, are models of gender equality. *Towards Equality* points out the pervasive derogatory images of women in Hinduism (p. 40). A woman "is called fickle-minded, sensual, seducer of men; given to falsehood, trickery, folly, greed, impurity and thoughtless action; root of all evil; inconsistent; and cruel." Her prescribed destiny is to be a faithful, subservient, and uncomplaining wife and mother: "In childhood a woman must be subject to her father, in youth to her husband, and when her lord is dead to her sons. A woman must never be independent" (pp. 40–41, citing Manu). Hindu law forbids polygamy, but in part because economically dependent and uneducated women do not have the means to move the courts on their own behalf, "bigamous marriages are still prevalent among Hindus" (p. 108). Because marriage is woman's destiny, widowhood is considered deeply inauspicious, and widows, unlike widowers, by and large are forced to live a restricted life (p. 42).

Islam, on the other hand, places women on an equal footing with men in the eyes of the Almighty, and the Quran is filled with injunctions aimed at bettering the lot of women. However, the codification of Muslim law (into the Shariat) has not been so kind to women. Over the centuries, the Quran has been interpreted in India so as to legitimize prevailing social norms that have placed women in an inferior legal, social, and religious position. (p. 43). For example, in law, whereas the testimony of a single male witness is respected, that of a single woman is not; her testimony must be corroborated by a second woman. Socially and economically, a Muslim woman is heavily dependent on men in part because of the insistence that her modesty and chastity be protected; her seclusion from men precludes her full participation in most educational and business fields (pp. 43–44).

With respect to the family, Muslim law allows women some important rights. Marriage is not religiously obligatory. It is a contract; thus divorce is allowed and there is no ban on a widow's remarriage. In social practice, however, both divorce and widows' remarriage is frowned upon. Furthermore, women's status within the family is gravely diminished by the legality and practice of polygamy, and by the fact that a husband can obtain a divorce simply by declaring it so (p. 44). Of course, the husband's "absolute and unlimited right to repudiate the marriage at his will" (known as talaq) is uniquely his; the wife has no corresponding right (p. 119).[16]

In India, certain social customs that are not strictly speaking religious, and which may indeed cut across religions, are also extremely harmful to women. *Towards Equality* was particularly attentive to the impact of patrilocality: throughout India, a girl upon marriage frequently goes to live in the home of her in-laws. At the very least, her family loyalties are expected to change upon marriage. Emotionally, as well as legally and economically, a girl is transferred upon marriage to another family. This one fact has a hugely negative impact on the well-being of girls and women.

Within the natal family, boys are more valued than girls. A son will remain within the family; a son will care for parents in old age. Parents' investment of emotional and financial resources in their son is, therefore, a investment in their own future. Simply put, a son is an asset. A daughter is a liability. Thus, parents do not make an equal investment in their daughters; the poor literacy rate for women as well as the adverse sex ratio described above may well be a result of this distinction. When resources are scarce they are more likely to go to a permanent son rather than to a transient daughter.

The transfer of the daughter from one family to another is usually accompanied by an exchange of cash and/or goods; a marriage is most often arranged by the parents and is in part a commercial transaction. Westerners are sometimes surprised to hear that arranged marriages still predominate among all classes in India. Just as interesting is that neither *Towards Equality* nor contemporary feminists cite arranged marriage *per se* as one cause of violence against women within the family or as a factor in sustaining women's inferior status. Indeed, according to *Towards Equality* the existence of caste in Hindu society, which traditionally limits one's choice of marriage partners to certain groups, as well as prescriptions within the Muslim community which may restrict marriage choice to certain socioeconomic categories or to particular categories of family relations "make arranged marriage the most desirable form of marriage. . . . Marriage cannot be left to the young if these restrictions and preferences are to work. The institution of arranged marriage thus fits well with the social structure" (p. 62). Contemporary feminists say that even among educated, urban youths, there is a preference for parents to pick a future spouse from one's own religion, region, community, and caste. Girls and boys generally grow up separated from each other; friendships between boys and girls are typically frowned upon. Thus, young people have little opportunity to meet and select their own marriage partners. These social patterns are not seen as a problem by most contemporary feminists; that marriage typically occurs in the absence of love or even friendship is not a movement issue.[17] Violence within marriage, including that which stems from exorbitant demands for dowry payments, *is* a movement issue. The commercial aspect of arranged marriage is condemned, but arranged marriage is not.

The transfer of payments upon marriage can work in one of two ways: when the payment is *to* the family of the bride, it is called bride-price; the money that is paid *by* the family of the bride is called dowry. The Dowry Prohibition Act of 1961 prohibits both types of transactions. In 1974 the CSWI declared that the Act had had no effect whatsoever (p. 76); this remains true today, despite new legislation to strengthen it.

In the system of bride-price, one family pays the other for their right to have authority over the bride; the husband's family in effect buys him a wife. The status relationship is clear; only women are bought and sold. But at least there is an acknowledgement that the woman is worth something and that her parents should be compensated for losing her. The woman thus has some status. Furthermore, as she has economic value, parents do not so desperately dread the birth of a daughter since upon marriage she will bring them some material return. Under the system of bride-price, a husband is less likely to treat his wife too harshly since, if she leaves, it will cost him to replace her (p. 70).

The practice of bride-price has been giving way, however, to the practice of dowry. The shift is probably not in women's best interest. Traditionally the prerogative of higher castes, the taking of dowry is being emulated by those of lower castes and status as they aspire to higher status.[18] Indeed, as a new middle class has developed in India the practice has spread. "Black money and unaccounted earnings have given impetus to dowry. . . . A new class of *nouveaux riches* has emerged that buys a daughter's future with dowry, to raise its own social status by entering into marriage alliances with families of high status." (p. 76)

Some contemporary feminists are re-thinking dowry and contend that it should be seen as a daughter's rightful inheritance from her father in an inheritance system in which women do not receive land. Others maintain, though, as did the CSWI, that the practice of dowry sends horrific messages about the worth of women. A woman is seen as parasitic, as a liability; thus a new family must be paid off to take her.

In practice, the reality can be just as awful as the image. In paying dowry, the parents of the girl are trying to buy her a good life with another family; but the bride then becomes a hostage to her in-laws' desire for continued material wealth. Even after the marriage, the bride's family is "under compulsion and heavy pressure" to continue giving gifts to the husband's family. "In the first few years of marriage, the girl's treatment in her husband's house is linked to these gifts" (p. 71).

In present-day India, "dowry deaths"—in which young brides are murdered by their husbands and/or in-laws—occur in the thousands each year. The murder is often preceded by demands for increased dowry payments; a dowry death may also result from the husband's desire to marry again and thus obtain a new dowry.

Far from being an anachronistic holdover from a bygone age, dowry has contemporary meaning within an increasingly capitalist and money conscious society. The rise in education in India has led not to a decrease in dowry demands, but rather, to an increase. An educated man is worth more in the dowry market than an uneducated one (p. 74).

There are more or less well-defined grades of dowry for men in different professions. For example men in the I.A.S. [Indian Administrative Service] and I.F.S. [Indian Foreign Service] . . . can easily expect to get in cash and kind at least a lakh [one hundred thousand] of rupees. Business executives rank next. Engineers and doctors stand lower than the business executives. This class seems to expect that marriage would bring them not only a partner but also all the things needed to set up a modern household, such as a car, refrigerator, radiogram. These groups . . . naturally influence those below. Thus a peon or a clerk would demand such things as a bicycle, a transistor, and a wrist watch. A scooter is a common . . . gift to the son-in-law in the groups at the middle level. In villages too there are similar demands. (p. 73)

The education of women does help to limit dowry, but only if the husband's family has the expectation that the new bride will pursue a career, and thus bring money into the family in that way. They may prefer, however, that she not; a non-working wife is a sign of her husband's wealth and contributes to his status.

The CSWI strongly criticized the ineffectual Dowry Prohibition Act of 1961 and made a number of suggestions for strengthening it. But the Committee spoke too of the need to arouse social consciousness "particularly amongst women, to enable them to understand that by encouraging dowry they are perpetuating the inequality of the sexes." It called for an improvement in women's self-image. Also critical to ending dowry, the CSWI argued, are increased opportunities for women's employment and a reassessment of the value of household work and homemaking. The Committee recognized that these are not tasks only for government; the responsibility for change, the report argued, must be shared by the community. *Towards Equality* is thus in part a call for movement activitity to mobilize public opinion, change oppressive social institutions and educate women as to their legal rights (see p. 101).

Economic Opportunity

Nor can government alone bring about the changes required to bring women fully into the economic development process, since opposition to increased participation by women in the economic life of the country derives in part from social mores which deem women's "proper" economic role to be strictly separate from men's (p. 149).

Nonetheless, *Towards Equality* strongly criticizes government's inattention to the particular and terrible problems that a "modernizing" economy has brought to women. With the shift from traditional forms of agriculture and production in household industry to an increasingly capitalist economy characterized by larger scale and organized economic activities, labor has ceased to be organized by family units and instead has become more competitive and individualized. As jobs became scarcer and more technical, women were handicapped by their lack of education and limited opportunity to acquire new skills; they were left behind in the labor market (p. 149). The Committee found that women are the greatest

victims of unemployment and underemployment, and that the proportion of women below the poverty line exceeds that of men (pp. 160–161).
Governmental measures since independence to remove women's educational handicap, generate employment for women, provide equal
remuneration, and end discrimination in hiring have been, according to
the CSWI, "extremely inadequate" (p. 230).

The report painstakingly and clearly documents women's growing position of inferiority in the economy. Since the beginning of the twentieth
century, the participation of women in the paid labor force declined in absolute numbers, in the percentage of female workers to the total female
population, and as a percentage of the total labor force. The decline of
women's participation in the industry and service fields means that
women have become increasingly dependent on agriculture, which by
and large pays lower wages than jobs in the other sectors. As significant to
understanding women's economic status is the fact that only a very small
percentage of women workers—approximately six percent—are in the organized sector. The other 94 percent work in what is called the unorganized sector. (81.4 percent are in agriculture; 12.6 percent in other occupations.) There, they are largely non-unionized, and are outside the reach
of most laws that seek to protect labor from exploitation and unsafe working conditions (pp. 156–157).

The organized sector of the Indian economy consists of all public sector
jobs and all jobs in the private sector that are non-agricultural and that
employ ten or more persons. These include jobs in factories, mines and
also, in the one exception to the "non-agricultural" category, on planta-
tions. While women's employment by the organized sector has increased
dramatically in numbers, moving from 1.37 million in 1962 to 2.14 million
in 1973, the overall size of the organized sector has increased correspond-
ingly, so that women in 1973 comprised 11 percent of all organized sector
employees, just as they had in 1962 (p. 184). The stability of women in the
organized sector is due to their increased employment by the *public* sector; the percentage of women in the organized sector employed privately
declined from 65 percent in 1962 to 53 percent in 1973 (p. 185).

In the organized sector of the economy, a number of laws exist that are
designed to protect workers in general and women in particular. *Towards
Equality* argues that the burden imposed on industry by such laws cannot
be held as the cause of the decline in the employment of women in private
industry, since the laws are for the most part simply ignored. Payments of
maternity benefits (guaranteed under the Maternity Benefits Act of 1961),
for example, are "negligible." Although required by law to erect separate
sanitary facilities for women and men, and to supply creches in establishments employing fifty or more women, "many employers still do not provide separate toilets or rest rooms. Where they do exist, the arrangements

are inadequate, without proper service and maintenance. Creches are very often only a room without proper arrangements" (p. 191). Nor can the requirement for equal pay for women and men workers be blamed for a cut back in women workers, since, it, too, is not honored.[19] Women's wages are held back by sex segregation in jobs: certain jobs are earmarked for women, and are paid low wages (p. 195). But even within the same category of job, including those that are completely unskilled, Committee members found stark wage differentials that convinced them that "prejudices, rather than skill or productivity differentials determine wage differences between the sexes" (p. 193).

Thus within the organized sector laws are, in practice, nearly useless for preserving the rights of women workers. For example, women agricultural workers in the organized sector could not hope to receive the same wages as men. In some states, agricultural labor does not fall under the Minimum Wages Act of 1948. In others, even when the state sets minimum wages, there is discrimination against women: the minimum wage for the same work as that performed by men was set lower by the state (p. 165). Another inequity arises when agricultural jobs traditionally performed by women (i.e. transplanting, threshing, harvesting) are assigned lower wages than those traditionally done by men (i.e. plowing) (p. 167).

In any case, government standards are usually irrelevant, since the minimum wage law is usually unimplemented.[20] India's National Commission on Labour, cited in *Towards Equality,* put the blame for this not on government but on "the poverty and illiteracy of agricultural labour, the casual nature of their employment and their ignorance of the law," all of which conditions, the CSWI point out, apply particularly to women (p. 165). Here, surely, is an implicit call for movement organizing. *Towards Equality* is even more explicit. No substantial improvement in the condition of female agricultural labor is possible, it argues, without "the organisation of labour . . . to improve the bargaining power of these workers, to prevent exploitation and low wages" (p. 169).

In closing its discussion of women's economic participation, the CSWI made a number of recommendations to the government. Most broadly, it urged the adoption of "a well defined policy to fulfill the Constitutional directives and Government's long term objective of [the] total involvement of women in national development." It made specific recommendations with regard to laws regulating maternity benefits, provision of creches, working time and the equalization of wages. It recommended more vocational training for women (pp. 230–233).

But, recognizing the limits of government activity, and in light of its understanding that women were critically hampered by lack of organization, the Committee also called on labor leaders to organize agricultural workers and others in the unorganized sector of the economy, and recommended that existing labor unions form women's wings to empower them within the unions, and to look after their interests as workers. As Chapters 4 and 7 show, this charge has been taken up by some existing unions, but most effectively by organizations whose raison d'etre is to empower women of the unorganized sector.

Women in Politics

The constitution of India provides for universal adult suffrage (Article 326) and Indian women have been active participants in every Indian election. Yet *Towards Equality* charges that women have had only limited impact on the political process. To be sure, women have been highly visible participants; they have served in both houses of Parliament and in the state legislatures, been governors and chief ministers of states, and served at the national level as ambassadors, cabinet members and, of course, in the case of Indira Gandhi, as prime minister.

However, despite the achievements of an elite few, women as a whole have been underrepresented throughout India in both appointed and elected positions; they have minimal power within the parties; and they participate in elections as candidates and as voters with less frequency than men (pp. 287–289).

None of these facts is unique to India. For example, the percentage of women in the Lok Sabha compares favorably with that in many western democracies. While in 1984, for example, the U.S. Congress and the British House of Commons each had fewer than five percent female members, female membership in the Lok Sabha has ranged from a low of 2.8 percent in the first, 1952 election, to a high of 8.5 percent in the 1984 election.[21] Still, *Towards Equality* criticized political parties for neglecting their duty to politically educate and mobilize women and for their failure to nominate more female candidates (p. 290).

As important as the level of female participation is the degree to which the interests of women are represented by the political process. According to CSWI findings, women are most concerned with problems that affect their daily lives. These include rising prices, the scarcity of essential commodities, hoarding and blackmarketing, unemployment, and poverty. However studies cited by *Towards Equality* show that many women believe electoral politics are ineffective in solving precisely these problems (p. 292); the Committee reported a growing disillusionment among women with the political process.

The presence of women in government had not alleviated this problem. The committee charged those women who had attained high positions in party hierarchies and political insitutions with being unrepresentative of women and unresponsive to women's interests. Women's entry into the political process, particularly at the state level, "depends more on their support within the party" than on support within the electorate. Female politicians aquire their positions "mainly through certain ascriptive channels" (p. 298); they are most often women of considerable economic means and members of prominent political families (p. 290). They have neither derived their strength from nor helped to develop a constituency concerned with problems that affect women specifically. As a result of this, and of their small numbers, the CSWI charged, they fail to voice the problems of women in the legislatures and in decision-making bodies within the parties.

Indeed, the authors of *Towards Equality* contended, the political elite as a whole had neglected the concerns of women, apparently believing them to have been solved by the constitutional and other protections adopted soon after independence. The report itself makes it clear that this is far from the case. Furthermore, "it is clear that despite certain legal and even institutional changes, the final legitimation for a successful reorganization of society lies in a revolution in norms and attitudes in the minds of the people" (p. 302). That change will occur, and the concern of political elites will be drawn to the problems of women, only when there is "an active women's movement" (p. 298). Again, here, the Committee explicitly called for movement activity to raise the consciousness of women and men, and ultimately to move the political system to be responsive to women's needs.

Health and Education

In deploring the health problems of Indian women, the CSWI blasted the government for the inadequacy of medical facilities and particularly of maternity services. (pp. 316–320). However, the Committee seemed to assign the greatest blame for women's poor health to a range of cultural norms that define women as "expendable assets" (p. 321). Women, for instance, serve food to the men of the family first, and then eat what is left over. "In families affected by poverty, this generally results in . . . greater malnutrition for the women" (p. 311). Frequent pregnancies and lactation contribute further to malnutrition (p. 314).

The high fertility rate is the product in part of the culturally-prescribed near universality of marriage coupled with an "insistence on the marriage of women in the early phase of their child bearing period." Large families, particularly those with several sons, are seen as a source of collective economic security. Each additional child, however, "is a burden on the mother, affecting her physical and mental health" (p. 311).

Women's undernourishment and high rate of fertility are coupled with cultural prescriptions for maintaining modesty, even secrecy, about physical matters: "they are unable to . . . discuss their health problems, if any, or even visit the doctor . . . particularly a male doctor" (p. 311). The overall impact is a "consistent neglect of female health" (p. 312).

Early proponents of the family planning movement in India had presented birth control as a way to improve the health and status of women, and the CSWI agreed that women must be released "from the bondage of . . . frequent childbirth." However, the Committee disagreed with the notion that greater use of birth control methods will raise women's status; instead, *Towards Equality* argues, it is the improved status of women that will prompt more use of birth control. Only with a "rise in the age of marriage, education, employment, better living conditions and greater general awareness" will women adopt family planning methods (pp. 321–322).

Thus education is seen as a critical tool for the improved status of women. Article 45 of the constitution directs the State to "endeavor to provide . . . free and compulsory education for all children until they complete the age of 14 years." When *Towards Equality* was written, this goal was still far from being met, particularly for girls. In 1968–69, only 57% of all girls aged 6–11 and 18% of all girls aged 11–14 were enrolled in school (compared to 93% and 45% for boys of these age groups). These aggregate statistics are somewhat misleading, since rural girls are much less likely to have access to educational resources. Secondary education is largely limited to girls from the upper and middle classes, mostly from urban areas. This is even more true of higher education (p. 240–241).

The Committee, in urging expanded literacy for women to achieve improvements in their health, greater employment opportunities, and the ability to exercise their legal rights, did not stop there. The CSWI urged too that the content of the curriculum be altered to challenge existing sex roles and cultural biases concerning women. Blasting the schools for reflecting and strenghtening "the traditional prejudices of inequality," *Towards Equality* calls for a revolution in the values taught in schools. "If education is to promote equality for women, it must make a deliberate, planned and sustained effort so that the new value of equality of the sexes can replace the traditional value system of inequality" (p. 282).

Raised Expectations

The Committee on the Status of Women in India raised expectations that government must act to improve women's lives, even as the perception grew that government's ability to do so was at best stagnant. The gap between the raised expectations and the capacity to meet them helped prompt the mobilization of concerned individuals to take up movement activity.[22]

Towards Equality was itself to become a major text of the emerging transformation in consciousness among educated women. Its compelling descriptions of the vast and disabling range of problems facing Indian women heightened demands for their amelioration, while its compilation of facts has provided heavy statistical ammunition, particularly for those who have chosen to work in the "rights" segment of the movement.

At the same time, *Towards Equality* marks a recognition that women's status cannot be improved through government action alone. The report consistently calls for changes in consciousness and in social structures beyond the reach of government. In doing so *Towards Equality* implicitly, and sometimes explicitly, recognizes that movement activity is essential, that the electoral process cannot perform the functions of personal and community empowerment and of ideological transformation as well as movement activity can.

The First Agitations for Women's Rights

It was the government's failure to protect women from violence that came to the forefront as the first target of the new post-emergency women's movement. Two issues, each of which will be discussed more extensively in Chapter 5, proved particularly mobilizing: dowry deaths and the rape of women in police custody.

Indira Gandhi's emergency seems, inadvertently, to have contributed to developing outrage about "dowry murder," in which a husband and/or his family threaten, beat, or even finally murder a (usually young) wife in the attempt to extort money from her parents in the years soon after marriage. During the emergency, Sanjay Gandhi issued his own five-point program designed to supplement his mother's twenty points. Among his dictums was "Never accept dowries as a condition for marriage." One prominent scholar and activist suggests that the attention thus focused on dowry may in part be responsible for the "completely unexpected and spontaneous explosion of women's anger against dowry murders" that occured in the late seventies.[23] Also contributing was the fact that, during the emergency, the press was stifled from writing about government abuses of civil liberties, even as the need to address human rights issues was never felt more keenly. As a result, dowry deaths became a topic of press coverage; human rights abuses could be covered if they were not explicitly concerned with government. Finally, of course, the emergency brought forth a new militancy over human rights issues generally, coupled with a deep skepticism over how much the government and the police could be relied upon to protect rights.

With the close of the emergency, a women's group closely associated with the new Janata government, Mahila Dakshata Samiti, began to systematically investigate cases of the "accidental" deaths—often by burning in alleged kitchen accidents—of young brides. Early in 1978, MDS published a report in which it alleged that many of these deaths, labeled suicide or accident by the police, were in fact murders; the report, in turn, was widely publicized in the national press.[24] Protests began, and press coverage of these protests generated still more protests. In 1979, MDS demanded the strengthening of the 1961 Prohibition of Dowry Act.[25]

In May of 1979, newspapers carried, not the usual short police blotter report of a woman's accidental death or suicide, but rather a full report of the burning of Tarvinder Kaur by her mother-in-law and sister-in-law. As she lay dying, Kaur made a statement to the police alleging that while she was watching television her in-laws doused her with kerosene and set her afire; the police nonetheless recorded the case as suicide. The papers interviewed her father, who said that she had been under constant presure from her husband's family to get more dowry from her parents so that her husband could expand his business.[26] As a result of this case, individual women and some who belonged to civil liberties and political groups joined together briefly under the name Stri Sangharsh (women's struggle). Although this group quickly splintered, the meeting seemed to provide the catalyst for what became the first widely publicized demonstration against "dowry murder" on June 1, 1979. The demonstrators, armed with leaflets proclaiming "Women are not for Burning," marched through New Delhi neighborhoods to the house where Kaur's murder took place, and there demanded the punishment of the murderers, and an end to dowry and to dowry deaths.[27] Other demonstrations followed: outside the homes of other suspected murderers; outside the police stations whose officials consistently failed to act; in other cities and towns throughout India.[28]

Agitational activity, including the creation of new autonomous women's organizations and newly coordinated efforts by a number of established women's groups, grew markedly in 1979 and 1980. Prompting the expanded mobilization was a Supreme Court decision in September 1979 in what became known as the Mathura rape case.[29] This decision was so egregiously contemptuous of women's rights that it sparked enormous reaction.

Mathura was a girl judged to be 14 to 16 years old when the incident occurred in 1972.[30] An orphan who lived with her brother, Mathura was a dalit (untouchable) and, like her brother, a laborer. She had met a young man, Ashok, and they planned to marry. Unfortunately, her brother did not approve of the match and on March 26, 1972, he went to the local police station and lodged a complaint that his sister, a minor, was being kidnapped by Ashok and his family (specifically Ashok's uncle and aunt). At nine o'clock that night, these three and Mathura were brought to the police station, and statements were taken from Mathura and Ashok. At that point, now ten-thirty p.m., the entire party—Mathura, her brother, Ashok, his aunt and uncle—were told to go. As they were leaving, however, one of the two policemen present caught hold of Mathura's hand and told her to remain. Soon after the others left, the lights in the station were turned off and the doors bolted.

Mathura stated in court that the policeman then took her into a latrine in the back of the police station. She claimed that she attempted to cry out, but was prevented from doing so. In the dark latrine, the officer loosened her underwear, turned on a flashlight, and stared at her genitals. He forced her first onto a cot and then onto the ground, where he raped her. The second policemen, who until then had been sitting nearby, then approached Mathura, fondled her, and attempted to rape her; his intoxication prevented him from penetrating her.

While these events took place inside the station, Mathura's brother and friends remained outside, becoming more and more anxious. They went to the rear of the building to see if they could gain entry, but the station was locked and completely dark. They called out her name but received no response. A crowd began to gather. Finally, one of the policemen appeared, and when Ashok's aunt asked where Mathura was, the officer replied that she had already left. Soon after he had gone, Mathura came out of the station. In the presence of the assembled group, she told her brother and friends that she had been raped.

The aunt took Mathura immediately to a local doctor, who did not examine her, but who advised them to file a complaint with the police department. The head constable, who had left the station earlier in the evening, was summoned from his home to find an angry crowd threatening to beat up the police officers Mathura had named and to burn down . the police station; under pressure, he accepted a statement from Mathura. The next day, approximately twenty hours after the incident, she was examined by a physician, who discovered no physical injuries, and no semen in her vagina; semen was however detected on her clothes, and on the clothes of the first police officer. The doctor also found that Mathura had had sexual intercourse in the past.

The police officer's defense at the trial was that since Mathura showed no physical injury it was apparent that the sexual intercourse was not forced but had occurred with her consent. In finding the policemen innocent, the Sessions Judge went one step further than even the defense had suggested; he hypothesized that the existence of semen on both the officer's and Mathura's clothes was not evidence that any intercourse had taken place between them; each, he said, could have had intercourse with other persons. After all, the doctor's report led him to conclude that Mathura was "habituated to sexual intercourse." However, if there *had* been intercourse between them, he saw no reason to think it was without her consent: "Mathura," he wrote, "could not very well have admitted that of her own free will she had surrendered her body to a police constable." He declared that she had made up a story of rape in order to "sound virtuous" before her lover Ashok.

On appeal, the High Court reversed the finding, and sentenced the first officer to five years' imprisonment and the second officer to one year. The Court was moved by a number of factors. The physical evidence of the semen on both the clothing of Mathura and the first officer was seen as strong circumstantial evidence. As important to the Court were a number of social factors that made the policeman's defense improbable: the court found it highly unlikely that, as the officers were strangers to her, Mathura would "make any overtures or invite the accused to satisfy her sexual desires." Nor did the court believe that she could have successfully resisted her assailants. The High Court concluded:

> On the other hand, taking advantage of the fact that Mathura was involved in a complaint filed by her brother and that she was alone in the police station at the dead hour of night, it is more probable that the initiative must have come from the accused and that [the] victim Mathura must not have been a willing party to the act of sexual intercourse. Her subsequent conduct in making a statement immediately, not only to her relatives but also to the members of the crowd, leave no manner of doubt that she was subjected to a forcible sexual intercourse.

In 1979, the Supreme Court of India reversed the decision of the High Court, and upheld the Sessions Court's verdict of innocent. The opinion writen by Justice Koshal found that as Mathura showed no evidence of injury, she must have consented. The Supreme Court also came up with a new twist: it is unlikely, the judges reasoned, that Mathura would have tried to shout and resist the policeman's advances, as she claimed, since when Mathura, her brother and her friends were leaving the police station, and the officer grabbed hold of her wrist and ordered her to stay, she did not even resist! Indeed, the Supreme Court hypothesized, Mathura was a completely willing participant:

> It would be preposterous to suggest that although she was in the company of her brother, she would be so overawed by the fact of the appellant being persons in authority and that she was in a police station that she would make no attempt to resist . . . Her conduct in meekly following [the officer] makes us feel that her consent [was not] passive submission.

Apparently, the justices of the Supreme Court found no reason to doubt that a *nice* girl—impoverished, powerless and frightened though she might be—would have resisted the orders of two armed police officers.[31]

Not everyone agreed. In September 1979, four highly regarded university law professors, two of them men, two women,[32] wrote "An Open Letter to the Chief Justice of India," protesting the Supreme Court decision. The tone of the letter is one of both outrage and shock at the absurdity of the Supreme Court's logic.

Your Lordship, this is an extraordinary decision sacrificing human rights of women under the law and the constitution. . . . Your Lordship, does the Indian Supreme Court expect a young girl, 14–16 years old, when trapped by two policemen inside the police station, to successfully raise alarm for help? Does it seriously expect the girl, a labourer, to put up such stiff resistance against well-built policemen so as to have substantial marks of physical injury? . . .

The fact remains that she was asked to remain in the police station even after her statement was recorded and her friends and relations were asked to leave. Why? . . .

Does the Court believe that Mathura was so flirtatious that even when her brother, her employer, and her lover were waiting outside the police station that she should not let go the opportunity of having fun with two policemen and that too in the area adjoining a police station latrine? . . .

One suspects that the court gathered an impression from Mathura's liaison with her lover that she was a person of easy virtue. Is the taboo against pre-marital sex so strong as to provide a licence to Indian police to rape young girls? . . .

The Court gives no consideration whatsoever to the socio-economic status, the lack of knowledge of legal rights, the age of victim, lack of access to legal services, and the fear . . . which haunts the poor and the exploited in Indian Police Stations. May we respectfully suggest that yourself [*sic*] and your distinguished colleagues visit incognito, wearing the visage of poverty, some police stations in villages adjoining Delhi?

The professors decried at length the complete reliance of the Supreme Court on the third paragraph of Section 275 of the Indian Penal Code, to the apparent exclusion of the second paragraph. The Penal Code defines rape as occurring when a man has sexual intercourse with a woman

First, Against her will. [or]
Secondly, Without her consent. [or]
Thirdly, With her consent when her consent has been obtained by putting her or any person in whom she is interested in fear of death or of hurt.

The Supreme Court, said the four lawyers, did not find evidence that Mathura was fearful of death or hurt; but, they said, what of the second criterion for rape, intercourse without her consent? The professors argued that the facts of the case showed that Mathura had *submitted*, not that she had *consented*.[33]

The lawyers were also critical of the Court for ignoring Section 160 of the Criminal Procedure Code, which declares that police officers may not interview a boy under the age of 15 or a female of any age in any place other than his or her residence; this despite the fact that as recently as 1978, Supreme Court Justice Krishna Iyer had specifically condemned the practice of calling women to police stations as a gross violation of section 160(1) of the Criminal Procedure Code.[34] Yet this issue was never addressed by the Court in the Mathura case.

All in all "An Open Letter to the Chief Justice of India" exposed the astonishing limits of the Court's willingness to extend human rights protections to women, the impossible standards of evidence that were required in rape cases, and the unfairness of the expectations placed on the poor, illiterate and powerless to move the courts on their own behalf.

"An Open Letter to the Chief Justice of India" was widely disseminated, and its outrage proved infectious. Other rape cases and cases of police abuse of women were also publicized and protested, including the case of Maya Tyagi, who was dragged through the streets of her town of Bhaghpat, U.P. in torn clothes to the police station for questioning, and that of Rameeza Bee, who was gang raped by policemen in Hyderabad; when her husband protested, the police beat him to death.[35]

The Rameeza Bee rape had taken place in April 1978, and was followed by angry riots in which crowds attacked Hyderabad police stations; twenty were killed by police gunfire. These events were widely reported in the all-India press, but, perhaps because of the four lawyers' public protest, and perhaps because of the accumulating anger, it was the Mathura case that generated the widest protests and the most interest at the level of government. But, in 1981, when the Sessions Court found the officers in the Rameeza Bee case innocent, several women's organizations—the Indian Federation of Women Lawyers, Vimochna, and Stree Shakti Sanghatana of Hyderabad—filed an appeal; for the first time, women's organizations were granted the *locus standi* to move a court in a rape trial. This signified the Supreme Court's agreement that rape was not a private matter, but a matter in the public interest; in 1978 the courts had not allowed women's organizations to file appeals in the Mathura case.[36] As a result of pressure from women's organization, the government of Andhra Pradesh also filed an appeal.[37] Unfortunately, however, the High Court upheld the acquittal of the eight police officers who were accused of the rape, holding that although Rameeza Bee had been raped beyond reasonable doubt, there was no evidence to indicate which of the officers had committed the rape.

In the aftermath of the Mathura case, demonstrations took place in cities and towns throughout India; International Women's Day, March 8, 1980, saw demonstrations in Bombay, Madras, Kanpur, Pune, Sangli District of Maharashtra, Ahmedabad, Hyderabad, Bangalore, and Delhi.[38] Lawyer's groups and civil liberties groups became involved; the People's Union for Democratic Rights published a pamphlet entitled *Rape, Society and the State* and an independent lawyers' collective published *The Rape Bill*.[39] Lawyers volunteered their services to women's organizations,[40] and, as will be discussed in Chapter 5, demands were presented to the government for the revision of the rape law.

Mobilized by anger over Mathura, new autonomous women's groups emerged or became mobilized. Bombay saw the creation of the Forum Against Rape (which later, indicating its broadening agenda, changed its name to Forum Against the Oppression of Women.) In New Delhi, women who had come together first in the group Stri Sangharsh to protest dowry deaths began a consciousness raising group; inspired further by the Mathura case and demonstrations surrounding it, this group evolved into Saheli, an organization dedicated to assisting battered women.[41] In Maharashtra, the Stri Mukti Andolan Sampark Samiti, a coordinating group of about thirty women's organizations (some connected to political parties, some autonomous) that first came together in 1979, collected ten thousand signatures on a petition calling for a review of the Mathura rape judgement.[42] The Balatkar Viodhi Manch (Platform Against Rape) came into being in the Vidarbha region of Maharashtra.[43] According to its founder, Seema Sakhare, the Mathura judgment "moved me to [travel] throughout Vidarbha and to make the womenfolk become aware of rape and rape law and social injustice. . . . That was the beginning of our Action group."[44] Existing women's organizations, too, began to focus their attention on issues of violence against women.

By the end of the 1970s, and with the dawn of the 1980s, a women's movement determined to protect and enhance women's rights had emerged onto the Indian scene. That much needed to be done to safeguard women's rights had become apparent; the anger with government's failure to protect women grew. The next chapter explores the resources that made it possible to transform these sentiments into movement activity, and the structural forms that the movement took.

Notes

1. Gail Omvedt, *We Will Smash This Prison* (London: Zed Press, 1980), p. 78.

2. Although it is not a formal arm of the Socialist Party, its leadership was nonetheless closely tied to the party. S. N. Tawale, "Profiles of Women in Maharashtra," in *Symbols of Power: Studies on the Political Status of Women in India*, ed. Vina Mazumdar (Bombay: Allied Publishers, 1979), p. 252.

3. NFIW, *For Equality: For a Just Social Order* (New Delhi: NFIW, 1984), p. 31.

4. Omvedt, pp. 78–81; and Nandita Gandhi, "When the Rolling Pins Hit the Streets." Unpublished paper prepared for the National Conference on Women's Studies, Chandigarh, October 1986, p. 7.

5. Nandita Gandhi, p. 8; and Jana Everett, "Approaches to the 'Woman Question' in India: From Maternalism to Mobilization," *Women's Studies International Quarterly* 4:2 (1981), p. 171.

6. Vina Mazumdar, "The Role of Research in Women's Development: A Case Study of the ICSSR Programme of Women's Studies," *Samya Shakti* 1:1 (1983), p. 24. Mazumdar was the Member-Secretary of the Committee.

7. Government of India, Department of Social Welfare, Ministry of Education and Social Welfare, *Towards Equality: Report of the Committee on the Status of Women in India* (New Delhi: 1974). Although dated December 1974, the report was in fact submitted in January 1975 and became available in May. Interview, Vina Mazumdar, 23 June 1986, New Delhi.

8. Jo Freeman, *The Politics of Women's Liberation* (New York: David McKay, 1975), p. 52.

9. Copies of government documents would ordinarily not be seen by the average reader. However, the Indian Council of Social Science Research brought out an inexpensive paperback summary of the report, making it much more accessible. *Status of Women in India: A Synopsis of the Report of the National Committee* (Bombay: Allied, 1975).

10. Vina Mazumdar reports that, during the Emergency, three women activists who were to become MPs in 1977—Mrinal Gore and Pramilla Dandavate of Janata and Ahilya Rangnekar of CPM—read and discussed *Towards Equality* while sharing a jail cell. They told her later that they had not known the situation for women was so appallingly bad. Interview, 23 June 1986.

11. For example, for every thousand men, there are 1054 women in the U.S. and 1037 in Japan; Indonesia has 1018 women for every thousand men, while the Philippines has 1010. *Towards Equality,* p. 15.

12. Government of India, Ministry of Social and Women's Welfare, *Women in India: Country Paper* (New Delhi 1985), p. 29. In a 1986 interview, C.P. Sujaya, the Joint Secretary of the Department of Women and Child Development revealed that, especially among poorer groups, the male/female ratio remains "quite startling." She cited Kaira District in Gujarat, an area where women have recently become active in the much-touted "dairy revolution," which offers them better economic opportunities. However, she said, in Kaira, a "model" district, there are only 878 women to every 1000 men. New Delhi, 23 June 1986.

13. Also known as the Sarda Act, the Child Marriage Restraint Act was passed in 1929 with a minimum age of marriage for males of 18 years and for females of 14 years; the latter was amended in 1949 to 15 years. *Towards Equality,* p. 111. In 1978, the Act was further amended, raising the minimum legal age at marriage to 18 years for girls and 21 for boys. *Women in India: Country Paper,* p. 14.

14. "Dowry Main Cause of Early Marriage in UP," *Indian Express* 9 May 1986.

15. *Women in India: Country Paper,* pp. 16, 43.

16. For *Towards Equality*'s assessment of Christian, Jain, Budddhist, Sikh, Zoroastrian, and Tribal religious custom and law, see pp. 47–50.

17. Interview, Maitraeyi Krishna Raj, Assoc. Director, SNDT Research Unit on Women's Studies, Bombay, 9 July 1986.

18. Dowry is also common among non-Hindu communities, including a number of Muslim and Christian communities. *Towards Equality*, pp. 71–75.

19. C.P. Sujaya acknowledges that the 1976 Equal Remuneration Act remains "on paper only." Interview, New Delhi, 23 June 1986.

20. Interview, C.P. Sujaya, 23 June 1986.

21. See Mary Fainsod Katzenstein, "Towards Equality," *Asian Survey* May 1978, p. 478 and Neerja Chowdhury, "The Khadi Image Goes," *The Statesman* 19 Jan. 1985.

22. This idea of relative deprivation is discussed by Ted Gurr in *Why Men Rebel* (Princeton: Princeton Univ. Press, 1970).

23. Vina Mazumdar, "The Role of Research in Women's Development: A Case Study of the ICSSR Programme of Women's Studies," *Samya Shakti* 1:1 (1983), p. 34.

24. Madhu Kishwar, "Introduction," in *In Search of Answers*, ed. Madhu Kishwar (London: Zed Press, 1984), p. 31.

25. Mahila Dakshata Samiti, *Report of Seminar on Amendment to the Prohibition of Dowry Act and Protection of Abandoned Women and Children* (New Delhi: MDS, 1979).

26. Manini Das, "Women Against Dowry," in *In Search of Answers*, ed. Madhu Kishwar, p. 222.

27. Reported in Das, pp. 222–223. See also Urvashi Butalia, "Indian Women Fight On." *Inside Asia*, no. 1 (1984), p. 26.

28. See, for example, *Manushi* no. 4 (1979-80), pp. 35–36 and *Manushi*, no. 5 (1980), pp. 31–34.

29. Officially, *Turkaram vs. the State of Maharashtra* (1979) 2 S.C.C. 143.

30. This account is drawn from several sources, all of which derived the facts of the case from the evidence that was presented in turn to the Sessions Court, the Bombay High Court (Nagpur Bench) and the Supreme Court. See Upendra Baxi, Vasudha Dhagamwar, Raghuntah Kelkar and Lotika Sarkar, "An Open Letter to the Chief Justice of India." Full text available in the Center for Education and Documentation, Bombay. Much of the text is also cited in the following two sources: "Rape: The Victim is the Accused," *Manushi*, no. 4 (1979-80), pp. 42–46; and Nandita Haksar, *Demystification of Law for Women* (New Delhi: Lancer, 1986), pp. 70–77.

31. The Justices also exhibited a double standard in which they expected Mathura to resist the officer's order to remain, but did not apparently expect her brother or lover to protest.

32. Upendra Baxi, Raghunath Kelkar and Lotika Sarkar were professors at the University of Delhi; Vasudha Dhagamwar taught at the University of Pune.

33. The rest of Section 275 defines intercourse as rape: "Fourthly, With her consent, when the man knows that he is not her husband, and that her consent is given because she believes that he is another man to whom she is . . . married. Fifthly, With her consent [but she is unsound of mind or intoxicated]. Sixthly, With or without her consent, when she is under sixteen years of age." Oddly, neither the Justices nor the four lawyers raised the issue of Mathura's age, which may well have been under sixteen.

34. *Nandini Satpathy* (1978 2 S.C.C. 424).

35. Sunil Sethi, "Controversial Code," *India Today* 31 Dec. 1983, pp. 134–135. Re: Rameeza Bee, see also Vimla Farooqui, "A Woman Destroyed," *Manushi* no.1 (1979), pp. 21–22; "Reports" *Manushi, no.* 8 (1981), p. 16; and "Rameeza Bee—Justice Denied," *Sangharsh* n.d., p. 2. (Sangharsh is a newspaper published by the Bangalore women's organization Vimochna.)

36. "More About Rameeza," *Sangharsh* n.d., p. 8.

37. "After The Protest," *Manushi* no. 19 (1983), pp. 20–21.

38. "We Will Not Live in Fear Anymore," *Manushi* no. 5 (1980), pp. 31–34; and *Saheli: The First Four Years* (New Delhi: Saheli, 1985), p. 3.

39. Vibhuti Patel, "Women's Liberation in India," *New Left Review* no. 163 (1985), p. 80.

40. "Other Women, Other Places," *CWDS Bulletin* 2:1 (1984), p. 8.

41. *Saheli: The First Four Years*, p. 3.

42. "Morcha to Kala Ghoda," *Sunday Observer* 23 March 1986, pp. 22–23.

43. "A Haven for Rape Victims," *Free Press Journal* 14 April 1984.

44. Seema Sakhare, "Our Fight for Socio-Legal Justice for Women in India." Paper read at the National Seminar on "A Decade of Women's Movement in India: A Review of Achievements and Issues." SNDT Univeristy, Bombay, 8–10 January 1985.

4

A Movement Emerges:
Resources and Structures

Chapter 2 explained what structural dislocations provided the opportunity for the development of movement activism, while Chapter 3 described ideological developments that helped spur activism on behalf of women, particularly the emergence of a keen recognition of the degraded status of women and of the state's complicity in maintaining it. These factors help explain *why* the movement emerged. This chapter turns to the question of *how* the movement emerged.

Resource mobilization theory points to three factors that are critical to movement emergence: leaders, communication networks, and existing organizational structures that give potential activists prior connections to others.[1] These resources do prove important in the case of Indian women, but as the theory's points of reference are exclusively western movements, it misses some other factors that emerge as equally critical to the development of women's movements in less developed countries. In countries where literacy is low and poverty is high an educated middle class can provide a readily politicized constituency, scholarly support and advocacy, and leadership; in India's women's movement educated women have been both a vital "conscience constituency,"[2] concerned with the future of poor women, and a group acting in its own self-interest. Additionally, what may be thought of as "international feminism"—both normative ideology and the influence of feminist ideas on economic development practices sponsored by governments, the United Nations and a range of non-governmental organizations—has provided a range of resources.

In investigating what resources have made the women's movement possible, it is again helpful to think in terms of the "rights" and "empowerment" tendencies within the movement, for while some of the inspiration and resources have been shared, others are not. The movement, after all, is, really a series of separate organizations, each with different emphases, which work cooperatively only on an *ad hoc* basis.

In addition to expanding upon resource mobilization theory, this investigation will demonstrate two propositions. First, the diversity in resources available to the different movement organizations, and their different organizational roots, portend the diversity in how they come to be structured, and what are their goals. Second, just as the analysis of why the movement emerged illustrated how closely tied the women's movement is to other Indian movement activity, so too this discussion of how the movement has developed will show that the women's movement is not and never has been isolated from other movements. It finds particular linkages to the international feminist movement, to other non-party movements in India, and also, in some cases, to Indian parties of the left.

Resources of the Rights Wing

Leadership and Preexisting Organizational Structures

Preexisting groups can be critical resources for generating a new movement. An organized group constitutes a set of individuals who are already predisposed to participation in public issues and who share a common set of values. Leaders are already in place; mobilization is facilitated by the existing structures of authority and communications.[3] In the mobilization of the Indian women's movement following the Emergency, new or newly revitalized movement organizations concerned with rights drew on several different types of existing political groups: political parties of the left, social service agencies and independent socialist organizations.[4]

Political Parties. Although much of the women's movement is composed of "autonomous" groups with no formal tie to any other organization or party, the largest national opposition political parties have women's organizations affiliated with them (some loosely, some closely); these must also be counted as important components of the women's movement. Resources provided by political parties made the emergence of these groups possible; the origins of these resources and the continuing party affiliation of the groups greatly influence their organizational structures and political strategies.

The largest organizations have already been mentioned: the National Federation of Indian Women (which has ties to the CPI); the All India Democratic Women's Association (affiliated with the CPM); the All India Coordination Committee of Working Women (which is the women's wing of CITU, Centre of Indian Trade Unions, also of the CPM); and Mahila Dakshata Samiti, an independent organization with close ties to the Janata party.

NFIW, formed in 1954, is the oldest of these. A number of its founders had been members of the All India Women's Conference, the largest women's organization in the struggle for independence. At that time, AIWC included members with widely diverse ideological predisposi- tions. After independence, as AIWC retained close ties with the Congress government, communist women broke with the organization, which they accused of being "pro-establishment" and "elitist."[5]

While not officially a part of the Communist Party of India, NFIW closely toes the CPI ideological and tactical line. For example, NFIW with- drew its support from the Anti-Price-Rise movement of the early 1970s and backed Indira Gandhi's declaration of emergency when the CPI did.[6] Thus, while technically an independent organization, it is with good rea- son that other activists regard NFIW as the women's arm of the CPI.

NFIW is a hierarchically structured organization whose stated goal is to struggle on behalf of poor and working class women. The means of do- ing so have been twofold. On the one hand are fairly traditional social service projects organized by middle-class women and delivered as serv- ices to poor women. These have included literacy classes, sewing classes, and some development of employment-generating projects.

The other means of struggle is "agitation" to influence government de- cision making. The General Secretary of NFIW speaks of the organization as a "pressure group" that "pushes" government and makes "demands." "We think you have to go to the streets."[7] The effort to enroll large num- bers of women in affiliated local organizations is in substantial part to build pressure on government to provide education, technical training, equal pay, and jobs for women, to prohibit dowry and to institute land re- form. Thus, although the organization prides itself on its militancy, its goal is to influence the creation and implementation of law.

NFIW was already functioning when the women's movement had its awakening in the late 1970s; since then, it has joined with other organiza- tions in broad coalitions around a number of issues specific to women, in- cluding anti-rape and anti-dowry activities. NFIW states categorically, however, that it is "not a feminist organization," by which it means that it rejects "the idea that women's struggle is against men."[8] The group ar- gues instead that women's rights are wholly dependent on socialism. In keeping with CPI ideology, it expects a socialist transformation to take place through parliamentary politics. Thus, its mobilization of poor women is an attempt not only to pass specific laws but to build an elec- toral force.

The two organizations affiliated with the CPM resulted from the raised consciousness about women sparked by the emerging women's move- ment. Calls for the organizing of women were heard at the founding con- vention of CITU in 1970, but not until the late 1970s did pressure by women within CITU and the CPM finally bring the All India Coordinating Committee of Working Women (AICCWW) and the All India Democratic Women's Association (AIDWA) into being;[9] obviously, without the CPM and CITU, they never would have existed.

AICCWW is the women's wing of CITU; its focus is to improve trade union policy regarding women and to bring more women into the trade union movement, particularly, of course, into CITU; in this they have enjoyed some success.[10] AIDWA is a membership organization[11] whose local affiliates organize around a range of problems at the local level including dowry and violence against women, price rises, and working women's grievances. The organizing of women is often facilitated through contacts made with their husbands through other CPM affiliates: CITU or the Democratic Youth Federation of India.[12] The founding of these women's organizations has prompted an expanded role for women in the main channels of the CPM, with the number of women in high levels of the CPM increasing.[13]

Like NFIW vis-à-vis the CPI, local AIDWA affiliates insist that they are not formally connected to the CPM.[14] The officers of the Delhi Janvadi Mahila Samiti (the Democratic Women's Association), for example, acknowledge that many of them are also members of CPM, but point out that most of the mass membership is not. They are insistent that the Janvadi Mahila Samiti is affiliated with AIDWA but not with the CPM. However, Vimal Ranadive, AIDWA's Vice-President, is also the General Secretary of AICCWW, which *is* a part of CPM's union, CITU. AIDWA activities are regularly reported upon in the AICCWW magazine, *The Voice of the Working Woman;* AIDWA conferences are presided over by CITU officials;[15] and again, as with the NFIW, local AIDWA groups tend to adhere to the parent party's political line. This coyness about their political affiliations, and thus about their long-term objectives of building up parties, earn women's groups associated with political parties the opprobrium of independent feminist groups. One activist in autonomous organizations describes the left political parties as "manipulative" and notes that autonomous women's groups remain "implacably opposed" to their approach.[16]

NFIW and AICCWW often work closely together, and share a similar analysis of the causes of women's oppression and of the need for "militant" agitation.[17] Like NFIW, the CPM affiliates believe that socialism in India will prove sufficient to improve women's lives, and disavow any connection to a *feminist* movement.

Nonetheless in a number of instances, NFIW, AIDWA and AICCWW have formed coalitions with autonomous groups around particular gender interests including rape, dowry, and dowry death. The coalitions form to mount a particular demonstration or send a delegation to speak to government leaders, and afterward they are dissolved. Thus, despite the differences that separate them from the autonomous women's organizations, the organizations affiliated with the left parties are very much a part of the women's movement.

Although it appears that both AICCWW and AIDWA seek to build the CPM, the daily activities of local AIDWA-affiliated groups are often not dissimilar to those of some of the autonomous organizations. Free legal clinics providing advice about dowry and family violence; anti-dowry demonstrations, including some held outside homes where brides have been killed or allegedly committed suicide; public rallies to influence government policies regarding maintenance for divorced Muslim women; and public denunciations of the police handling of cases of violence against women are all part of AIDWA's repertoire.[18]

The roots of the Mahila Dakshata Samiti (Women's Vigilance Committee) are in the Anti-Price-Rise movement in the early 1970s; it enjoys a close relationship to the Janata party. Here again, it was the prior existence of political groups, and the experience and leadership of some prominent women, that helped this organization to take shape just after the ending of the emergency.

As discussed in Chapter 3, Socialist women began the Anti-Price-Rise movement in coalition with women from the two communist parties. In addition to the experience gained in that movement, Pramila Dandavate, the President of MDS, credits J.P. Narayan's call for Total Revolution and the report of the Committee on the Status of Women in India with widening the participants' horizons.[19] Then there was the emergency itself; the Socialist leaders of the Anti-Price-Rise movement were among those imprisoned. Upon their release, and Indira Gandhi's announcement of the upcoming election, the Socialists became active in the new Janata party. At the same time, in 1977, the Socialist Anti-Price-Rise organization that had existed in New Delhi prior to the Emergency was transformed into the Mahila Dakshata Samiti, a name suggested by J.P. Narayan.[20] In keeping with its roots in the Anti-Price-Rise movement, the group adopted as its symbol a woman's fist holding a rolling pin. MDS's first president was Dr. Sushila Nayyar, an elder stateswoman of the Janata Party, who had once been Mahatma Gandhi's personal physician. Mrinal Gore and Pramila Dandavate were among the founding members; both had been on the Joint Action Committee of the Anti-Price-Rise Movement and both became Janata MPs.

As an organization in sympathy with the Janata party, Mahila Dakshata Samiti is comfortable with parliamentary politics. In contrast to the autonomous women's groups which have little faith in these institutions, MDS believes that lobbying within the parties and the legislatures for new laws and better implementation of the law will be fruitful. Also needed is agitation; according to Pramila Dandavate, even sympathetic legislators may be unable to push for women's causes without the assistance of pressure from the outside. Indeed, she insists that despite the overlap in membership of prominent Janata women, MDS is *not* an arm of Janata, but instead is an independent pressure group that lobbies not only the Congress leadership, but also Janata leadership.[21] While this may be true in terms of their formal organizational affiliation, the overlapping membership, the shared political outlook, and the shared circumstances of their births mark MDS and Janata as closely related.

MDS has concentrated its educational and agitational efforts into three organizational wings: consumer protection; actions opposing dowry and working for the protection of women's rights; and a less well-defined concern with the general status of women. In the areas of consumer protection and dowry, MDS has sponsored a number of symposia that have attracted important political leaders, jurists, scholars and journalists. In 1977-78, MDS initiated the first study of dowry deaths; its 1978 report, widely publicized by the press, revealed that many of the deaths routinely recorded by the police and reported in the press as suicides were, in fact, murders. Subsequent to this, the press began more and more to discuss the phenomenon that has become known as "dowry death."[22] It was MDS that organized the first demonstration against dowry death, in October 1978, and it initiated the creation of the Dahej Virodhi Chetana Manch, the wide coalition of women's groups opposed to dowry that marched on the Lok Sabha in August 1982.[23] The organization has also lobbied parliament to create family courts and preserve maintenance for Muslim women upon divorce.

Social Service Agencies. Two of the oldest women's groups in India, the Young Women's Christian Association and the All India Women's Conference became participants in the new women's movement of the 1970s and '80s. Here it was not the case of the resources of one organization helping to spawn another, but rather, in the case of the YWCA, a growing radicalization of an existing organization allowing for the use of its resources for new purposes. AIWC, too, while retaining a more staid outlook, has also been caught up in the tide of contemporary movement issues, and has lent its resources to some causes.

The YWCA was founded in England in 1855; twenty years later, India's YWCA was founded by British "mem sahibs" who started sewing classes and Bible study groups. In the first decade of the twentieth century, secretarial classes were introduced for single women; married women could choose from among classes in home decorating, cooking and sewing. The concern with decent housing for working women that had prompted the founding of the YWCA in England was duplicated in India; the Bombay YWCA built its first hostel in 1887.

Today, the YWCA has 67 centers all over India; while classes and service projects continue, there have also been enormous changes since the early 1980s.[24] The National Secretary of the YWCA, Ivy Khan, explains that the YWCA is moving away from a welfare orientation:

> Historically, the YWCA was one group of people doing something for another group of people. But times and concepts change. We now think you can't do things for other people; they must take it because it's their right. You have to make them understand that it's their right to claim what's theirs: that's our goal.[25]

With this shift in philosophy, actions have also changed. The YWCA pushes for improved legislation; the leadership has worked for anti-dowry laws, demonstrated against the Muslim Women's Bill (which will be discussed in chapter 6), lobbied successfully for reforms in Christian inheritance laws, and drafted a memorandum to the government opposing the use of amniocentesis for sex determination. The Y has helped to organize demonstrations and has participated in demonstrations organized by other groups.

The tradition of providing housing for working women has remained and, at least in some branches, become radicalized: the Bombay YWCA now provides housing for low-income women and women "in distress"—battered women and others leaving their husbands. The Bombay Y also works in conjunction with autonomous groups, including the Women's Centre, to provide counseling and support for these women.[26] While the autonomous organizations may have helped to radicalize members of the YWCA, the Y provides resources; most of the Ys have some kind of income-generating project, such as the international guest houses in Delhi and Bombay. They have the hostels and the staff which can be reoriented to new uses. And, when it comes to government lobbying, they have nothing if not an image of respectability.

On the scale of respectability, none can match the All India Women's Conference, which seems to have lost something of the feisty spirit it had during the nationalist struggle. Founded in 1927, AIWC fought first for the enfranchisement of women and then for revisions in personal (e.g. family) law.[27] In addition to lobbying for women's rights, AIWC also undertook some social work activities—it set up hostels for working women, "rescue homes" for prostitutes, and encouraged schools for girls—but these were secondary to its role as a lobbying body for the legal and political rights of women.[28]

Since independence, AIWC has turned more toward social services, running schools, libraries and hostels for working women; sponsoring family planning clinics; offering charity to needy children; running programs for the mentally retarded; and operating homes for the aged and indigent.[29] Because its philosophy continues to be so evidently a "maternalist" one,[30] rather than one that encourages the empowerment of women, AIWC has not been a significant factor in the women's movement of the 1970s and '80s. Still, on occasion, it has used its resources to lobby government officials regarding issues of concern to other movement organizations: the elimination of dowry, the establishment of family courts, and greater legal protection against rape and dowry death.

Typical of AIWC activities was its participation along with the other large women's organizations—NFIW, AIDWA, AICCWW, the YWCA—some women MPs, and representatives of the research community in a 1980 meeting held at AIWC headquarters. These groups demanded a meeting with the Deputy Chairman of the Planning Commission in order to plead for greater attention to women's needs in the Sixth Five Year Plan.[31] The word had been leaked that the proposed plan barely included mention of women, much less a systematic plan for their uplift. The flavor of the meeting is recalled by one participant, who reports that "the poor man came to the meeting and walked into an angry barrage of elderly women shouting at him, 'we won't have it!' "[32] They were rewarded with a promise that the draft plan would provide more avenues for employment to women and also try to safeguard women's rights; in fact, the Sixth Plan did, for the first time, include a chapter on women and development.

Thus, while AIWC has not been in the forefront of activism, it has at times been a participant in the new efforts being made. Its long history and its participation in the nationalist movement still provide it with a cachet of respectability that can be, and has been, put to use, particularly to be heard at the upper levels of government.

Leftist Movements. Many of the women involved in autonomous organizations were formerly associated with independent radical organizations or with the revolutionary-minded Communist Party of India (Marxist-Leninist). Their break from male-dominated organizations was partly inspired by Western feminist ideas,[33] as women began to expect greater respect for women and for issues pertaining to women within these organizations. Instead, they found leftist organizations unrelentingly sexist: the sexism was personally directed at them as women activists, and the organizations "were utterly insensitive to the oppression of women."[34] A number of women activists also rejected the hierarchical organizational style dominant in the left, preferring instead a more consensual approach to decision making. Many of the women who left these organizations for ones with a greater, if not exclusive, concentration on women, continue to regard themselves as operating within a socialist or Marxist ideological framework, but generally add the word "feminist" to their self-description.[35]

Vimochna, in the city of Bangalore, is an example of an autonomous organization whose members were first exposed to political ideas and actions and who gained organizational skills through association with leftist organizations. Vimochna grew directly out of the Society for Informal Education and Development Studies (SIEDS), founded in 1976.[36] This group was created by educated leftist activists and scholars who were disillusioned with existing radical politics. Some of the members had been expelled from the CPM for raising critical questions, others were supporters of the CPI(M-L) who had become disillusioned with that party over questions of means and ends, while still others belonged to Trotskyite groups. They were brought together by a belief that Marxist categories were insufficient to explain and rectify Indian conditions, and by a critique of the existing communist parties for failing to see a relationship between the hierarchical organizational means upon which they relied and the likely centralized ends that would result.

SIEDS operates as a decentralized collective, with members choosing to focus their energies on different projects. In 1979, some of the women in the collective began meeting, and found a welcome respite from the fact that, in the meetings of the whole collective, it was almost solely men who spoke. The women's organization, Vimochna, became formalized, and began to work first on cases of violence against women.

Although members of the group continue to work with individual victims of violence, and to educate poor women about women's issues, much of the work of the group now concerns media and cultural politics. In addition to sponsoring an annual women's film festival, the group publishes an occasional journal in English, *Sangharsh,* that is highly theoretical and intellectual; a bimonthly newsletter called "Vimochna Varthapatra," in Kannada, the language of Karnataka, which publishes investigative reports and articles on violence against women as well as more theoretical material; and a bimonthly English-language news sheet, "Krithi."[37] Vimochna also contains a street theater group that writes plays about dowry, housing, and other women's problems, and performs them on street corners. In conjunction with the Women and Media Group of Bombay, Vimochna successfully protested an hour-long talk show on the national television network, Doodarshan, for perpetuating negative stereotypes of women; the show was withdrawn after a few months.[38] Along with the SIEDS collective, Vimochna also runs a women's bookstore, Streelekha, described as "a woman's place," but explicitly open to publications on peace, development, ecology, and on movements of workers, Dalits, and peasants.[39]

As a part of a broader collective, Vimochna is very much influenced by, and influences, the view that effective radical action must necessarily link together a number of movements. Within SIEDS is a group focusing on workers' issues, one working on peace issues, a "peoples' rights commit-tee" that is a human rights group, and one that works on environmental issues. Thus, Vimochna's work on behalf of women is seen as part of a broader agenda of social change to be brought about through movement politics.

The members of other autonomous groups also had experience work-ing in radical political groups. The first of the new wave of women's groups to appear in the 1970s was the Progressive Women's Organization (POW) of Hyderabad. It was founded in 1974 by students at Osmania University who were connected to the CPI(M-L); the new group was an independent one, and began with campaigns against dowry and sexual harrassment (called "eve teasing" in India).[40] POW's manifesto, however, makes plain its authors' grounding in Marxist thought: the section that explains why women are oppressed is an unattributed synopsis of Engels' *The Origin of the Family, Private Property and the State*, and the POW pledges itself, among other tasks, to "uphold and propagate scientific so-cialism," fight against the feudal economy, and unite with the toiling masses against foreign exploitation. Unlike Marxist organizations, how-ever, the manifesto also denounces economic and cultural patterns that specifically oppress women. POW demanded the abolition of prostitution and obscenity (defined as the depiction of women as degrading sex ob-jects), and called for improvements in and implementation of laws regard-ing inheritance, child marriage, dowry, equal pay and maternity and creche facilities.[41]

The Socialist Women's Group was formed in Bombay in 1977. Many had a Trotskyite background; others were members of left political par-ties.[42] In April 1978 the group organized a workshop for women activists to which women from Delhi and five other cities came; out of this meeting came the proposal to create a feminist journal with a "Marxist point of view" to be brought out in both Hindi and English on a bimonthly basis. It was proposed that the paper "publish articles from women all over the country on their struggles and experiences" as well as theoretical articles. While it would attempt to "relate to all women," its focus would be on the lower middle-class and working-class women.[43] It was also suggested that a more modest newsletter be created. *Feminist Network* was the first effort in that direction; six issues were published in mimeographed form beginning in July 1978. This newsletter ceased publication when the envi-sioned magazine, titled *Manushi*, (Woman) began publishing in New Delhi in January 1979; those putting out the *Feminist Network* threw their support to *Manushi*.[44]

The founders of many autonomous women's organizations were thus not novices in political activity, but had experience in radical organiza-tions. What drove these activists into autonomous organizations was their disagreement with a Marxist perspective that they came to see as too narrow and a style of organizing they saw as too undemocratic. Still, it was their participation in these older groups that brought them into politics and gave them the skills necessary to begin new organizations.

A Communications Network and a Sympathetic Press

Jo Freeman's *The Politics of Women's Liberation* demonstrates that a communications network was key to the founding of the U.S. feminist movement.[45] The same is certainly true of the Indian case. Here, there were existing communications among groups that became mobilized for new activities; the network quickly expanded to include newly formed movement organizations. In addition, there was an extremely sympathetic national press that facilitated communications among the activists, and also between the activists and government, and the activists and interested citizens.

Chapter 3 described large public demonstrations beginning in 1979 demanding better police and court protection with regard to both dowry death and rape. On March 8, 1980 (International Women's Day), in New Delhi, a coalition of 12 organizations came together to protest government actions in the Mathura rape case. The action in Delhi was not unique; a larger march was organized in Bombay by the Forum Against Rape, and other demonstrations occurred in cities across the country, including Madras, Pune, Bangalore and Hyderabad.[46] By 1982 the Delhi coalition, called the Dahej Virodhi Chetana Manch, had grown to about thirty organizations.[47]

It was possible to organize these demonstrations because of the ease of communication that was already present among the existing groups as well as the channels that were opened up among the newer, autonomous groups; as early as April 1978, activists from Delhi, Bombay, Kanpur, Poona, Sangamner, Ahmedabad and Varanasi had met together in Bombay;[48] in 1979 an all-Maharashtra coordination committee of women's organizations, Stri Mukti Andolan Sampark Samiti, was formed.[49] In New Delhi, groups with disparate ideologies would come together at the headquarters of the YWCA to plan demonstration tactics. National conferences were soon organized: in November 1980, "Perspectives for the Women's Liberation Movement in India," a national conference of autonomous women's groups, was held in Bombay.[50] This was followed in April 1981 by the First National Conference on Women's Studies at Bombay's SNDT Women's University, which was attended by some 380 delegates.[51] In December 1985, 85 women's groups were represented at the "Perspectives for the Autonomous Women's Movement in India" conference.[52]

That the groups communicate and cooperate on specific campaigns and around specific issues should not be taken to mean that these groups are in any way centrally organized. Different groups take initiative over different issues or for particular demonstrations; there is no central coordinating body. In this decentralized movement, where cooperation among the various movement organizations around particular issues and events is strictly *ad hoc,* communication takes on heightened importance.

Many organizations have created newsletters, bulletins or full-fledged journals and magazines. Early among the autonomous organizations was the mimeographed English-language *Feminist Network,* which gave way to the much more professionally presented magazine *Manushi,* publishing alternately in Hindi and English, and enjoying a distribution of 10,000,[53] which has continued to serve as a communications medium for individual activists and movement organizations. *Manushi's* editors, Madhu Kishwar and Ruth Vanita, view it not as primarily a generator of ideological theory but rather as a communications link among activists in women's organizations and in democratic rights groups. They publish many reports of women's struggles around the country, and it is their intention that activists will learn from the methods and self-evaluations of others.[54] The "letters" column of the magazine conveys the sense that this in fact does occur.

While *Mansushi* is the best known abroad of the Indian women's journals, it is not the movement's only voice. Other independent feminist journals have been published, in several different languages. Among the most important are *Sabla,* in Bengali, published in Calcutta; *Apni Azade ke liye* and *Aawaz Aurat Ki,* both published in Patna (Hindi); *Samata* in Bangalore (Kannada); *Anusaya* in Ahmedabad (Gujarati); *Bauja* in Pune (Marathi); and *Maitreyi* in Bombay and *Shackles and Women* in Punjab, both in English.[55] In addition, many autonomous organizations put out their own newsletters. For example, Saheli in New Delhi publishes the *Saheli Newsletter,* while the Women's Centre in Bombay puts out *Womennews* and a Marathi-language newsletter. Among the party-affiliated women's groups, publishing ventures are also common, with AICCWW responsible for *The Voice of the Working Woman,* and NFIW printing the *NFIW Bulletin.* The AIWC puts out *Roshini,* while SEWA publishes *We, the Self Employed.* The Centre for Women's Development Studies publishes a scholarly journal, *Samya Shakti,* and also a more newsy *Bulletin of the Centre for Women's Development Studies.* Similarly, in addition to the many scholarly studies it sponsors, the Research Centre on Women's Studies of SNDT Women's University issues the *RCSW News Letter.* Many of these bulletins repeat news of events first printed elsewhere, run brief summaries of protests around the country, announce conferences and meetings, and tell readers where they may obtain various types of resources. Thus, there is certainly no dearth of movement literature, or of means of communicating among groups.

The mainstream press—particularly the English-language press—has been a vital communications link among movement activists and between the movement and the general public and members of government. Since the emergency, the press has hammered away at a number of women's issues. Discrimination in law, women's poor health, illiteracy, low pay and inadequate employment: all have been sympathetically discussed in the press through reports, editorials and continuing columns. Of greatest importance has been the press' attention to violence against women, particularly domestic violence, which moved from being virtually unreported to being splashed on the front pages. Dowry deaths, previously hidden in the police reports as suicides, were exposed as murders. The issue was thus brought dramatically not only to broad public attention, but specifically to the attention of government officials.

The reasons for this interest by the press are not hard to fathom. In the wake of the emergency's repression of all civil liberties, the press became highly attuned to issues of human rights; one of the clearest indications of this was the explosion of writing about women. Additionally, the activists who began to take up women's issues after the Emergency were elites who had easy access to the press: they were already the leaders of organizations, party officials, published authors, scholars; they were savvy and they were credible.[56] They could plant ideas for articles, and at the very least get their demonstrations and press conferences covered. Finally, there were a growing number of women journalists who successfully clamored to cover these issues, and who have done so with insight and conviction.[57]

This is not to say press coverage has been all activists wish it would be; there is a notable failure to follow up on cases of violence against women and a tendency to favor urban-based movement activity and urban women's issues. Still, it has been an effective tool in the building of public sentiment and in pushing government officials to pay attention to women's issues.

The support for women's issues in the English-language press is not always replicated in other languages. For example, northern activists complain that little positive is to be found in the Gujarati or Hindi press, although in keeping with the more liberal consciousness of Maharashtra, the Marathi press is more supportive.[58] While these positions do bear on the creation of broad public opinion, the English-language press is probably the most compelling in the short run to elites of the central government.

Age Cohort of Educated Women

Educated women were essential to the emergence of the women's movement. In 1947, 23,000 Indian women were enrolled in institutions of higher education. A generation after independence, that number had increased to 900,000.[59] While this is small when compared to the size of the population, educated women are concentrated in urban areas, and thus have more impact there than their numbers, seen on a national scale, would imply.

Educated women in India have been involved in politics since the days of the nationalist movement. With the achievement of independence, the first generation of women leaders joined with their male Congress colleagues and became supporters of and participants in the new parliamentary structures.

The educated women of the 1970s were different. As described in Chapter 2, broad disillusionment had set in concerning the capacity of existing institutions to adequately address the problems of development generally and to safeguard human rights, and this feeling was deepened by the Emergency. The exposure of educated women to feminist ideas from the West added to the radicalism that grew because of the domestic crisis. The works of Simone de Beauvoir, Shulamith Firestone, Kate Millet, Juliet Mitchell, Susan Brownmiller, and Alice Walker, among others, are well known, as is The Boston Women's Health Collective's *Our Bodies Ourselves*, which was sold to Indian readers through *Manushi*.[60]

Educated women in the 1970s also seemed to have had a sense of entitlement that made them different from their predecessors. As a result of the influence of Western feminist ideas, as well as a growing liberalism in Indian middle-class families about women being educated, the newly educated felt they had a *right* to their education and to political participation;[61] when they were denied this in student politics, political organizations and parties, they were unwilling to accept inequality.

As educated people, elites in Indian society, the women not only developed a belief in their own rights, but also a sense of political efficacy; these are people who believe they can make a difference. In addition, the educated women of the 1970s acquired a set of intellectual skills that have been important to movement development. They develop ideas; they write; they produce scholarship; they generate publicity. Their skills have enabled them to appeal to international and government sources of funding, to speak to (and become a part of) the national media and to create their own media; they have established feminist libraries and "think tanks" that provide scholarly assistance to movement activists and government agencies. In short, education inspired many activists to take up movement politics, and it gave them the means to pursue that goal.

International Resources

It has already been argued that both Western feminist ideas and the attention focused on women by International Women's Year had a significant influence on the rights wing of the movement. But the international influences are filtered through an Indian lens.

Some Western feminist concerns—notably about sexuality—have had limited or no appeal in India. Lesbianism is not acknowledged to be a political issue or even to exist within the movement. Indian feminists recoil from any suggestion that they are anti-family or anti-male, and so lesbianism remains in India a problem that has no name.

However, other Western ideas have been welcomed: the politicization and denunciation of violence against women (particularly domestic violence) has had particular resonance.[62] Although sexuality *per se* has not been an issue, the identification of women's health and reproductive rights as political issues has made an impact.[63] In India, though, the health issue that has most mobilized political action is one that is unfamiliar in the West; it is the problem of amniocentesis being widely used not to determine genetic disorder, but rather to determine the sex of the fetus in order to then abort female fetuses.[64] Also of deep concern is the safety of injectible contraceptives, a Western-inspired problem, indeed, since that is where the drugs are developed and manufactured; the battle against them draws on data gathered by Western academic and feminist sources who have opposed the use of these drugs.

In addition to ideological influence, international sources have provided concrete financial resources. Funding has gone to organizations struggling for women's legal rights and to autonomous organizations that provide assistance to victims of violence. For example, the Women's Centre in Bombay, which provides temporary shelter, job counseling, and psychological counseling to battered women, was founded by six women in 1981. Initially a modest organization operating out of a member's apartment, it began to grow. By 1983, the group was receiving funding from Oxfam and the Unitarian Universalist Service Committee.[65] It moved into an office space, and began to build a library and sponsor conferences for activists. A 1984 workshop, funded by Oxfam, drew together representatives from twenty-five women's organizations that provide assistance to "women in distress."[66]

International agencies have also supported research activities and women's studies. The first National Conference on Women's Studies received support from a number of international sources: UNICEF, UNESCO, the International Labor Organization and the Ford Foundation all contributed. The Ford Foundation has provided funds, too, to SNDT Women's History Archive, the Indian Association for Women's Studies and the Centre for Women's Development Studies. CWDS has also received funding from the ILO.[67]

International funding has been of even greater significance to women's organizations that work for economic development and empowerment at the grass roots. This subject will be examined after a brief look at the structure of the rights wing of the women's movement.

The Structure of the Rights Wing

Different organizational structures are appropriate to different goals; *how* a movement (and a movement organization) is organized will have an impact on *what* a movement (and a movement organization) may achieve. The nature of the resources that help to bring a movement into being, including strongly held beliefs, helps to shape a movement's structure and its goals.

The development of several women's organizations out of major opposition parties is a case in point. Both the CPM and the CPI believe that the solution to India's problems is a state socialism, so they struggle to achieve state power; their analysis of Indian conditions dictates that they act through parliamentary means. The women's organizations that have grown out of these parties (NFIW and AIDWA) share this strategy. Thus, agitational activities are a major tactical weapon; these simultaneously serve to publicize grievances, demonstrate the inadequacies of government and possibly move it to act, and increase the visibility of the organization and party.

While these organizations are helpful to women in a variety of gender specific ways, they also serve the CPI and CPM aim of building a working class movement. For example, leaders of the Delhi unit of AIDWA spoke proudly of their accomplishment of organizing the wives of male textile workers, women who had formerly "held their striking men back." In contrast, by 1986, in the midst of a textile strike, the women were, they said, acting "with very militant demands . . . in solidarity with the men."[68]

The large memberships of these organizations and their hierarchical structures confer on their national leaderships considerable clout; they have access to high government bureaucrats and to elected officials, including the Prime Minister.[69] To a large extent, the women are organized in order to be available for agitation; they are mobilized to be a pressure group against the incumbent government and a constituency for communist party politics. But while this structure is very useful for influencing law and government policy, it is less useful from the perspective of empowering the membership. The members give clout to the *leadership*; it is the leaders who have power, who are recognized elites and who can engage in elite politics.

Much the same statement, of course, may be made about the leaders of the older social service organizations, the YWCA and AIWC. While their activities on behalf of women are important parts of their mission, their positions at the heads of these large organizations give them direct access to government decision makers—access that can be insured, if necessary, by helping to organize agitational activities among their membership.

Mahila Dakshata Samiti is a much smaller organization than either NFIW or AIDWA, and functions largely as an elite-based interest group. Because of its leaders' connection to Janata, their own prestige as political elites, and the organization's financial resources, they have been able to organize symposia featuring distinguished jurists, politicians, and academicians. These have influenced the public debate on legal issues such as dowry and maintenance for Muslim women.

As is true of the other party-affiliated organizations, MDS' desire to influence public opinion and government behavior is coupled with a keen desire to oust Congress from power. At least some activists who have shared MDS's concern for women have been dismayed by the intensity of the quest for party ascendancy.[70] Many women's activists do not believe that placing another party in power will have a dramatic impact on the status of women, and they resent an organization using women's issues for party ends.

The autonomous organizations, often developed by women who have rejected party politics, are usually non-hierarchical and collective in style. Their activities often bridge the "rights" and "empowerment" wings of the movement. They do seek to build public consciousness by generating publicity around issues of concern to women (primarily violence and health issues); lobby members of government and agitate for revised legislation; and assist women through the maze of police and law courts. In addition, they seek in their internal practice to give women new confidence and new skills.

In contrast to the parties, the autonomous organizations do not seek state power. Their rhetoric stresses the need to empower the grass roots and end social hierarchies; the language is reminiscent of Western new social movements and of socialist feminism in particular. Here is one example:

A struggle for socialism means . . . *not only* the abolition of the dominance of one class over another, but the abolition of *all* dominance, all hierarchies, all subordination—between classes, sexes, races, etc. . . . *Revolution* is the *process* through which . . . a new morality can be worked out.[71]

New Delhi's Saheli is one of the autonomous organizations that emphasizes process in its work. Made up of several full-time paid staff members and 25 to 30 volunteers, Saheli was founded by women who had participated in agitations against dowry deaths and the Mathura rape case. The organization counsels battered women and those who fear being murdered by their husbands and in-laws; it offers legal advice, too, to the parents and siblings of burning victims. After several years of sheltering women in the homes of volunteers, it has been able to create a small short-stay home for those women who choose to leave their husbands. Saheli also tries to find the women paid work. In addition to its activities of counseling and assisting approximately 200 individuals each year, Saheli helps to organize demonstrations in the capital against the inadequacy of laws protecting women.[72]

While most of the funding for Saheli comes through individual donations, and while Saheli considers the ideal to be private sources of funding because these infringe least on the autonomy of the group, the shelter is funded by the Ministry of Social Welfare. The collective did decide to solicit government monies and to accept institutional funds some specific activities or projects. A Joint Secretary in the Department of Women and Child Development told me that Saheli would like assistance to create more and better accommodations, but that the government insists on more reports and studies than Saheli has been able to provide.[73] Saheli itself describes the regulations that must be met to receive most government funds as "insurmountable."[74] An organization determined to avoid bureaucratization finds it hard to communicate effectively with the bureaucracy that is government.

The group operates as a collective. Responsibilities and tasks are rotated among small sub-groups. Major decisions are made collectively; or, at least, this is the ideal. A paper written by Saheli in 1986 acknowledged many problems with the collective decision-making process: differential expertise among members, tensions between old and new members, inefficiencies that result from the maximum rotation of tasks so that members can learn as many skills as possible, too much time spent deciding trivial matters while important ones are neglected.[75] As a result, the group has experimented with a new structure, in which sub-groups that undertake particular tasks make the decisions about those tasks; no longer does the whole collective control (or purport to control) decisions about everything.

Despite the problems of operating with collective decision making, no thought has been given to moving to a more hierarchical mode of organization. The belief in maximizing participation at all levels of decision making is fundamental to the groups' desire to match process with desired outcome. The same Saheli paper that reflects on its structure contrasts the collective structure with the alternatives found in centralized parties, trade unions, and voluntary organizations with clearly defined executives and staff, and finds all three to be flawed. The centralist party "suffers from a hierarchy which is not going to be destroyed after the revolution"; in unions "leadership gets well entrenched" and inevitably becomes, as Robert Michels predicted, oligarchical; within voluntary organizations, there is often tension between a staff that seeks greater input into decision making and an executive that seeks to retain power over the organization for itself.[76] Thus, the paper concludes, none of these alternatives are truly democratic; none conform to Saheli's belief "that given the right environment" all can rise to the same, or roughly the same, level of consciousness and skill.

As in most of the autonomous organizations, while the members of Saheli seek to help women who come to them with concrete problems, to raise their consciousness and ultimately to empower them, they simultaneously seek to empower those who are within. Thus, at a national conference of eighty-five autonomous organizations held in 1985, in addition to workshops exploring specific issues like personal law and women's health; communications among the groups and how to use the mainstream media; and the relationship of the autonomous organizations to the police and courts, there was also a workshop on the "politics of personal growth."[77] The workshop rested on the assumption that those working within the autonomous organizations had "grown as persons, become conscious, got strength, confidence and the courage to act"; participants discussed how best to expand these private triumphs into their public work.

The quest of the autonomous organizations for rights and empowerment is limited by their small numbers and tiny membership; their insistence on collective decision making dictates that the organizations must remain relatively small in size. To be effective, then, on any but a very local scale, they must grow in number. While at present autonomous organizations exist all over India,[78] India is a big place. Fortunately for the women's movement, these autonomous organizations are not the only groups seeking empowerment. We turn now to the resources and structures of the "empowerment" wing of the movement.

Resources and Structures
of Rural Empowerment Movements

Both urban and rural empowerment movements work among the very poor; here, the economic and social empowerment of women is seen as the prerequisite to the attainment and full enjoyment of political rights.

Although the goals of urban and rural empowerment organizations are similar, there are differences in their origins. The urban empowerment groups share some history with the rights wing—notably individual leaders who are experienced in party or labor union work. In contrast, the early rural movements spring from entirely different roots than the rights wing of the movement, namely small scale movements among the rural poor—some of them with Gandhian roots, some of them more radical.

Rural organizing for empowerment was inspired by several developments, both national and international, which came together in mutually reinforcing ways in the 1970s. On the international level, development sponsors had come to see intensive community organizing as a prerequisite to the efficacious use of resources; community empowerment became an explicit part of their agenda. Add to this the fact that, by the mid-1970s, at the beginning of the UN's decade for women, international agencies were themselves being influenced by feminist ideas. So, at the same time that development agencies were turning their attention to community development, they were also realizing that women are a significant part of the community and could no longer be ignored.[79] As a consequence, international agencies began looking for non-governmental organizations that were doing community organizing among women and that had the capacity to absorb and use funds.

Simultaneously, in the 1970s, there was an upsurge in community organizing among the rural poor by Indian activists. The voluntary groups, discussed in Chapter 2, had no expectation that government alone could accomplish the tasks of development and empowerment, and believed movement activity was vital to those ends.

The Ideology and Practice
of Early Grass-Roots Movements of Women

The ideological and tactical inspiration provided by these nonparty, grass-roots movements was crucial to the emergence and growth of women's rural empowerment groups.[80] A number of them have organized women within their communities, both because their participation is seen as critical to the future of the community as a whole, and because of a recognition of the specific gender-related needs of women. Included among these are several Maharashtra-based organizations that organize tribals—Shramik Sanghatana in Dhule District and Bhoomi Sena in Thane District beginning in the early 1970s, and Kashtakari Sanghatana in Thane in the late 1970s—and that have received substantial public notice.[81]

Their emphasis is less on moving government and more on creating structures and educating for direct political participation in decisions that affect the local community. Each of these movements has been characterized by a refusal to align with political parties, which they regard as opportunistic and ideologically rigid. Instead, actions aimed at government and the landlord class are undertaken locally, after the intensive discussion, politicization and strategizing that occurs in several forums: *shibirs* or "camps for collective reflection"[82] at which men and women, or women alone, gather to share experiences, build new ideological understandings, and formulate strategy; in the Tarun Mandals, or youth leagues; and in workers' associations—all characterized by a non-hierarchical style of organization and by group decision making. Actions have included marches, demonstrations, and strikes aimed at government representatives and landlords for increased wages and employment and the abolition of bonded labor; activities to enhance community economic power, such as the obtaining and managing of bank loans and collective savings funds; and also campaigns, particularly by women, against social ills, such as gambling, alcoholism, and the payment of bride price.[83] There has been a particular focus on the link between the economic exploitation common to the community as a whole and the sexual violence that is the particular victimizer of women and is visited upon them both by the men of their own families and by men who hold economic or state power over them, such as landlords, money-lenders, and police.[84]

Another early movement that has served as an inspiration to further activism is the Chipko movement in the Uttarkhand region of Uttar Pradesh. Widespread deforestaton, first by unchecked commercial interests and later under government auspices, had created an economic crisis for the local people who occupied the forests and drew their sustenance from them. The impact was paticularly great for women. Male migration to the plains is common, and it is women who do nearly all the work of cultivation.[85] It is also women who gather fodder, fuel, and water, tasks made much more time-consuming as the forests become denuded.[86]

The Chipko movement began under the leadership of C.P. Bhatt and other male Sarvodaya workers, organized as the Dashauli Gram Swarajy Mandal (DGSM); initial demands were for local participation in the management of the forests and limits on their commercial exploitation. Despite the fact that it was women's jobs that had been made the most difficult by the years of deforestation, the initial focus of the Sarvodaya workers was on organizing the men of the community.

In 1973, protests by the DGSM successfully prevented the Forest Department from allotting rights to a set of ash trees to a company from the plains, which intended to use the wood for tennis rackets, and persuaded the Forest Department to grant the DGSM rights to a smaller number of trees for the manufacture of farm tools. Still, in 1974, the government made plans to allow the cutting of 2,500 trees in the Reni forest. Bhatt suggested that, when the time came, the people hug the trees (Chipko means "to hug") to protect them. When the lumber company arrived at the forest, the men of the community were nearly all away, and it was the women of the area who quickly mobilized, confronted the contractors' men, and forced them to back down. A subsequent report by the U.P. government declared that the Reni forest should become a protected area.

It was this action that caused the Chipko movement to be known as a women's movement, even though, here, the women were acting in concert with the wishes of the men of their community. The tactic was imitated in other villages in the area throughout the late 1970s. The Sarvodaya workers, realizing that the women were a valuable political force, took to educating and involving them in public activities; women, who had never before done so, began to attend village meetings and to demand a voice.

As their participation grew, so too did the confidence and motivation of the women. This was particularly evident in an incident in Dongri Paintoli village. Here, the members of the all-male village council agreed to allow the U.P. government to fell a local forest, in return for which the government would provide the village with a new road, secondary school, hospital, and electricity. The women of the village, who lacked formal political power, nonetheless declared that they did not accept the decision of the village council and would fight the cutting of the trees. They were, in turn, threatened by the men. Nonetheless, when, in February 1980, the tree cutters arrived, the women came out in large numbers and succeeded in driving the workmen away; within a month, the government banned the felling of trees in the area.

The Chipko movement added a new dimension to the perception of what constitutes "women's issues." The way in which economic development is to transpire so as to best fill human needs and the importance of environmental conservation were introduced as issues of central concern to women. While the movement created problems, particularly the sharpening of disagreements beteeen women and the men of their communities,[87] it also heightened women's participation in public forums and their awareness of their own potentialites. Both in its expression of the empowerment of women and in the public issues it proclaimed as of concern to women, the Chipko movement was an important inspiration to the empowerment wing of the women's movement.

International Resources

These early organizing efforts involving women had no connection to international development agencies. However, with the ending of the emergency, all kinds of grass roots activity, including rural organizing, expanded. New groups gained access to international funds; some were developed from the outset with international help. There are a number of examples: Working in three villages in Andhra Pradesh, the Comprehensive Rural Operations Service Society organizes laborers and marginal farmers to gain the collective bargaining power necessary to acquire government funds for economic development; other purposes are to educate and to increase self-esteem. CROSS has mobilized women to participate in mixed groups with men, and it has also created women's associations. These have fostered women's participatory and leadership skills and struggled to stop violence against women. CROSS receives funding from several agencies, including Christian Aid and Bread for the World.[88] The Centre for Women's Development Studies (CWDS), located in New Delhi, has begun small income generating projects among tribal women in West Bengal and in the Punjab; funding comes from the International Labour Organization and from the Indian government.[89] The Self Employed Women's Association (SEWA), which will be discussed extensively below, sponsors a number of rural development projects under the name SEWA-Jaago ("awakening"); SEWA receives funding from the ILO, World Bank, Oxfam, Ford and NOVIB (Netherlands).[90] Similarly, in 1980, Working Women's Forum, located in Madras, began to organize landless rural women to receive bank loans and other government inputs. In addition to assistance from the Indian government, WWF receives funding from, among other donors, the Indo-German Social Service Society, the Rabo Bank Netherlands, the ILO, the FAO, Ford and Oxfam.[91]

Of course, only those organizations that are sufficiently well known and bureaucratized themselves can receive international funding; by law, such organizations must be officially registered with and recognized by the Indian government. There are many movement organizations at work in rural areas that are much smaller than those named above and that reject becoming bureaucratized and registered and/or the principle of accepting funds from government or from international sources.

Urban Activists Organizing Rural Movements

The leadership of urban- or town-based activists is another critical resource in the founding of rural movement organizatons. SEWA, WWF, and, on a much smaller scale, CWDS are all hierarchically structured urban organizations that have expanded their outreach into rural areas. But more radical movement organizations—those that adhere to a decentralized mode, are based among tribals, Dalits, and the poor, and are explicitly socialist or communist in ideology (although non-party)—are also generally the product, too, of educated urban leadership. For example, Shramik Sanghatana, one of the models for movement organizing, was founded by educated urban activists who built on the initial social welfare work of a Sarvodaya group.[92] Kashtakari Sanghatana, an organization of landless tribals in Thane District, Maharashtra, was founded by a Jesuit priest and a young, educated woman activist who had been involved in missionary work.[93] The J.P. movement inspired the creation of Chhatra Yuva Sangharsh Vahini in the city of Patna. From its founding in 1975 until 1977, the organization concentrated on building public opinion against the Congress and the Emergency. With Congress' defeat in 1977, the group turned its attention to the longer term task of building J.P.'s "total revolution"; toward this end, the young urban activists decided to organize landless labor, and selected Bodhgaya, Bihar as the site of their activities. In the context of their organizing, the urban activists paid special attention to the task of organizing women.[94] One more example will suffice: The massive textile strike in Bombay in the early 1980s drove many recent immigrants back to their villages in search of work. In the Khanapur taluka of Sangli district, Maharashtra, it was these returned workers, more sophisticated and urbane than their rural relations, who began to organize a movement, Mukti Sangharsh, to struggle for more work and better wages from Maharashtra's employment guarantee scheme; many of those employed by the scheme, and many of those organized, were women.[95]

Rural empowerment movements do not spontaneously spring up among the poor and illiterate. Rural movements have links to urban ideas and events and to political changes at the center; urban connections and educated urban leadership are usually essential to their formation. The picture sometimes drawn in the West of India's toiling rural masses as somehow timeless and immutable is incorrect; political currents rock the rural areas as surely as the urban ones. In terms of the women's movement, the political distinction of consequence is less the urban/rural "divide" than the organizational goal of long-term empowerment versus that of immediately influencing the state.

Resources and Structures of Urban Empowerment

There are three women's organizations in India that bear special mention for their work among the urban self-employed, or, as they are often called, workers in the "informal" or "unorganized" sector. These are the Self Employed Women's Association of Ahmedabad; Working Women's Forum in Madras; and Annapurna Mahila Mandal in Bombay.

Women in the urban informal sector work at a variety of tasks, most of them yielding extremely low pay. They are domestic servants; rag pickers; vegetable vendors; piece-workers at sewing, at biri (cigarette) rolling, at papad (crackers) baking; haulers; quilt makers; paper pickers; broom makers. Although India has many laws designed to protect workers, such as minimum-wage laws, and women workers in particular, such as the Equal

Remuneration Act (1976) and the Maternity Benefit Act (1961), these do not apply to the unorganized sector. And the vast majority of women who work—well over ninety percent—do so in the unorganized sector.[96]

This percentage has been increasing, as women have been forced out of the organized sector through a combination of increased mechanization and women's limited access to skills training. Technology has replaced unskilled laborers, particularly in textile factories and mines, and it is women who have been let go; both the percentage of women throughout India who work for remuneration and the percentage of women as members of the total labor force have declined.[97] The decline is particularly striking in the organized sector. In 1925, women were 20 percent of all workers in cotton mills nationally; 15 percent of all jute workers; and 38 percent of all who worked in the mines. By 1975, women were 2.5, 2.0, and 5.0 percent of the workers in those respective industries.[98]

As women have been forced out of paid factory labor in the cities,[99] they have been forced to become self-employed, or to work at exploitative rates at non-unionized jobs outside of government control. SEWA, WWF, and Annapurna each act as a combination trade union/credit advancing/ social service providing agency for the informal sector worker. While these organizations are sometimes criticized by autonomous feminist organizations for not concentrating on gender issues, and by communist groups for offering an insufficient challenge to the existing political and economic systems, I will argue in Chapter 7 that their work places them unquestionably within the empowerment segment of the women's movement: their goals include helping women to help themselves by assisting them to fight for decent wages or to build their businesses, to improve their educations, and to develop unity, self-confidence and group power. These groups succeed better than most.

This section describes the resources that helped them emerge and the organizational structures that govern their work.

Self Employed Women's Association

Along with Working Women's Forum, the Self Employed Women's Association is one of the largest and most successful movement organizations. SEWA (the acronym means "service" in Gujarati), had its beginnings in the labor union movement. Its midwife was the Textile Labour Association (TLA) of Ahmedabad, India's oldest and largest textile workers union.[100]

TLA has a venerable history. It was founded in 1917 by Mahatma Gandhi, Shankarlal Banker and Ansuyaben Sarabhai. The last was a young woman, daughter of an extremely wealthy Ahmedabad millowner, who had been educated in England and who upon her return took up the cause of the poor laborers, particularly millworkers, of Ahmedabad. In 1917, she asked Mahatma Gandhi to help mediate a dispute between the millowners and the workers. The result was India's first large-scale strike by textile workers, followed by a compromise decision that established the worth of arbitration.[101]

In 1954, TLA established a women's wing. Its focus was not working women, although there were plenty of these,[102] but rather on providing welfare activities and training for the wives and daughters of male mill workers. Beginning with classes in sewing, TLA expanded its activities to classes in knitting, embroidery, spinning, press composition, typing and stenography; by the late sixties, one thousand women a year received training. TLA did not, however, offer them any assistance in finding employment.

In 1969 TLA hired Ela Bhatt, a lawyer who was active in social work and union activities, to head up the women's wing. In response to complaints made by female tailors of exploitation by contractors, Bhatt initiated a study of their work. During their research, organizers received an education, learning how completely unprotected—"by unionization, by legislation, by government, and by society"[103]—the women were; at the same time, the organizers became known to the working women.

As a result, in 1971, a group of women who pulled carts in the cloth market approached TLA and asked for assistance in obtaining housing; migrants, the women were living in the streets. In exploring their situation Bhatt and her staff also met with a group of forty women who earned their livings as headloaders—carrying bales of cloth on their heads from the wholesaler to the retailers—who complained of their low wages, and of the fact that since no written records were kept on how many trips they made, they were often cheated out of wages. Organizers from TLA called a meeting for women who worked in the cloth markets. Following this, Ela Bhatt wrote an article for a local newspaper describing the grievances of the workers and their mistreatment by the merchants. The merchants countered with their own publicity, in which they claimed their treatment of the workers was always fair. In a tactic reminiscent of the Gandhian style of moral persuasiveness (which does not shrink from implicit threats of public mortification), Ela Bhatt had the merchants' claims printed up on small cards which were then distributed to the headloaders to use to remind merchants of their public commitment to fairness.

The news of this action prompted more women to approach the TLA. The next group were dealers in used garments. At a meeting organized by TLA, one dealer suggested that the women form a permanent association. TLA agreed and offered support: the staff of TLA's women's wing became, in one swift move, the SEWA staff. Although the TLA president became SEWA's president, Ela Bhatt, whose salary was still paid by TLA, became its General Secretary. TLA provided rent-free office space and an initial loan of five thousand rupees.[104] Thus it was the initiative of the working women combined with the material resources and leadership of TLA's women's wing that resulted in the formation of SEWA in December 1971.

Since its founding, SEWA has grown into an organization of over 40,000 dues-paying members[105] whose goal is to gain visibility, protection, and a "fair deal" for women workers of the unorganized sector. Toward this end, it insisted on becoming a registered trade union, arguing that a union can exist not only to negotiate with an employer, but also to foster the workers' "development." Overcoming the objections of the Labour Commission and the Gujarat Labour Department, SEWA prevailed and in April 1972, SEWA became a registered trade union of self-employed women workers.[106]

The SEWA Union bargains on behalf of its members with contractors and acts as an interest group with regard to economic development issues. It is particularly active in seeking state implementation of laws. The Union operates a legal-aid division that represents individual complainants, and it has moved the courts to challenge widespread instances of police harassment and hostile actions of municipal governments.[107]

SEWA has also provided women with the resources necessary to gain a sounder economic footing. In order to provide inexpensive sources of credit and release the women from their indebtedness to moneylenders and traders, SEWA in 1974 drew on monies available to low income workers through the nationalized banks to establish the SEWA Cooperative Bank. Despite dire predictions that poor uneducated women would fail to repay the loans, the bank has had the extraordinarily high recovery rate of ninety-eight percent.[108] The SEWA organizers recognized, too, that the utter lack of social services available to women workers in the unorganized sector severely hampered their movement toward economic self-sufficiency. As a result, they began the SEWA Mahila Trust.[109] This has provided the women with health care, maternity benefits, economic assistance for widows, life insurance and some day-care facilities. Its experiments in these areas have been noted with interest by both the Indian government and international agencies since, in the words of Sebstad's study for the Agency for International Development, "SEWA has demonstrated that it is possible for the government or other public insitutions to deliver similar types of programs to the self-employed through voluntary or workers' organizations."[110]

Perhaps most importantly, SEWA has created economic cooperatives through which women obtain supplies, organize production, and market their own goods. Although a first effort at organizing *papad* makers failed, there has been greater success with a cooperative of block printers and one of *chindi* workers.[111] As of 1978, SEWA also began creating income-generating projects for women in rural areas.[112] *Khadi* (hand loom) spinning and weaving and dairy cooperatives have been started with SEWA money and institutional support.

These projects, which will be described in greater detail in Chapter 7, are in part about economic growth, but they are also about democratization, participation, and empowerment.

Although SEWA was first organized in a representational model, there has been an increasing attention to participatory democracy within SEWA ranks. This has been true both at the level of the organization as a whole, and particularly true for those involved in the cooperatives. This decreasing centralization and corresponding emphasis on the empowerment of the individual women members accounts in part for differences between SEWA and TLA that broke them apart in 1981.

Tensions arose early between TLA and SEWA over the process of decision making, as SEWA leaders expressed a preference for broadened participation for both members and organizers. In contrast, TLA is an organization run from the top down, with decisions commonly made by a small group of leaders. The insistence on obedience was particularly contrary to the agenda of empowerment SEWA has for women: through their work in SEWA women should not only gain economically but also develop self-confidence, pride, and assertiveness.

The differences came to a head in 1980 when TLA president A.N. Buch, who was also the president of SEWA, disciplined a SEWA organizer for "indiscipline." Bhatt and other SEWA organizers came to her defense, prompting Buch to charge them all with insubordination; he argued that as "staff" and "employees" they had no right to question his authority. The SEWA organizers refused to back down, and Buch resigned from SEWA.

The conflict deepened as SEWA's scope expanded from traditional union activities into income generating activities and the development of women-run cooperatives. Other factors leading to SEWA's expulsion had to do with the militancy of SEWA's tactics; TLA leaders did not feel comfortable with SEWA's confrontations with police and municipal leaders. The final break occurred in the wake of riots against *harijans* (untouchables) that took place in Ahmedabad in 1981. Beginning with protests by students and then professionals against reservations for *harijans* in schools, the situation soon degenerated into violence. TLA chose not to take a stand on the issue. Bhatt and SEWA came out in support of the policy of reservations, and urged TLA to do likewise. Again citing "indiscipline," TLA expelled SEWA, and withdrew seven hundred thousand rupees from the SEWA bank, nearly causing its collapse.[113]

SEWA's dedication to expanding cooperative ventures for women in both urban and rural areas may be seen as an effort to build empowerment. The leadership sees these alternative economic structures as a laboratory for a more broadly cooperative economic system. Although still a modest effort, the movement toward cooperatives is part of a long-range dream. The expectation is that, after being started up with the help of organizers and outside funds, the cooperatives will be turned over to the women who work in them; the women should make the decisions and control the resources that affect their futures. So far, this plan is working: according to Renana Jhabvala, SEWA's Secretary, cooperatives that have been in existence for more than three years have become self-supporting.

In the process of organizing economic cooperatives, SEWA workers also address social issues of importance to women, including dowry and rape, and emphasize the critical importance of unity, organization, and self-reliance for solving these problems. Organizers stress the participatory nature of their enterprise: the goal of SEWA's leaders is to be dispensable, and for the movement to be run entirely by its members. In the words of Ela Bhatt, "I and my colleagues think of ourselves as matchsticks only. Matchsticks are used to light a lamp; [they are] useless once their appointed task is over."[114]

Working Women's Forum

The other Indian women's organization that rivals SEWA in its reach and effectiveness in empowering women economically, socially, and politically is Working Women's Forum. Founded in 1978 in Madras, it has expanded to rural areas in Tamil Nadu, as well as to cities and towns in Andhra Pradesh and Karnataka. All told, WWF has as many as 40,000 members.[115]

Like SEWA and Bombay's Annapurna Mahila Mandal, WWF, too, owes its founding in substantial part to the energies, skill, political experience and political connectedness of its founder. By the late 1970s, Jaya Arunachalam had long experience working as an organizer in the poorest areas of the city of Madras. She served there as a Congress Party activist and was also engaged in relief work through Congress and through a voluntary organization called the Vidhya Bharati Trust, of which she was Executive Secretary.[116] In these capacities, she developed a sophisticated knowledge of national and state political processes and such practical skills as fundraising and public relations, as well as a deep understanding of local problems and an extensive network of connections with women in the poorest neighborhoods of Madras.

In late 1977, the monsoons brought severe flooding to Madras, and Arunachalam undertook relief work in the slums. At the same time, in part as a result of the split in the Congress Party after the Emergency, in part as a result of her talks with the poor women, she began to reevaluate her role as a party organizer. The women among whom she was working were largely self-employed and complained of being exploited by money-lenders. They demonstrated little interest in party politics; their concern lay instead in their capacity to earn a living. As one of Arunachalam's co-workers later recalled,

> We found we were doing wrong by calling women to political rallies. . . . We offered nothing in return. By meeting the women in small groups we found out that each and every woman is engaged in some occupation and in-debted to the money lenders. We decided to organize women around eco-nomic concerns.[117]

Arunachalam withdrew from Congress Party activity in early 1978, and together with several co-workers began to organize the Working Women's Forum.

Her long political experience and her connections became of impor-tance immediately both in organizing the poor women and in obtaining financial resources with which to build the organization. The initial fund-ing came from the Vidhya Bharati Trust, which in Arunachalam's words "mothered" the Forum. Through the Trust, she developed contacts with the Indo-German Social Service Society, which provides the bulk of the Forum's budget and has been the Forum's most important continuing funding source. WWF has received additional financial resources from an impressive range of international groups—including the Ford Founda-tion, Rabo Bank Netherlands, Oxfam-America, Appropriate Technology International, USAID, and the FAO—as well as from the Family Planning Foundation of India.[118]

Apparently, Arunachalam was not familiar with the workings of SEWA. Despite this, she developed an organization whose goals and methods are strikingly similar. Her discussions with Madras' self-employed women made clear that affordable credit was their main priori-ty. As a result, the major activity of the Forum is to facilitate the lending of money from India's nationalized banks to self-employed poor women. Working Women's Forum has identified some 65 petty businesses and trades operated by its members in Madras, but the majority are engaged in four areas: vegetable vending, managing snack stalls, trading cut cloth, or fruit and flower selling. Prior to the formation of the Forum the four per-cent per annum loans that the nationalized banks are supposed to offer to the so-called "weaker sections" of society were rarely made available to these women, for the banks did not regard their trading activities as legiti-mate businesses. They also were reluctant to process very small loans.[119]

WWF has linked the self-employed women to government resources by creating an administrative structure to facilitate the lending process. Through WWF, self-employed women are organized into neighborhood groups of about twenty members each. These groups are the mechanism through which the members apply to the government for loans, and they serve as the guarantor of the loans for the government. The members of a group apply together for a loan, and they are mutually responsible for its repayment. A group leader, elected by the group, collects money either daily or weekly from each member and sees to it that the loan is repaid on schedule. This structure has proved to be very successful: six years after the organization was formed, over 36,000 loans had been given out, with a repayment rate of 89.4 percent.[120]

The mutual responsibility imposed by the loan group serves not only an economic purpose but a social one: The Forum seeks to empower its members through the process of working together collectively. The organizational structure of the Forum is simple, designed to encourage grass-roots decision making and participation.[121] The neighborhood groups meet at least once a month and are the organizational foundation of the Forum. All Forum activities, which include day care facilities, night classes for members and for their children, and classes in health care and family planning, are run by and through the groups. At their monthly meetings, members voice their problems and suggestions; the local leaders iron out administrative problems. Periodically, groups from several nearby localities get together for a larger session, and there are annual meetings of the entire Madras membership as well.

Decisions affecting the organization as a whole are made by the Governing Board of the Forum, which is composed of the several hundred elected group leaders. The leaders themselves are products of the grass roots: they come from the neighborhoods, and serve voluntarily. Most of these women are not educated and, of course, they are poor. Some of them were the ones who first got their groups together. They are expected to act as intermediaries between their groups and the Board, bringing the opinion of their group members forward, and conveying to them the decisions and ideology of the Forum.

True to its desire to remain a grass-roots organization, there is a minimum of paid staff in Working Women's Forum. The structure above the Board is very small. Jaya Arunachalam, as President, continues to play a critical role in obtaining financial resources from institutional donors and banks. She is assisted by six high level administrators (one general secretary, two vice-presidents, and three area organizers) and a small field staff, most of whom were neighborhood leaders of particular skill who have been trained as organizers. But although the organization as a whole is structured so as to emphasize local decision making and selfgovernance, still the hierarchy does provide some strong ideological influence.

This is aimed largely at analyzing and attacking social problems that hinder the advancement of poor women. While the organization is unaligned with any political party, it does not eschew attempts to influence public policy with reference to economic needs and public services; there have been demonstrations, for example, for the construction of thatched stalls and public toilets for women in the markets, and for an end to police harassment of vendors. The membership is also mobilized to demonstrate publicly with regard to social issues, notably to condemn dowry and to fight for family planning resources. The organization is ideologically committed to opposing communalism and encourages the integration of different castes and religious communities in the neighborhood loan groups and among the organizers.

Thus, in Working Women's Forum we again find an organization in which the major activity is an economic program aimed at helping its women members to gain economically. But, here, too, the overall goals are more ambitious: economic self-sufficiency is viewed as one critical aspect of a broader empowerment that includes the breaking of restrictive social structures, the building of self-confidence, and an increase in participation in decision making about one's life and community.

Annapurna Mahila Mandal

Annapurna Mahila Mandal is the third of the large organizations that work among poor, self-employed urban women. Two major resources made the emergence of Annapurna possible.[122] The first was the initiative and political expertise of one woman, Prema Purao, its founder. The second was the state's interest in providing bank loans to the self-employed poor. Annapurna's continued growth has been facilitated by its tightly structured organization and its early efficiency, which made it attractive to both international agencies seeking to fund viable non-governmental organizations and to the Indian government.

It was Purao who urged the nationalized banks to give low interest credit to self-employed women and who organized the women so that they could receive the loans. Purao had been a member of the CPI and an organizer for its union, AITUC, for 25 years before starting Annapurna. She was also a member of the National Federation of Indian Women, and during the Anti-Price-Rise Movement she acted as treasurer of its organizing committee. Despite this CPI background, and the fact that she was married to a CPI activist, Purao says that she left the CPI in 1973, and indeed Annapurna is apparently not connected to the CPI;[123] she claims, too, that the members of Annapurna are too busily engaged in "concrete work" to spend much time on agitational activities.[124] Aside from the efforts the leadership makes to lobby government officials, that claim appears to be true; Annapurna's organizing is not apparently aimed at creating an agitational force that will serve the interests of a political party in the manner of NFIW or AIDWA.

Annapurna Mahila Mandal began as a voluntary agency to organize and procure bank loans for self-employed *khanawallis* (food providers);[125] it has since expanded to provide some social services and to generate additional small-scale employment projects. *Khanawallis* are women who in their own homes cook two meals a day for men who have left their families in their villages and have migrated to the city, alone, to work; the men often live in barracks-like facilities. During a textile strike in 1973, the women continued to feed their customers, who now could not pay, despite the fact that this meant sinking into ever increasing debt. It was while organizing the male workers that Purao became aware of the *khanawallis*; she has commented that she suddenly realized that "these women were enabling the workers to continue their struggle. And I realized that as trade unionists we had never looked into the problems of these women."[126]

In 1975, she was approached by a woman who said that she was returning to her village since she was unable to repay her moneylender; her overwhelming indebtedness was hardly surprising, since *khanawallis* were customarily charged as much as 120 percent interest per annum for the loans they needed to purchase supplies.[127] At the suggestion of her husband, Purao approached the Bank of Baroda to see if she could arrange low cost loans for the women.

Purao served as the intermediary between the state's resources and the *khanawallis*, and Annapurna has continued to serve that function by helping to facilitate both the conferring of loans and their repayment. The first loans of Rs. 1500 (approximately U.S. $200) went to fourteen women in 1976. In a structure similar to that arrived at independently by WWF, Annapurna puts together neighborhood groups of ten to fifteen women; while the bank loans go to individuals, the group has to guarantee the loan. The failure of an individual to repay deprives her group's members of future loans; thus, the members are accountable to each other, and there is enormous social pressure to repay.[128] In addition, to help assure a high rate of repayment, an Annapurna staffer accompanies the bank's cash collectors on their rounds, and has the cash collector spend one day a month in each of their local centers. Annapurna further tries to guarantee repayment by taking 200 rupees off the top of every loan of 1500 rupees; this money is placed in a savings account that is used to make loan payments if a creditor falls behind. These strategies have been enormously successful: during Annapurna's first five years, loans were recovered at the rate of 90 percent, compared to a recovery rate of 30 percent for similar loans throughout the country as a whole.[129]

The organization's success in helping the state to loan to self-employed women has generated the interest and support of several foreign agencies, including Oxfam, the Ford Foundation, and Swedish and Norwegian aid agencies, and the continuing support of the Indian government. In 1983, contributions from these bodies enabled Annapurna to open a "multipurpose center" and to expand its social services to include legal assistance, a small health clinic, and a few rooms for those fleeing domestic violence.[130]

Annapurna as a whole is hierarchically structured, with more layers separating the grass roots from the leadership than in WWF. Each individual member (there are now 15,000 of them)[131] belongs to a loan group; these are in turn joined together into some twenty larger units. The smallest organizational unit, the loan group, elects two to three representatives to serve on the area committee, which in turn elects several representatives to the AMM Executive Council, comprised of fifty to sixty members. Atop the Executive Council is an Office Bearers group of about fifteen that meets more regularly; this group includes the Secretary of AMM, Prema Purao, who continues to lead the organization. There is also a hired staff of administrators, who are generally of middle class background, and thus somewhat distanced from the *khanawallis*.[132]

These three urban-based organizations of self-employed women have much in common. All owe their existence in substantial part to the political expertise and party or trade union connections of energetic, educated leaders. These leaders, in turn, have mobilized resources from the government of India and from state governments—resources that were already available in theory, but not in fact. Only through collective organizing could self-employed women demand and receive what was rightfully theirs.

SEWA, Working Women's Forum, and Annapurna Mahila Mandal have also all enjoyed great success in attracting the resources of an international development community anxious to assist women but requiring rationalized organizational structures with identifiable and responsible leaders through which to channel their funds. The desire for local self-governance as a means toward empowerment has thus had to be balanced against this bureaucratic necessity.

Chapter 7 will explore in more detail how these groups have helped empower the self-employed women who are their members.

Notes

1. For a summary of these points, see Doug McAdam, John D. McCarthy and Meyer N. Zald, "Social Movements," in *Handbook of Sociology* ed. Neil J. Smelser (Beverly Hills, CA: Sage, 1988), pp. 715–716.

2. John D. McCarthy and Mayer N. Zald. "Resource Mobilization and Social Movements: A Partial Theory," *American Journal of Sociology* 82 (1977), p. 1222.

3. See Bert Useem, "Solidarity, Breakdown Model and the Boston Anti-Busing Movement." *American Sociological Review* 45 (1980) pp. 357–369.

4. Labor unions also served as midwives to some women's organizations, but these will be discussed in the section below which concerns urban empowerment organizations.

5. Manju Gandhi, "National Federation of Indian Women (NFIW): Work and Issues Taken Up During the Decade." Unpublished paper presented at the National Seminar on a Decade of Women's Movement in India: A Review of Achievements and Issues; Research Unit on Women's Studies, SNDT Women's University, 8 to 10 January, 1985, p. 2; *For Equality: For a Just Social Order* (New Delhi: NFIW, 1984), p. 16. "National Federation of Indian Women," *HOW*, 4:2–3 (1981) p. 14.

6. Jana Everett, "Approaches to the 'Woman Question' in India: From Maternalism to Mobilization," *Women's Studies International Quarterly* 4:2 (1981), p. 171.

7. Interview, Vimla Farooqui, New Delhi, 19 June 1986.

8. Interview, Vimla Farooqui; *For Equality*, p. 27.

9. Interview, Vimal Ranadive, Secretary, AICCWW and Vice President, AIDWA. New Delhi, 18 June 1986.

10. Interview Vina Mazumdar, New Delhi, 23 June 1986. For example, the *CWDS Bulletin*, 1:2, 1983, p. 9 reports on AICCWW organizing a CITU-affiliated union among workers in Kanak Industries, a garment manufacturer in Bombay.

11. The largest number of members, who total 115,000, is in Kerala and West Bengal, where the CPM has been very strong, and in Tamil Nadu. Interview, Vimal Ranadive. Ranadive is married to B. T. Ranadive, president of CITU.

12. A coordinated campaign with DYFI was conducted in New Delhi to protest poor conditions in the resettlement communities that were created by the government on the outskirts of New Delhi when Rajiv Gandhi tore down slum areas in the center of town. Interview, officers of the Delhi Janvadi Mahila Samiti, New Delhi, 21 June 1986.

13. Interview, Vimal Ranadive.

14. Interview with two officers of the Delhi Janvadi Mahila Samiti.

15. "AIDWA Calls for Massive Anti-Price Hike Stir," *The Voice of the Working Woman*, March 1986, p. 8.

16. Vibhuti Patel, "Women's Liberation in India," *New Left Review* no. 153 (1985), p. 86.

17. Interviews, Vimla Farooqui and Vimal Ranadive.

18. "Delhi Janwadi Majila Samiti Holds it First State Conference," *The Voice of the Working Woman* July–Aug 1982, pp. 11–12; "Anti-Dowry Cell Called a Mockery," *Times of India* 5 June 1983; and Interview with officers of Delhi Janvadi Mahila Samiti, 21 June 1986.

19. Pramila Dandavate, "President's Note," in Mahila Dakshata Samiti, *Biennial Report, 1984-85: Report of the Workshop on Relevance of Law to Women; An Introspection of Action and Future Perspectives* (New Delhi, 1985).

20. Everett, "Approaches to the 'Woman Question' . . . ," p. 170.

21. Interview, Pramila Dandavate, New Delhi, 23 July 1986.

22. Madhu Kishwar, "Introduction," in *In Search of Answers* ed. Kishwar and Ruth Vanita (London: Zed Books, 1984), p. 31.

23. Mahila Dakshata Samiti, *Biennial Report, 1984-85*, p. 6; see also "Two Big Anti-Dowry Demonstrations," *Manushi* no. 12 (1982), p. 47

24. Flavia, "The Relationship Between Women's Institutions and Social Movements." Paper presented at the workshop: Institutional Approaches to Helping Women in Distress, organized by Women's Centre and Nirmala Niketan, 1984, Bombay; Interview, Susie Methai of the Bombay YWCA, 14 July 1986.

25. Interview, Ivy Khan, New Delhi, 4 August 1986.

26. Interview, Susie Methai.

27. Beginning in the 1940s, AIWC fought for the creation of a uniform civil code that would guarantee to all Indian women equal rights in inheritance, marriage, and guardianship, consent of both parties for marriage, the prohibition of polygamy and the legitimization of divorce. However, the Congress formulated a *Hindu Code Bill*, which was finally enacted in 1955, and then with unequal rights to inheritance. Flavia, "The Relationship Between Women's Institution and Social Movements," pp. 12–14. For a detailed treatment of AIWC during the pre-independence period see Jana Everett, *Women and Social Change in India* (New Delhi: Heritage Publishers, 1985); and Geraldine Forbes, "From Purdah to Politics: The Social Feminism of the All-India Women's Organizations," in *Separate Worlds*, ed. Hanna Papanek and Gail Minault (Delhi: Chanakya Publications, 1982.)

28. Forbes, "From Purdah," p. 229.

29. All India Women's Conference, *Annual Report, 1983* (New Delhi).

30. Jana Everett, "Approaches to the 'Woman Question' in India: From Maternalism to Mobilization," pp. 169–78. In her 1983 Presidential Address the AIWC president approvingly quoted Napolean's dictum, "Give me good mothers and I can give you a good nation." *AIWC Annual Report, 1983*, p. 46.

31. *AIWC Annual Report, 1983* p. 94.

32. Interview, Vina Mazumdar, 23 June 1986.

33. Vasanth Kannabiran and Veena Shatrugna, "The Relocation of Political Practice—The Stree Shakti Sangathana Experience," *Lokayan Bulletin* 4:6 (1986), p. 24; Interview, Vibhuti Patel, Bombay, 5 July 1986; and Nandita Gandhi, "Women's Movement in India: Proposing an Alternative Perspective," (New Delhi: Lokayan paper, n.d.), p. 42.

34. Neera Desai and Vibhuti Patel, *Indian Women: Change and Challenge in the International Decade 1975-1985* (Bombay: Popular Prakashan, 1985), p. 65.

35. In Bangalore, Vimochna describes itself as "socialist feminist"; "Editorial," *Sangharsh* n.d., p. 2. In Hyderabad, Stree Shakti Sanghathana is "Marxist-feminist"; Kannabiran and Shatrugna, "The Relocation," p. 24. And in Bombay in the late 1970s the Socialist Women's Group put out a newsletter called *Feminist Network*.

36. As the organization was founded in the midst of the Emergency, it took a name that sounded "vague and respectable." This fact, and the following account, are derived from an interview with a founding member of both SIEDS and Vimochna, Corinne Kumar d'Souza, New Delhi, 25 July 1986.

37. "Vimochna: Forum for Women's Rights." pamphlet, n.d.

38. The name of the ill-fated show was "It's a Woman's World." Interview, Kalpana Sharma, Bombay, 18 July 1986. Sharma is a member of the Women and Media Group.

39. "Streelekha: A Woman's Book Place." pamphlet, n.d.

40. Gail Omvedt, "Women in Popular Movements: India and Thailand During the Decade of Women." A Report Prepared for the UNRISD Popular Participation Programme, June 1985, unpublished, p. 13; and Interview, Vibhuti Patel.

41. "Draft Manifesto of the Progressive Organisation of Women,"in *Reaching for Half the Sky: A Reader in Women's Movement* (Baroda: Antar Rahtriya Prakashan, 1985), pp. 105–113.

42. Omvedt, "Women in Popular Movements," p. 15; and Interview, Vibhuti Patel.

43. *Feminist Network* no. 1 (1978), p. 10.

44. Vibhuti Patel, "Women's Liberation in India," pp. 79–80.

45. (New York: David McKay Co., 1975), pp. 63–67.

46. "We Will Not live in Fear Any More," *Manushi* no.5 (1980), pp. 31–34.

47. "Two Big Anti-Dowry Demonstrations," *Manushi* no. 12 (1982), pp. 47–48.

48. *Feminist Network,* July 1978, p. 2.

49. Vibhuti Patel, "Indian Women on Warpath," in *Reaching for Half the Sky* (Baroda: Antar Rashtriya Prakashan, 1985), p. 22. See also Jyoti Punwani, "Morcha to Kala Ghoda," *The Sunday Observer* 23 March 1986.

50. *Womennews,* 2:2 (1985), p. 14.

51. *Report of the National Conference on Women's Studies* (Bombay: Sreemati Nathibai Damodar Thackersey Women's University, April 20–24, 1981).

52. *Report, National Conference: Perspectives for the Autonomous Women's Movement in India,* (Bombay, December 1985), p. 5.

53. Two thousand issues are distributed abroad. The English language edition subsidizes the Hindi edition, which has a distribution of two to three thousand. Interview, Ruth Vanita.

54. Interview, Madhu Kishwar; and "Madhu Interviewed," *Spare Rib* [London] no. 145 (1984), p. 8.

55. Patel, "Indian Women on Warpath."

56. See Urvashi Butalia, "Indian Women and the New Movement" *Women's Studies International Forum* 8:2 (1985), p. 132. Madhu Kishwar, "Introduction," in *In Search of Answers,* p. 31, cites the role MDS played in helping to "sensitize" journalists, who began to give systematic coverage to women's actions concerning dowry death.

57. Notable among them have been Shahnaz Anklesaria's column "Woman and the Law" and Neerja Chowdhury's "Woman's World," both in *The Statesman,* and Kalpana Sharma writing in *The Indian Express.*

58. "Report of Workshop on Communication Network," *Report of National Conference on Perspectives for the Autonomous Women's Movement in India,* p. 14.

59. *Towards Equality,* pp. 239, 241; and Government of India, Ministry of Social and Women's Welfare, *Women in India: Country Paper* (New Delhi, 1985), pp. 43-45.

60. See *Manushi,* no. 1 (1979), p. 30 for advertisement for *Our Bodies Ourselves.* One project of the Stree Shakti Sangathana of Hyderabad, a Marxist-feminist

group, was to translate *Our Bodies Ourselves* into Telegu and rework it to make it more pertinent to Telegu readers. Vasanth Kannabiran and Veena Shatrugna, "The Relocation of Political Practice," p. 33.

61. Interview, Vibhuti Patel.

62. Dorothy Stein makes the point that the reasoning leading up to the Dowry Prohibition Act of 1961, which came prior to the contemporary women's movement either in India or in the West, was "but slightly influenced by the emerging evidence of harassment and cruelty to young wives in the course of demands for augmented payments from her parents. . . . Rather, it focused on the particular social and economic stresses placed on the families of young girls who are required to provide these goods." "Burning Widows, Burning Brides: the Perils of Daughterhood in India," *Pacific Affairs* 61:3 (1988), p. 465.

63. In 1987 an editorial collective in Bombay published *In Search of Our Bodies: A Feminist Look at Women, Health and Reproduction in India* (Bombay: Shakti). The extensive bibliography lists in addition to many Indian sources such standard Western feminist authors as Phyllis Chesler, Mary Daly, Barbara Ehrenreich and Deirdre English, Gena Corea, Linda Gordon, Ellen Frankfort, Rayna Rapp and Jo Freeman. The section of the bibliography entitled "Women's health: Theory and Politics" lists only Western sources. Another indication of international influence is that funding for the book came from the Unitarian Universalist Service Committee.

64. One oft-cited study in Bombay reported that of 8000 abortions performed after sex-determination tests, 7,999 were of female fetuses; the exception was one Jewish woman who wanted a girl. Ameeta Mishra, "Amniocentesis, Law and the Female Child," paper prepared for *Equality, Development and Peace: The Women's Decade in Review, Women's NGO Consultation* (New Delhi: 3–4 April 1985), p. 2.

65. Sharmila Joshi, "The Awakening Feminists," *Imprint* April 1986, p. 67.

66. *A Move Towards Cooperation Between Women's Institutions. Report of a Workshop on "Institutional Approaches to Women in Social Distress"* (Bombay, 1985), p. 3.

67. *Report of the National Conference on Women's Studies* (Bombay: SNDT Women's University, 1981), p. 5. Memo provided by Viji Srinivasan, Program Officer, Ford Foundation, New Delhi; and Interview, Vina Mazumdar.

68. Interview, two officers of the Delhi Janvadi Mahila Samiti, New Delhi, 21 June 1986.

69. The annual reports of the major party-affiliated women's organizations and the large independent organizations are replete with reports of meetings and deputations. See, for example, *All India Women's Conference Annual Report, 1983* and National Federation of Indian Women, *Eleventh Congress, 1984.*

70. Interview, Sumbul Rizvi, an attorney who formerly worked with MDS, New York, 8 June 1989. She left the organization because she felt that each issue was approached first from the angle of how it could be used against Congress, and helped to found an autonomous organization, the Women Lawyers Action and Research Collective.

71. "Declaration of Socialist Women's Group—Bombay," 1977, in *Reaching for Half the Sky,* p. 100. Emphasis in the original.

72. Saheli, *Saheli: The First Four Years* and interview with four members of Saheli, New Delhi, 11 June 1986. In response to my request for an interview, I was told that

it is the policy of the collective that one individual cannot serve as a spokesperson for the group; four members agreed to meet with me.

73. Interview, C. P. Sujaya, New Delhi, 23 June 1986.

74. Saheli, *Saheli: The First Four Years*, p. 15.

75. Saheli, "Women's Organisations: A Perspective." Paper delivered at the National Conference on Women's Studies October 1986, Punjab University, Chandigarh.

76. Ibid., pp. 26–29.

77. *National Conference, Perspectives for the Autonomous Women's Movement in India: A Report*. (Bombay, 1985).

78. Organizations from the following states and cities attended the 1985 conference: Andhra Pradesh, Assam, Bihar, Delhi, Goa, Gujarat, Karnataka, Kerala, Maharashtra, Nagaland, Orissa, Punjab, Tamil Nadu, Uttar Pradesh, and West Bengal.

79. According to Viji Srinivasan, who from 1980 to 1986 was a Program Officer in the New Delhi office of the Ford Foundation, women program officers were hired in all eight Ford field offices at the request of Franklin Thomas, who became president of the Ford Foundation in 1979. In 1980 the New Delhi office began to develop programs explicitly for women. Interview, New Delhi, 28 July 1986.

80. For example, in their paper, "Rural Women's Mobilization: The Khanapur Taluka Experience" (Bombay, SNDT University, National Seminar on A Decade of Women's Movement in India: A Review of Achievements and Issues) Gail Omvedt and Nagmani Rao cite the "decade of struggle and experiences of rural mass organizations like Shramik Sanghatana and others" as a factor in the founding and ideological predispositions of the Mukti Sangharsh, a rural women's movement begun in 1983. p. 6.

81. Some of the following discussion appeared in Calman, "Women and Movement Politics in India," *Asian Survey* 29:10 (October 1989) pp. 954–956. © by The Regents of the University of California, reprinted by permission of the Regents.

82. According to Bhoomi Sena activists. See G.V.S. de Silva, et al., *Bhoomi Sena: A Struggle for People's Power* (Bombay: National instiute of Bank Management, 1978).

83. See Leslie J. Calman, *Protest in Democratic India* (Boulder, CO: Westview Press, 1985), chapter 8; Jana Everett, "We were in the Forefront of the Fight," *South Asia Bulletin* 6:1 (1986); and Amrita Basu, "Two Faces of Protest."

84. Gail Omvedt raises this point in "Women in Popular Movements," p. 16. See also Sujata Gotoskar-Kanhare, "Organising Working Class Women," *How* 5:1 (1982), pp. 11–14.

85. The following account is drawn largely from Shobhita Jain, "Women and People's Ecological Movement: A Case Study of Women's Role in the Chipko Movement in Uttar Pradesh," *Economic and Political Weekly* 13 October 1984, pp. 1788–1794.

86. See Bina Agarwal, *Cold Hearths and Barren Slopes: The Woodfuel Crisis in the Third World* (New Delhi: Allied, 1986).

87. For a critical appraisal of the Chipko movement, see Kumud Sharma, Balaji Pandey and Kusum Nautiyal, "The Chipko Movement in the Uttarkhand Region, Uttar Pradesh, India: Women's Role and Participation," in *Rural Development and*

Women: Lessons from the Field ed. Shimwaayi Muntemba (Geneva: International Labour Office, 1985), pp. 173–193.

88. *Towards Empowerment* ed. Khamla Bhasin (New Delhi: FAO, 1985), pp. 74–83. Part of this discussion is drawn from Maria Mies, "Landless Women Organise," *Manushi* 3:3 (1983), pp. 11–19, rpt. in Bhasin.

89. Interview, Vina Mazumdar (Director CWDS) and Interview, Meena Gupta, Director, Ministry of Labor, New Delhi, 24 July 1986.

90. *Ford Foundation Annual Report,* p. 27. Interview, Marty Chen, 10 June 1986; and Neera Desai and Vibhuti Patel, *Indian Women: Change and Challenge in the International Decade 1975-1985,* p. 54.

91. Marty Chen, *The Working Women's Forum: Organizing for Credit and Change* (New York: SEEDS, 1983); Interview, Viji Srinivasan.

92. Calman, *Protest,* pp. 165–167.

93. Kashtakari Sanghatna, "Kashtakari Sanghatna (The Warli Uprising Revisited," in *Agrarian Struggles in India After Independence* ed. A.R.Desai (Delhi: Oxford, 1986), p. 428.

94. "'Zameen Kenkar? Jote Onkar!' The Story of Women's Participation in the Bodhgaya Struggle," *Manushi* 3:2 (1983), pp. 2–16.

95. Omvedt and Rao, "Rural Women's Mobilization," pp. 1–6.

96. See Kalpana Sharma, "Weaving a Warped Policy," *Indian Express* 23 May 1985; and Maitrayee Mukhopadhyay, *Silver Shackles: Women and Development in India* (Oxford: Oxfam, 1984), p. 49. 60% of the workers in the unorganized sector are women. Government of India, Ministry of Social and Women's Welfare, *Women in India: Country Paper* (New Delhi: 1985), p. 76.

97. In 1961, women were 32% of all workers; in 1981, they were 26%. In 1961 28% of all women worked for remuneration; in 1981 20% did. These figures were shared by Meena Gupta, Director, Ministry of Labour, Interview, New Delhi, 24 July 1986.

98. Renana Jhabvala, *Closing Doors: A Study of the Decline in Women Workers in the Textile Mills of Ahmedabad* (Ahmedabad: SETU, 1985), p. 7.

99. Much the same phenomena has occurred in rural areas touched by the green revolution; in general, when agriculture shifts from subsistence to commercial, women lose out. Interview, Meena Gupta; and Mukhopadhyay, *Silver Shackles,* p. 52.

100. This account of SEWA is drawn largely from the following sources: Devaki Jain, *Women's Quest for Power* (District Ghaziabad: Vikas, 1980); Jennifer Sebstad, *Struggle and Development Among Self Employed Women: A Report on the Self Employed Women's Association, Ahmedabad, India* (Washington, D.C.: AID, 1982); and Interview, Renana Jhabvala, Secretary of SEWA, Ahmedabad, 30 June 1986.

101. For more on the Ahmedabad strike see Judith Brown, *Gandhi's Rise to Power: Indian Politics 1915–1922* (London: Cambridge Univ. Press, 1972), pp. 111–122.

102. As of 1950, women comprised about 25% of the millworkers, but that number has been rapidly declining; by 1969 women were only 4 to 5% of the workers in the mills, and by 1975, only about 2% of the mill workers were women. Sebstad, p. 30; Interview, Jhabvala.

103. Jain, *Women's Quest,* p. 23.

104. Ibid., p. 24.

105. *Shramshakti: Report of the National Commission on Self Employed Women and Women in the Informal Sector* (New Delhi: Gov't of India, 1988), p. 221.

106. Jain, *Women's Quest*, pp. 24–25.

107. For instance, in 1983 SEWA filed a writ petition in the Supreme Court, successfully challenging a ban that had been imposed on *toplawalis*, the women vegetable vendors who sell their goods just outside Ahmedabad's Manek Chowk [market]. The women had been the victims of police harrassment and attempted bribery. "The court directed the municipal corporation and the police to formulate a scheme in consultation with SEWA to accommodate the women vendors." "Working for Women," *India Today* 28 Feb. 1985, pp. 134–135. See also Shahnaz Anklesaria, "United They Gain Face," *Statesman* 19 Dec. 1983.

108. "Working for Women," p. 135.

109. While funds for this venture came from a variety of sources, including private donations and various philanthropies, the largest sum was the Rs. 176,000 (U.S. $20,000) that Bhatt received from her 1977 Magsaysay award. Sebstad, p. 68.

110. Sebstad, p. 68. SEWA has received funding from a number of international organizations, including Oxfam, the Ford Foundation and the International Confederation of Free Trade Unions, as well a number of foreign governments, including Norway, Sweden, the Netherlands and Luxembourg. Ibid., pp. 258–259.

111. A *papad* is a kind of large cracker made from lentil flour. *Chindi* refers to scraps of cloth gathered from local mills and then sewn into quilts.

112. International influence is seen again as the introduction of income-generating projects was in part inspired by a six week seminar on rural women at the Institute of Development Studies, Sussex, Great Britain. Ela Bhatt attended this seminar in early 1978. In addition, funding for SEWA's first rural income generating project was provided by the International Confederation of Free Trade Unions. Sebstad, p. 145.

113. Interview, Jhabvala, and press release issued by SEWA, April 1981.

114. Cited in Tushar Bhatt, "Good Samaritans," *Sunday,* 2-8 December 1984, p. 45

115. *Shramshakti*, p. 222.

116. Jason Brown, "Forum," in *Opinions*, (Madras: Working Women's Forum, 1984).

117. Cited in Marty Chen, *The Working Women's Forum: Organizing for Credit and Change*, p. 2.

118. Chen, p. 20; and Sidney Jones, "Women's Programs in India: Would they Work Here?" Inter-Office Memorandum, Ford Foundation, dated 7 March 1980, rpt. in *Opinions*.

119. Chen, pp. 6–8 discusses this and the structure of WWF.

120. According to a Bank of India study, cited in Nandini Azad, "Reaching Out to Women Workers Through Grassroots Delivery Systems," *Indian and Foreign Review* 21:22 (1984), p. 13.

121. This discussion is derived from Chen, pp. 5–8, 14–15, and 19–20.

122. The following account is drawn from several sources: Prema Purao, "Annapoorna Mahila Mandal," *How* 4:2–3 (1981), pp. 11–13; Prema Purao and Mira Savara, *Annapurna Mahila Mandal* (Bombay, AMM: n.d.); *Annapurna Mahila*

Mandal: Report of Activities from January to September 1984 (Bombay, AMM: 1984); Jana Everett and Mira Savara, "Bank Loans to the Poor in Bombay: Do Women Benefit?" *Signs* 10:2 (1984), pp. 272–290; Jana Everett and Mira Savara, "Class and Gender: The Organizational Involvement of Urban Working Class Women in India," paper prepared for Annual Meeting of the Association for Asian Studies, March 1989.

123. Jana Everett reports that at least up until 1982, some local meetings of Annapurna were held in a CPI storefront; however, it was her impression, too, that there was no significant connection between the two. Telephone interview, 20 June 1989.

124. Interview, Prema Purao, Bombay, 11 July 1986.

125. *Annapurna* is the goddess of food. The name of the group means the goddess of food's women's circle.

126. Quoted in Everett and Savara, "Bank Loans to the Poor in Bombay," p. 283.

127. Purao and Savara, *Annapurna Mahila Mandal*, p. 1.

128. Purao and Savara, Ibid, p. 6.

129. Everett and Savara, "Bank Loans to the Poor," p.285. Annapurna literature claims rates of well over 90 percent; Everett and Savara found that 90 percent of Annapurna loans were repaid on time (p.289).

One study of Annapurna has severely criticized it for collecting fees from members at the time loans are made, and thus leaving the *khanawallis* less money to work with. See Sharayu Mhatre, Sulabha Brahme and Govind Kelkar, *Bank Credit to Women: A Study of Kanavals or Working Class Lunch Suppliers* (Bombay: National Institute of Bank Management, 1980). But taking into account all fees and interest, the first time borrower must pay Rs. 180 for the Rs. 1500 loan, or 12%. After that, her fees to Annapurna are only Rs. 12 per loan.

Is it worth it? Even for the borrower who gets nothing else from Annapurna, and who takes only one loan, it appears to be so. A rate of 12%, after all, is obviously a vast improvement over the moneylenders' rates which range to as much as 120% per annum.

130. Annapurna Mahila Mandal, *Report of Activities*, pp. 6–19.

131. *Shramskakti*, p. 222.

132. Everett and Savara, "Class and Gender," p. 11.

PART TWO

Effectiveness and Potential

5

Ending Violence Against Women

The next three chapters will assess how effective the organizational structures of the Indian women's movement have been and are likely to be in the near future. With respect to the rights wing, this poses some problems of judgment. The attainment of "rights" on paper is easily measured, but the reality of rights is a much more difficult matter. An apparent victory in obtaining a new law may, in fact, be close to meaningless in terms of impact. As Joseph Gusfield has written in a different context, "the achievement of legislation or favorable legal decision by no means implies that the *behavior* under concern has changed."[1] This is eminently true of India, where high government officials freely admit that important pieces of legislation exist "only on paper."[2] While the women's movement has been successful in improving legislation in a number of areas, it appears that, so far, little in the way of behavior—by citizens and by the state, particularly the police—has changed.

But a movement, even one that seeks mainly to move government and to obtain rights, must also be judged by its success in changing attitudes. Thus, in addition to evaluating concrete achievements, the analyst must also look for ideological shifts in both civil and political society that might ultimately bear fruit.

The goal of the rights wing of the movement is to pressure the government to create laws that will protect and expand women's rights. In this, it has enjoyed only very modest success. A number of laws pertaining to violence against women have been changed for the better, but they are still far from what the activists want, and very far from effecting behavioral change. Similarly, there have been some successful attempts to amend personal law in favor of women; but the overwhelming fact is the inability of the women's movement to move the state toward the adoption of a uniform civil code. Instead, we find state cooperation in the reassertion of patriarchal religious mores.

The assumption of rights activists is that the state can force a difference in behavior through legal change. The evidence, thus far, is that it cannot.

Not only are most ordinary Indian citizens steeped in a set of social beliefs and economic structures that mandate women's inferior status in the family and society, but so too are the Indian police officers, lawyers, and jurists who interpret the law.

The value of the campaigns for new laws may derive less from the change in law itself than from the public debate and subsequent consciousness raising and mobilization of women and men that are generated by the campaigns. Demonstrations outside parliament or outside the homes of alleged murderers of women; deputations to highranking politicians; news conferences held by women's organizations: all these receive wide and sympathetic coverage, particularly regarding issues of violence against women. The rights wing of the movement has without question succeeded in taking a range of women's problems that have for millennia been hidden within the family and bringing them into public view; debates about women's independence, once unthinkable, are now commonplace.

The achievement of a new law, then, should be seen as a beginning, as a means of mobilizing support and generating new thinking; the laws themselves, however, given the lack of resources, the continuing societal resistance to women's rights, and the apparent lack of political will on the part of the state to enforce them, are not terribly useful except as they legitimize new societal goals. While it is a positive step, the passage of law must not be confused with an immediate change in reality.

In short, even for the rights wing of the women's movement, what most distinguishes it from politics-as-usual is its ability to raise questions and to change attitudes; fighting for new law can be empowering, but less because the law empowers than because the struggle empowers.

Violence Against Women: Rape

A Philanderer of 22, Phul Singh, *overpowered by sex stress* in excess, hoisted himself into his cousin's house next door, and . . . overpowered the *temptingly lonely prosecutrix* of 24, raped her in hurried heat, and made an urgent exit, having fulfilled his erotic sortie. / . .

A *hypersexed* homo sapien cannot be rehabilitated by humiliating or harsh treatment. . . . The appellant has no vicious antecedents except this fugitive *randy molestation*. . . . We must design a curative course for this prisoner to rid him of his *aphrodisiac overflow* and restore him into safe citizenship. . . . Given correctional courses through meditational therapy . . . his *erotic aberration* may wither away [*sic*].[3]

The above is an excerpt from a decision rendered in 1980 by Supreme Court Justice Krishna Iyer, a man often active on behalf of women's issues, reducing the sentence of a convicted rapist from four years to one. (The emphasis is added.) That a jurist friend of the women's movement perceived rape as a manifestation of "randiness" and eroticism indicates the depth of gender bias against which the women's movement has had to struggle in its battle to criminalize the violence against women that is rape.

Rape of course has long been criminalized, on paper, in the Indian Penal Code; but, because of the attitudes of the police and the judiciary, the possibility of obtaining a conviction has been almost nil. As described in Chapter 3, it was the state's de facto acceptance of rape as evidenced in the Mathura and the Rameeza Bee cases that sparked enormous movement activity in 1979 and 1980. Let us offer one additional example of judicial reasoning.[4] In 1977, in *Pratap Misra and Others versus the State of Orissa*, the Supreme Court overturned the rape convictions of three men; they had been found guilty in Sessions Court and their convictions had been upheld in the High Court. However, Justices P.N. Bhagwati and S.M. Faizal Ali saw the case differently. The Sessions and High Courts believed the following: the three men had burst into a vacation lodge, and forcibly dragged a woman's male companion 15 feet away; two of them held him while the third raped her. She was then raped by a second of the three men. She was five months' pregnant at the time, and a few days later miscarried. In the Sessions and High Courts the three were found guilty not only of rape, but of wrongfully confining the companion, causing the miscarriage, and also of injuring a forest service employee who, with several of his colleagues, had come upon the scene of the two men holding the sobbing companion and had attempted to question them.

The defendants argued that neither of the rapes ever happened; no intercourse ever took place. The Supreme Court rejected that defense, believing it to be a lie, but created one of its own, one that the defense had never dared put forward: the Justices decided that the woman and her companion had consented to the intercourse. Their reasoning was that she was a woman of "bad character."[5] Furthermore, they argued, "The admitted position is that the prosecutrix is a fully grown up lady, habituated to sexual intercourse and was pregnant. She was experienced . . . It is also admitted that she was a midwife and had served in that capacity with a doctor." "Admitting" these facts was tantamount, in the Justices' minds, to acknowledging that she could not be raped. They quoted "medical experts" who were of the opinion that "it is very difficult to rape single-handed a grown up and experienced woman without meeting the stiffest possible resistance from her." They were also influenced by the scientifically "inescapable conclusion" that if she had been raped, she would definitely have suffered a miscarriage immediately, and not several days later.

The outburst of agitation and protest in 1979 and 1980 brought a response in August 1980: the government introduced into the Lok Sabha a

Criminal Law (Amendment) Bill. Four months later, the Bill was referred to a Joint Committee of both houses of parliament; the 84th Law Commission was also established by the government to conduct hearings and make recommendations; and in December 1983, the Bill was finally passed. The interval between its introduction and its passage allowed plenty of time for interested parties to make known their desires and reservations. Women's organizations, whose agitations were responsible for the government taking action, nonetheless had reason to be seriously disappointed with the outcome. The bill was focused almost solely on custodial rape, and even here, most of their suggestions and the suggestions of the Law Commission were ignored.[6]

The most positive aspect of the new law is a direct response to the Mathura and Rameeza Bee cases: in the event of an accusation of custodial rape—that is, when a rape is alleged to have been committed by a man in authority, including a police officer, a jail or women's hostel superintendent, or a hospital staff member—the burden of proof that the incident was not a rape now lies with the accused. If, in these circumstances, the woman says she did not consent, she is to be believed. Further, the law also makes punishable intercourse "not amounting to rape" which occurs after a public official "takes advantage of his official position and induces or seduces" a woman in his custody to have sexual intercourse.

In other words, any sexual intercourse between a public official and a woman in his custody is now suspect; the punishment varies from a minimum of ten years to life for a custodial rapist, to less than five years (no stated minimum) for a custodial "seducer." How the court is to interpret the difference remains to be seen, but, if its past leniency is any guide, it may be conjectured that the court will find more cases of "seduction" than rape.

Although the burden of proof was shifted in the event of custodial rape, women's groups remain skeptical that many such cases will ever reach trial, since evidence can so easily be destroyed by the police or other officials. The Law Commission appointed by the government, along with women's activists, had suggested some changes designed to preserve evidence and thus facilitate prosecutions. It had urged that a police officer in charge of a police station who refuses to record any information that is reported to him shall be punished with imprisonment of one year and/or a fine. But the new law does not ensure that the police will report a rape case if a complaint is made to them. The Law Commission also urged that the law contain a directive that both the man accused of rape and the victim be medically examined without delay. This recommendation, too, did not find its way into the new law.

The Law Commission also made a number of recommendations, which met with the approval of women's groups, for preventative measures designed to limit the number of custodial rapes that occur. It is plain from these suggestions that neither the women's groups nor the Commission had any confidence in the integrity of the police. And indeed, judging from continuing reports in the Indian press about rapes in police custody, or police rapes that take place in the context of putting down social or political unrest, there appears to be precious little reason to trust the police.[7]

The recommendations included the following: (1) A woman should be interrogated only in her own home, and a relative or friend or representative of a women's welfare organization should be with her. (2) No woman should be arrested at night. If she must be arrested after sundown, the arresting officer must obtain permission from a superior. (3) Once a woman is arrested, she should not be kept in a police station, but rather in a women's detention center or welfare institution. None of these suggestions made their way into the new law, a fact which indicates an apparently greater confidence in the police by the parliament than by the women's groups and Law Commission.

Women's groups and advocates also complained that the definition of "custodial" rape was too narrow, and did not encompass those who have other, unofficial forms of power over women, particularly economic power. Under the new law, the minimum sentence for custodial rape is ten years; that for other rapes was increased from two years to seven years (although in either event, the court may, with cause, choose to impose a lesser sentence). Many women argue the difference implies that private individuals like landlords and employers do not also have coercive power that they abuse. Geeta Mukherjee, a CPI MP, had tried to expand the meaning of custodial rape to include "power rape," or economic rape. She and others pointed out that rape seems to be most often committed against economically powerless women, particularly tribals and landless laborers, often by landlords, contractors, employers, money-lenders or the bullies who are hired by them to keep workers in line.[8]

Another omission which angered feminists is that the new law does not forbid the examination of a rape victim's past sexual history.[9] As was seen in the example of *Pratap Misra* . . . cited above and in the Mathura case, it is common in rape cases for a woman who is sexually "experienced" to be deemed of "loose character"; the assumption is that such a woman consented. The suggestion by feminists and, again, by the Law Commission, that the victim's past history be left out of the court room was designed to overcome this judicial prejudice; the suggestion, however, was denied.

Nor were feminists satisfied with the law's provisions on marital rape. Although a number of women's organizations had demanded that forced intercourse by a man with his wife without her consent should be considered rape, the law explicitly states, "Sexual intercourse by a man with his own wife, the wife not being under fifteen years of age, is not rape." The two exceptions to the continued legalization of marital rape are these: if the wife is under fifteen, the husband may be prosecuted for rape. But no minimum punishment is provided by the law if the wife is over *twelve* years of age; the maximum is two years. Also, a husband's forced intercourse with a wife who is legally separated from him is made a crime punishable by up to two years' imprisonment.

The most controversial aspect of the new law is that it abrogates the freedom of the press to cover rape trials. Rape trials are to be held *in camera*, and it is illegal "for any person to print or publish any matter in relation to any proceeding" concerning rape. In addition, the Act makes it a criminal offense, punishable by two years' imprisonment and a fine, to print or publish the name of a rape victim or any information which "may make known the identity" of such a person.

Some women's organizations had requested *in camera* trials, but they wanted access granted to concerned social workers, members of women's organizations and the press; their goal was to keep out intimidating or prurient-minded members of the public. Also, some had asked that the name of the victim not be printed, in order to protect her privacy.[10]

The blanket ban on press coverage greatly dismayed all segments of feminist opinion, the civil liberties organizations, the press, and Opposition MPs, who walked out in protest following the rejection of an amendment that would have allowed the press freedom to report rape cases with the exception of the victim's name.[11] Women's groups repeatedly pointed out that it was precisely the publicity and the pressure that had been generated by women's groups and the press that had moved the government to create a new law. They contended that there is a need to continue to mobilize public interest about rape in order to transform attitudes; the stifling of the press seems designed to limit further progress.

They argued, too, that the ban on any information relating to the victim was misguided; the reputations of the victims of rape would already be damaged in their local communities, and the severe prejudice they would encounter would not be made any worse by publicity.[12] They pointed out, too, that with no press coverage and no publicity by women's organizations, the absurd and sexist logic of courtroom decisions, so frequently encountered in rape cases, cannot readily be exposed. No press coverage, *in camera* trials, and the failure to prohibit examination of the victim's past sexual life do indeed seem to portend a continuation of gross judicial prejudice.

Thus, the passage of the Criminal Law (Amendment) Act in 1983 was hardly a feminist victory. The fact that parliament felt compelled to act in some way, to at least give the appearance of tightening up law and government actions with respect to the crime of rape, signifies a small triumph: segments of the public consciousness had been raised and pressure mobilized. Judicial decisions rife with gender discrimination had been held up to public ridicule, and parliament had acted to correct the inadequacies of courts and police. However, the reality is that the law itself is but a small step forward in the areas of custodial rape and consent, and a big step backward with regard to freedom of the press and the ability of the movement to continue to mobilize public opinion around the issue of rape.

Violence in the Family: Dowry and Dowry Death

"Wife allegedly burnt": Usha Rani, a 22-year-old housewife, and her parents were set on fire in their house on Monday night, allegedly by her husband Nahar Singh, an auto-rickshaw driver . . . A case of attempted murder was registered. (*Statesman*, 4 June 1986.)

"Young woman burns herself": Meenu burnt herself to death in East Delhi last night. The police said that the woman decided to end her life as her family found it difficult to make both ends meet. . . . The woman had a nine-month-old daughter. (*Times of India*, 5 June 1986.)

"Haryana official victim of dowry": Mrs. Dimpy Dalal, a senior officer of the Haryana Government, died of burns in her in-laws' house on Tuesday night, according to her relatives. Her husband Capt. Ajit Singh Lamba of the Army was arrested on a charge of abetment to suicide. In her dying declaration, she stated she had been tortured by her husband and in-laws for not bringing enough dowry. (*Statesman*, 6 June 1986.)

"Commits Suicide": A 28-year-old woman allegedly burnt herself to death because she could not stand the harassment by her husband. The couple had three children aged between 18 months and five years. The police have registered a case of abetment to suicide against the husband, an employee of the New Delhi government. (*Times of India*, 6 June 1986.)

"Dowry Death": A young bride was allegedly killed by her in-laws for not bringing adequate dowry according to a First Information Report (FIR) lodged with the Manpur police station. The victim was thrown into a well by her relatives. (*Times of India*, 7 June 1986.)

"Bring a Car or Drown Yourself": "Why don't you go and drown yourself?" For over a year 23-year-old Shanta had been repeatedly told this by her in-laws, and on May 10 she walked out of her home early in the morning and did just this. (*Statesman*, 8 June 1986.)

Sampuran Singh of Tilak Nagar tried to burn his wife Harbhajan Kaur to death in his house yesterday following an altercation between the two. (*Hindustan Times*, 11 June 1986.)

"Burnt for a Refrigerator": A young life was lost because of the rapacity of the in-laws. It began when the newly married Nirmal (24 years old) was unable to bring a refrigerator as part of her dowry. Nirmal was burnt to death. (*Statesman*, 11 June 1986.)

The above is a typical week's newspaper reporting in the nation's capital. The deaths of young married women are common, regularly reported upon since the women's movement drew attention to them in the late 1970s, and continue unabated. Indeed, they may be on the rise.

The battering and harassment that culminates, in thousands of cases, in murder result from women's subordination in the family and in society, a subordination that state structures uphold. The "dominant form of family structure concentrates immense unchecked power in the hands of men."[13] Some salient facts: most marriages, among all communities in India, are arranged, a practice which is defended not only on the ground that boys and girls have little opportunity for social interaction growing up, but also as a means to find a mate from one's own community and caste. Often, the bride and groom barely know each other, if they know each other at all, before marriage; there is no pretense of affection between the two. The emotional isolation of the bride is exacerbated by the fact that in most communities the bride goes, sometimes a great distance from her natal family, to live with her husband's family; the most common family type is the patrilineal, patrilocal family of at least two generations. This family is characterized by the subordination of women to men, and of younger people to older people; in north India the new bride is most commonly referred to as "daughter-in-law," not as "wife."[14] A new bride is thus at the bottom of the power structure, expected to conform to the desires of her in-laws, to be submissive to them and to her husband.[15] Her future happiness and well-being depend almost entirely on the good will of her new family—people she does not know, and who, with increased urbanization, may be virtually unknown to her relatives as well.[16]

Despite these poorly stacked odds, it is almost unthinkable for an Indian woman of any community not to marry. As a *Hindustan Times* editorial lamented, one thing that all the religious communities in India can agree on is that marriage for a woman is a *sine qua non.* "A woman living alone is viewed with hostility and contempt even when she is supporting herself."[17] Divorce is also gravely frowned upon. Two thousand years ago the Hindu law-giver Manu wrote that "A woman must never be independent." This dictum is largely believed today; worse, it is acted upon by those in authority. For example, the Crimes Against Women Cell, set up by the New Delhi police in 1983 in response to protests by women's groups that the police were inadequately investigating violent domestic crimes against women, frequently engages in family counseling. Its head, Kanwaljit Deol, has said that when a woman comes to her complaining of ill treatment in her home the primary aim of her department is in all cases to to bring about a reconciliation between husband and wife. One officer of the Cell said that she considered it a religious duty for her to reconcile couples; most officers believe that divorce is a disaster for a woman and should be avoided at almost all costs.[18] As long as the idea of a woman who is independent and unmarried is so culturally abhorrent, women in India will never be free.

Even if the marital family becomes a site of unbearable mental or physical cruelty, it is the rare woman who has the skills and the employment opportunities that would allow her to support herself (and her children) if she left, and the courage to face the social hostility that would result from her decision. Her only option may be to return to her natal family; and, often, it is her parents who assure her that life in the new family will get better, and who urge her to stay there. In addition to the disgrace divorce brings on the family, they do not want to have wasted the dowry they paid, and may not be able to afford either to support the divorced daughter or to produce the dowry necessary for a new marriage.

Matrimonial advertisements take up pages in the Sunday newspapers and make clear what is valued in men and in women: the gender stereotypes are stark. Both in the ads placed by the parents of women and in the ads placed by potential grooms, women are invariably described by their physical characteristics; the words "fair," "beautiful," and "slim" recur again and again. Certain admired feminine social characteristics are also commonly described: "charming," "good natured," and, most often, "homely" (which in India means home-loving). Their educations and occupations nowadays are also mentioned; the conspicuously mentioned "convent educated" signifies Westernized, but feminine; and their earning power may be considered an aspect of their dowry.[19] The men are most prominently described by their education, occupation, income and family wealth; physical descriptions usually extend only to height and weight, if that. One man is described as a "a qualified engineer with postgraudate degree from USA, 27 1/2, 174 cms., having industry and business establishments in Delhi and Calcutta." Another has a "high income from small scale industrial unit, Father Class I Officer"; a third is a "Bengali engineer M.B.A., managerial executive in company, in mid-thirties, with income around a lakh [100,000 rupees] annually"; while a fourth advertises himself as a "tall, slim, Jat Sikh, Class-I, Gazetted Officer, Govt of India."[20] As the ads make clear, the men are to provide and to control, the women to charm and obey.

Depending on their religious tradition, women have varying degrees of legal rights to inherit parental property; in practice, a woman nearly always inherits considerably less than her brothers, or nothing at all. But at the time of marriage, she brings a dowry. Some scholars have argued that this dowry constitutes a form of inheritance, and is thus beneficial to women.[21] Madhu Kishwar, who early on argued for a boycott of dowry, and some other women's movement activists have also taken to arguing that until women receive equal inheritance rights, "we have no rights to ask them to sacrifice the inadequate compensation they get by way of dowry."[22] However, others point out that, in practice, the dowry gifts are not given to the daughter, but to her new husband and, most particularly, to his parents; the money is under their control and used for their purposes, not hers. Furthermore, the daughter receives only what her parents can afford to or are willing to give at the time of her marriage; her brothers are entitled to inherit *all* the family wealth. The inheritance a boy receives is income producing—land, a business if there is one—while a girl's dowry consists of consumer goods—jewelry, clothes and, increasingly, sewing machines, stereos, refrigerators, televisions, motorcycles and the like, in addition to cash; land is virtually never given. Thus, it is a mistake to confuse dowry with inheritance; indeed, to argue their similarity is, in Ursula Sharma's words, "a convenient fiction which serves to obscure a real difference between men's and women's relationship to property." What dowry does, in fact, is to purchase "the cancellation of the daughter's automatic right to inherit."[23]

The Committee on the Status of Women in India pointed to another way in which the custom of dowry profoundly harms women: it imposes on the natal family a burden that is in part responsible for the pervasive favoring of boys over girls. Boys are family assets; they represent social security for parents in their old age. Girls are financial liabilities; because of dowry, they hurt the natal family's financial well-being. There is a saying in India that a girl is just "held in trust" by her parents; she is destined to be someone else's asset. It can hardly be denied that this financial difference leads not only to the psychological devaluation of women, but to their lack of access to scarce resources among the poor, to the preference for boys that with modern technology results in the abortion of girl fetuses, and to the horror of the prospect of a divorce that would both throw the woman back on the financial resources of her natal family and force them to try to come up with yet another dowry. Dowry places such a burden on the poor that it contributes to instances of female infanticide.[24] It is surprising that a contemporary activist like Madhu Kishwar neglects these aspects of dowry in rethinking its desirability. It is surprising, too, that the women's movement has no argument with the arranged marriage system of which dowry is an integral, although unadvertised, part, and has never brought up the need for state-sponsored social security as a means of limiting the preference for boys. Given India's economic condition, the latter is perhaps utopian; but it is never even mentioned as a long-term goal or, as far as I know, taken into account as part of the analysis of the oppression of women.

Ending dowry has been a central focus of the rights wing of the movement, mostly because of the drama and horror of the phenomenon of so-called "dowry deaths," in which a woman is murdered by her inlaws and/or husband after what are generally repeated demands for more dowry. When the demands fail, murdering her allows the husband to marry again and acquire a new dowry; as grisly and incredible as this sounds, it happens with regularity.[25]

The victims of "dowry death" are, as a result of the women's movement, now understood, too, to include those women who have committed suicide after being mentally and physically tortured by their in-laws; suicide seems the only recourse when they find themselves unable to face the terrible social stigma of divorce, have no alternative means of support, and have their appeals to come home rejected by their parents.

Although the focus on dowry obscures some of the other socioeconomic and religious causes of women's subordination, the women's movement must be credited with raising social and governmental consciousness about the evils that derive from the demands for dowry; it is a start. The phenomenon, however, in practice continues to grow. Registered cases of dowry deaths nationwide numbered 990 in 1985, 1,319 in 1986 and 1,790 in the first ten months of 1987.[26] But those are only the cases that are registered as murders, and the deaths of young women are almost never so designated. Instead, the police label them "accidents" or "suicides."

If, then, instead of looking to registered dowry deaths, we look to the frequency of violent deaths of young women, we see a much more frightening picture. A memorandum from 13 women's organizations to the Lieutenant Governor of Delhi on December 2, 1983, claimed that the number of young brides who died of burns in New Delhi had shot up from 311 in 1977 to 610 in 1982.[27] In 1983, the Anti-Dowry Cell of the Delhi police reported 690 deaths of women by burning.[28] In 1984, there were some 600 deaths; however only eight of these were classified as murder by the Anti-Dowry Cell.[29] While cases in and near the nation's capital receive the most publicity, there is abundant evidence of dowry murders elsewhere. A study reported in *Economic and Political Weekly* found that 34.2 percent of accidental deaths in urban Maharashtra and 64.9 percent of those in Greater Bombay in 1984 were due to burns. The highest percentage of deaths by "accidents" were in women aged 15 to 44. The researcher examined all the death and post-mortem certificates issued by the Coroner and found a fact indicative of the unwillingness of the authorities to label dowry deaths as murder: "not a single of these certificates gives a cause that can provide even a minimum of a hint of how these accidents were caused."[30]

Nor are "accidental" deaths of women confined to urban areas. Over 1200 cases of suspicious deaths of young married women were reported

to The Achil Bharatiya Hunda Virodhi Chalwal, an anti-dowry organization located in the Vidarbha region of Maharashtra, which encompasses
ten largely rural districts. The deaths—labeled accidents, murders and
suicides—occurred due to burning, poisoning, drowning or strangula-
tion. All the cases reported were of women who died within the first
seven years of their marriages; the largest number of deaths (745) occurred within the first year of marriage, and almost three-fourths of the
victims (930) were between the ages of fifteen and twenty-five. Neerja
Chowdhury, author of the "Woman's World" column in *The Statesman*,
found these facts particularly disquieting, since "Maharashtra has been
considered relatively more progressive from the point of view of women's
status than other States."[31]

Most dowry deaths do seem to occur in northern India. The official
statistics of registered dowry murders from 1982 to 1984 record Uttar
Pradesh with the highest number (446), followed by Haryana (165), Punjab (122), Delhi (112), Rajasthan (83) and Maharashtra (76).[32] However,
dowry deaths have spread to other areas. In 1987, 10 deaths were reported
in Jammu and Kashmir. More dramatic, according to government figures,
has been the spread southward; registered dowry deaths in Andhra
Pradesh leaped from 13 in 1985, to 79 in 1986, to 166 in the first seven
months of 1987. In Tamil Nadu, the number jumped from 12 in 1985 to 38
in 1986. In Karnataka, there were 22 registered dowry deaths in 1984, and
the number is on the rise: there were 50 in 1987. Deaths have also been
reported in Kerala, the state where women are most highly educated, in
the small towns and villages of Gujarat, in Orissa, and in West Bengal.[33]
As these numbers represent only those cases which the police identified
as dowry deaths, the number of women dying violent deaths in what the
police call "suicides" and "accidents" is no doubt far greater.

Rather than being a vestige of the past, the practice of dowry is expanding into more and more communities and castes. With the spread of
capitalism in India and with a growing middle class, dowry takes on new
dimensions, becoming a means for the acquisition of consumer goods
and/or the capital that will seed a new family business venture or pay for
the husband's education. Dowry death is in part a product of upward mo-
bility; and it seems to be especially prevalent among the lower-middle
and middle classes.[34]

The giving and receiving of dowry also is a way in which lower castes
emulate upper castes; it is a modern form of sanskritization.[35] There is
now bride-burning among the scheduled castes, and even among some
tribals, both communities in which women historically have enjoyed
more equality than in the upper castes.[36] And, although less common than
among Hindus, dowry and dowry death also occur among Muslims and
among Christians.[37]

Movement Agitations for New Laws and Better Enforcement

The feminist movement has fought dowry, dowry death and other forms of violence against women in the family by demanding both better laws and better law enforcement. The two are integrally connected, because the "better" laws are by and large efforts to close the loopholes in previous laws that enabled criminals to escape and police and courts to more easily interpret the law to conform with their own gender biases.

Agitational activity has taken a number of forms, and has been prolific. The anti-dowry protests of 1979 and 1980 resulted in the appointment in January 1981 of a joint committee of parliament to review the Prohibition of Dowry Act, 1961; but the joint committee did not announce its findings until 1982, and government took no action in the meantime. In July 1982, Mahila Dakshata Samiti invited a number of other groups to join in a committee that would coordinate the struggle against dowry. Known as Dahej Virodhi Chetana Manch (DVCM), or Forum to Combat the Dowry Menace, it included the major organizations associated with opposition political parties—NFIW, AICCWW, AIDWA—as well as the YWCA, AIWC, a number of student groups, representatives from *Manushi*, the Centre for Women's Development Studies, the War Widows' Association, and the All-India Federation of Consumer Organizations.[38] DVCM cut through broad political and ideological differences among women's groups, and under its auspices many protests took place, resulting in considerable publicity. In August 1982, DVCM marched on parliament, demanding revisions in the Prohibition of Dowry Act, 1961.[39] In the same month, the joint committee issued its report, which was received favorably by women's groups; but its recommendations languished. Women's groups continued to protest, demanding that parliament act.

In February 1983 an anti-dowry conference was held in the AIWC hall, with 30 voluntary groups in attendance.[40] The following month, the prime minister received a delegation of women MPs and representatives of DVCM, who urged her to promote passage of a new dowry prohibition act and amendments to the Criminal Procedure Code; she gave assurances that she would do so.[41] By July 1983, parliament still had not acted, and the DVCM announced plans for ten days of demonstrations to mobilize public support for a new antidowry bill. A few days later the Union Ministry of Social Welfare agreed to give financial assistance to voluntary organizations who run short stay homes for battered women. On August 8, there was the beginning of the first legal breakthrough: the Criminal Law (Amendment) Bill was introduced; this would amend the Indian Penal Code and the Code of Criminal Procedure to make cruelty to a woman by her husband or in-laws a punishable crime.[42] However, angry that the promised dowry amendment had still not been introduced, DCVM again demonstrated outside parliament. The demonstration was organized by five women's groups—MDS, AIDWA, AICCWW, NFIW and the YWCA—of which four were associated with oppostion parties.[43]

The Criminal Law (Second Amendment) Bill was finally passed by the Lok Sabha in December 1983; a comprehensive anti-dowry amendment, however, had still not been introduced, and demonstrations continued. On April 24, NFIW demonstrated outside parliament, and 144 were arrested. DVCM called for a "protest day" to demand the introduction and passage of such an amendment; it urged women to bring their *thalis* (metal plates) and spoons to generate a din that "may awaken the Government from its slumber."[44]

Finally, on May 9, 1984, the government introduced the long-awaited Dowry Prohibition (Amendment) Bill; the Bill, however, was immediately denounced by non-Congress women activists in the parliament[45] and by most women's organizations. The legislative victory, then, was extremely limited; a new law was passed, but was only a slight improvement on the old (1961) version; it fell far short not only of movement demands, but also of the recommendations of the parliamentary joint committee.

Before examining the legislation, let us first make note of other agitational tactics the movement has pursued. In addition to working for improved legislation by meeting with the prime minister, petitioning and demonstrating outside parliament, holding press conferences and generating favorable publicity in the press, movement organizations have also acted with relation to the courts: they have demonstrated outside courts that have acquitted accused dowry murderers, petitioned state governments to file appeals in certain dowry murder cases, and petitioned the courts directly.[46]

Women's groups and civil liberties groups have also conducted their own investigations into deaths the police have deemed suicides or accidents, and used the results to pressure higher authorities to intervene in local police matters; often, getting the attention of officials requires organized demonstrations as well. This was the case, for instance, in a village near Bangalore in January 1983, when the body of an 18-year-old, Pushpavathi, who had been married for eight months, was found hanging from the ceiling of her home; her in-laws insisted that her death was a suicide. The police refused for three days to register Pushpavathi's parents' complaint that she had been murdered; when they finally did, they showed no inclination to act on it.

The case was reported in the press and a women's group, Manini, sent a team of volunteers to investigate. From talking with neighbors and the parents of the young woman, they learned that, upon her marriage, her in-laws had demanded Rs.3000 in dowry; her parents had paid 1500, and the demands continued, accompanied by explicit threats on her safety if the demands were not met. The neighbors pointed out that the ceiling of the room in which she had allegedly hung herself was only 6 feet high; and that the feet of the corpse were touching the ground. They believed she had been killed by her in-laws and her body hung up to make it look like a suicide. Also, her mother-in-law insisted that Pushpavathi had been alone in the house that night because the rest of the family members slept in an outdoor shed; the neighbors pointed out that the shed was too small to have accommodated them.

Manini organized a protest demonstration with two other Bangalore organizations, Vimochna and the Centre for Social Studies. As a result of these efforts, the group met with the superintendent of police and the deputy inspector general of police for the Bangalore district, and the investigation was taken out of the hands of the local police.[47]

A similar story occurred in a town near Nagpur. Here, five days after her marriage, Chandra Sindhwi was burned to death; the local police registered the case as a suicide, although her parents registered a murder case against her in-laws. A team of eighteen volunteers from several women's organizations, including Chhatra Yuva Sangharsh Vahini, Sahjivan and Dahej Virodhi Samiti, went to the village to investigate. Her in-laws did not claim the death was a suicide; they said her sari had accidentally caught fire in the kitchen. But, the activists found, the story was implausible: why had she not run for help from the kitchen on the first floor to the bathroom near the kitchen, instead of to the one on the top floor of the house? Why had no family member heard her screams or come to her aid? Why did the police ignore the postmortem report which found 12 marks on her back caused by the blow of some heavy object?

Women's groups held demonstrations, demanding that the case be removed from the jurisdiction of the local police and given instead to the Central Bureau of Investigation. The chief minister of Maharashtra complied with this demand. As a result, thirty-four days after Chandra Sindwi's death, her father-in-law and eldest brother-in-law were arrested.[48]

In the Punjab, one death the police declared an accident was questioned by a commission of enquiry composed of members of the Punjab Human Rights Committee, the People's Union for Civil Liberties, a local advocate and two local officials. Their investigation led them to conclude that the woman had been murdered. They successfully petitioned the prime minister, who ordered the Ministry of Home Affairs to intervene.[49] In another case in the Punjab, an investigative report by a women's organization, the Jamhuri Adhikar Sabha, disclosed that still another "suicide" was most likely a murder; as a result of its report and continued public pressure, including a protest meeting, the police finally took action against the in-laws.[50]

These are but a few examples of protests aimed at forcing local police departments to do their jobs correctly. One high union government official told me that she regularly receives calls from bereaved parents asking her help in getting local police departments to investigate their daughters' deaths. Her belief is that police are reluctant to register married women's deaths as cases of murder, or even as illegal cruelty to wives under Criminal Procedure Code section 498a, since both of these charges are very difficult to prove; rather than have a number of unsolved cases on their records, the police would prefer to declare a suicide or accident and close the case.[51]

As we turn now to a discussion of the new laws that have been put into place with respect to dowry, it is well to keep in mind, then, that if the past is any guide, loopholes in these laws will continue to be used by the police to avoid filing cases of murder. Since even the new laws are filled with such loopholes, this does not bode well.

New Legal Measures to Safeguard Women

As a result of lobbying and agitation by the women's movement, a joint committee of parliament, with 21 MPs from a number of different parties, was appointed in January 1981 to suggest ways to end the giving of dowry (which had been outlawed since the Dowry Prohibition Act of 1961, but with no effect) and to prosecute those responsible for "dowry deaths." The report of the committee, which was nearly unanimous, was presented to parliament on 11 August 1982, but over a year passed before any legislative action was taken on its recommendations. Finally, two new laws came into being: the Criminal Law (Second Amendment) Act of 1983 became law in December 1983, and the Dowry Prohibition (Amendment) Act of 1984 came into effect in October of 1985. The former came closest to meeting both the demands of the women's movement and the suggestions of the parliamentary committee; the Dowry Prohibition (Amendment) Act, in contrast, was a major disappointment.

The purpose of the Criminal Law (Second Amendment) Act of 1983[52] is to encourage the prosecution and conviction of dowry murderers by (1) expanding the categories under which prosecutions may take place, (2) forcing the police to investigate suspicious cases, and (3) loosening some of the evidentiary requirements for a finding of guilty. It attempts to accomplish these goals through amendments to the Indian Penal Code, the Code of Criminal Procedure, and the Indian Evidence Act.

The first task was addressed by adding a section 498a to the Indian Penal Code: this makes *cruelty* to a woman by her husband or any of his relatives a crime punishable by up to three years' imprisonment, plus a fine. Cruelty is defined in two ways. The first is "conduct of such a nature as is likely to drive the woman to commit suicide or to cause grave injury or danger to life, limb or health (whether mental or physical) of the woman." This is a significant departure from previous law in that it makes *mental* cruelty, not just physical abuse, a punishable crime.[53] The second definition of cruelty ties it directly to continuing demands for dowry; cruelty means harassment of the woman with a view to coercing her, or any person related to her, to meet an unlawful demand for any property; or harassment because she or her relatives have failed to meet such demands. Again, cruelty need not be a physical act, but may include psychological threats.

Through the efforts of women's organizations, the careless or hostile attitude of the police to complaints of dowry death had become well known to lawmakers, and the 1983 Act included several provisions designed either to force the police to investigate or to allow private citizens to petition the courts directly. Women's organizations had complained that critical evidence was often covered up; most importantly, the body of the victim was often cremated before it could be examined by physicians or even seen by the woman's relatives. In earlier law, police officers were granted considerable discretion to judge if "there is any doubt regarding the cause of death"; and only if so, to order a medical examination of the body. The 1983 Act specifies that an officer *must* order a post mortem in any death of a woman who has been married for less than seven years in the event of suicide, of circumstances that create "a reasonable suspicion that some other person committed an offense" against her, or when any relative of hers makes such a request.

In addition, under the 1983 Act, there is recourse for investigation aside from the police: magistrates are empowered to hold enquiries into the cause of death of any woman who dies in the circumstances just described. Finally, by way of increasing pressure to investigate, any court can take up a case of cruelty under Section 498a *either* upon the receipt of a police report *or* upon a complaint made by the parents, siblings, or other blood relatives of the deceased. Again, there is a way for private citizens to circumvent police reluctance to intervene.

The final way in which the Criminal Law (Second Amendment) Act of 1983 attempts to strengthen efforts to prosecute dowry death is with an amendment to the Indian Evidence Act (section 113-A). In the event of the suicide of a woman who has been married for less than seven years, where it can be shown that her husband or his relatives had "subjected her to cruelty," the court "may presume" that "such suicide had been abetted by her husband" or by his relatives; abetment to suicide is a criminal offense.

For the most part, the Criminal Law (Amendment) Act of 1983 was welcomed by women's organizations and feminist commentators as strengthening the possibilities for the prosecution of dowry deaths, or deaths inspired, more generally, by the abuse of women within their marriage home. There were, however, some valid complaints that the bill did not go far enough. While it was considered an important advance that the courts would consider a complaint of cruelty made by the deceased relatives, feminists asked why the bill did not make an allowance for complaints to be made by registered women's organizations;[54] one of these, after all, is frequently the body to whom grieving relatives first turn for assistance, and such a body may have better resources for pursing a case than does the family. Furthermore, the joint committee of parliament had so recommended.

Another complaint about the Act was that it had nothing at all to say about the confused legal status of dying declarations: who must record them, and under what circumstances they will be considered valid evidence.[55] The courts regularly make a practice of dismissing a woman's dying declaration because a magistrate was not present, or because the woman was in too much pain to be believed. For example, in a 1984 case,[56] a Delhi High Court dismissed three separate declarations Shanni Kaur made as she lay dying of burns in a Delhi hospital; in each of the three statements she said her husband had poured kerosene on her and burned her. The first declaration was disbelieved by the court on the grounds that the doctor to whom the statement was made, and who recorded it, had not yet examined her to ensure she was "fit enough" to make the statement. The second declaration, made to the police, was dismissed because the judges suspected the police of recording the statement with a view to getting a reward. The *third* dying declaration was made to a second doctor, who *had* examined Shanni Kaur and found her fit to make a statement. But the court held that since she was "crying with pain" her statement could not be believed. The 1983 Act did nothing to dismiss the apparent judicial assumption that women are untrustworthy or to lend greater evidentiary weight to the declarations of dying women.

Writing in *The Statesman*,[57] Shahnaz Anklesaria made another good point about the limitations of the act for protecting women: Who is to care for a woman and her children if she complains of a husband's cruelty and he, as a result, goes to jail? One state, Orissa, empowers its courts to make provision for monthly payments to a woman in this circumstance,[58] but other states and the union government do not. How likely is a woman to send her husband to jail if she has no other means of support?

Even greater criticism was leveled at the 1983 Act for making no direct assault on dowry. The issue of dowry was finally addressed, after several years' delay, in what proved to be the very disappointing Dowry Prohibition (Amendment) Act of 1984. Feminists, women's organizations, and the English-language press bitterly denounced several aspects of the Act, which for the most part ignored the suggestions that had been made by the joint committee of parliament.[59] In the new law: (1) the definition of dowry is too filled with loopholes to allow for prosecution, (2) no ceiling is put on the amount of gifts that may be given, (3) the giving of dowry is equated with the demand for dowry, (4) the punishment provided is too weak, and (5) there is no provision for enforcement.

In 1961 the Dowry Prohibition Act had outlawed the giving or taking of dowry *in consideration of marriage;* in other words, in order to prove a crime, the dowry had to be shown to be a condition of the husband's agreement to marry. This was virtually impossible to do, since it could be claimed that the girl's parents had not given dowry, but rather "gifts" inspired by love of their daughter and her new husband.

The 1984 amendment was scarcely an improvement.[60] In the new language, the giving and taking of dowry *in connection with the marriage* is outlawed. The idea here was to take note of the fact that dowry demands often continue after a marriage has taken place. However, the vagueness of the language leaves intact the same problem that was present in the 1961 Act: it can be claimed that "gifts," not dowry, were received.

Indeed, the 1984 Act encourages this fiction by refusing to set a limit on the amount of gifts that can be given. Section 3 exempts from the prohibition of dowry any "presents" given to the bride or bridegroom at marriage "without any demand having been made on that behalf." The bride and bridegroom must make a written list of such presents, which should be "of a customary nature"; their value must not be "excessive having regard to the financial status of the person by whom. . . such presents are given."

This section has the effect of virtually nullifying the alleged purpose of the amendment, for, in practice, unlimited "gifts" are to be allowed. Although the joint commitee had recommended a gift limit of 20 percent of the bride's family's income during the previous year, in the Act what is "excessive" is nowhere defined. Nor is the meaning of "customary nature." All the new law does then, really, is to urge voluntary restraint. But as one commentator points out, the 1984 Act could easily have the opposite effect; it "may even encourage competition among upper class parents of [marriageable daughters], each trying to prove by giving hefty presents that his 'financial status' is greater than that of others."[61] In addition, by allowing gifts of a "customary nature," the Act appears to condone, rather than condemn, dowry.

Another criticism of the 1984 Act is that it treats the giver and the demander of dowry equally. Again, the joint committee had recommended against this, urging that the giver of dowry should not be prosecuted. And, indeed, common sense dictates that "no person, however much victimized, will go to the police knowing that he, too, can be arrested."[62] Nonetheless, the law is written in such a way as to discourage rather than encourage prosecution.

The Act provides that an individual found guilty of giving or receiving dowry must receive a prison term of between six months and two years, plus a fine of Rs. 10,000 or the value of the dowry, whichever is higher; the court is enabled, however, to take into account "adequate and special reasons" and so deliver a sentence of less than six months. In New Delhi, nine women's and civil liberties organizations called for a minimum prison sentence of one year.[63]

There were a few bright spots: under the new law, the giving or taking of dowry was made a cognizable offense, meaning that the police may make arrests without first obtaining a warrant. In addition, courts will take cognizance of an offense if registered by the police, if a complaint is made by a relative of a person involved, or if a complaint is made by a "recognized welfare institution or organization"; unlike in the 1983 Criminal (Second Amendment) Act, here the role of women's and civil liberties organizations is recognized.

But critics of the new bill were not satisfied with the implementation machinery created to set it in motion: not surprising, since there was none. The joint committee had recommended that state governments should appoint dowry prohibition officers for local areas, who should in turn be associated with an advisory board of women social workers.[64] This recommendation was not taken up by parliament. Instead, the instrument for the enforcement of the Act is supposed to be the list of presents given to the bride and bridegroom; any other presents will be considered illegal dowry. Putting aside for the moment the obvious ease of falsifying such a list, and the fact that there is no limit set on the value of "presents" that may be received (and thus the whole exercise seems to prove nothing), let us focus only on the question of what governmental body is to monitor and enforce this instrument. In an interview in December 1985, Margaret Alva, Union Minister for Women's Welfare, was asked about her plans for the new law. She responded:

> Well, to begin with implementation, the enforcement of the dowry act has been transferred from the Home Ministry to the Ministry of Women's Welfare. The infrastructure has got to be created by us. It is not just a question of law and order, or a question of police, it is the question of human resource development, you know, the question of women, their thinking, educating them and so on and so forth.[65]

Despite the fact that it was obvious to many observers that "successful administration of the Act will require a gigantic enforcement organization,"[66] it is clear from Alva's words that the government had at the time of the law's passage no plans to facilitate its implementation.

A small move towards implementation—at least on paper—did come in August 1986, when parliament passed another amendment to the Dowry Prohibition Act. This accepted the recommendations of the 1982 Committee and provided for the appointment of "dowry prohibition officers" by the states. The new amendment also significantly raised the punishment for the taking of dowry to a minimum of five years. Finally the new bill has made dowry murder a crime listed in the Indian penal code.[67]

Thus it can be concluded that the rights wing of the women's movement had generated enough publicity, concern, and pressure to move the government to act in a way that would give it the appearance of fighting dowry death, and even, indeed, to take some small steps in that direction. But legislative action has so far fallen far short of what the women's movement desires. While there have been some celebrated court victories for women's organizations—most notably the Supreme Court's upholding in 1985 of the conviction of the murderers of Sudha Goel[68]—the number of convictions is still infinitesimal.

It is apparent that, given prevailing social norms, the sexism of the police and of the courts, the conservative nature of the state, and the lack of political will to enforce laws that threaten the structure of the patriarchal family, changes in law *per se* have only very limited utility. In the short run, the laws do seem to create some small heightening of consciousness in the police force and the courts, and among a part of the public. Indeed, the generating of discussion around the issues, including the public debate that accompanies the introduction and passage of the new laws, is of more importance than are the feeble laws themselves. Until there is a greater and more widespread raising of public consciousness, and accompanying social pressure, new improved laws will be of little practical significance.

Raising Consciousness About Violence

Fortunately, the rights wing of the movement does embrace an additional strategy designed to help women resist the violence against them, and it is here that the distinction between the rights and empowerment wings becomes bridged. Groups such as Saheli in New Delhi and the Women's Centre in Bombay, while active in agitational work and the generation of publicity for new law, also seek to empower individual women in order to enable them, psychologically and financially, to leave dangerous homes.

As we have seen, for a woman to leave her abusive husband or inlaws takes enormous courage; she will often receive no help from her parents, will find it difficult if not impossible to re-marry, and will face widespread social opprobrium. If she has children, and leaves her home without them, she is likely to lose those children.

She will also be confronted with overwhelming practical problems. Where will she live? How will she earn a living? It is extremely uncommon for an Indian woman to live alone; in addition to the considerable social pressures against it, women are afraid of harassment and violence, and, in any case, can rarely afford to rent an apartment or own a home. Nor can they readily share an apartment or house with another woman; landlords are suspicious and usually unwilling to rent to women.[69] Thus nearly all women, even unmarried urban professionals, live in a family setting.[70] Those who do not live with their natal family still rarely live on their own. If they are in urban areas, and they are working women or students, they may get a room in a women's "hostel." These are most often run by social service agencies, or sometimes by the government, and closely resemble American dormitories of the pre–"sexual revolution" era. In the women's hostel run by AIWC in New Delhi, for example, notices on the hall bulletin boards are addressed to the "inmates" and signed by the "warden." Even making allowances for the differences between U.S. and Indian English, this usage reflects a good deal of the flavor of the place.[71]

A woman who escapes from a bad marriage and, often, from battering, cannot expect a court to award her ownership of the marital home; there is no community property in Indian law, and the home is considered her husband's property, even if she helped to finance it. If she is in a rural area, the land (and the home on it) belongs to men; wives and daughters do not inherit land.[72] The small maintenance she may be awarded for child support at the time of divorce will not be enough to finance housing;[73] prior to the divorce, of course, she will receive no maintenance of any kind.

Consequently, if her natal family will not welcome her, a woman's ability to find a place to live is extremely limited. In a country of over eight hundred million people, the government operates twenty-six short-stay homes for battered women.[74] Even if a woman can afford to live in a hostel, it is virtually impossible for her to be admitted to one if she has children with her. In 1985, the government opened Delhi's only shelter for women with children.[75] In 1986, the Bombay YWCA was planning to save a few rooms for women with children in the new hostel it was building; this would constitute a first in Bombay, a city of over eight million.[76]

Thus, for a woman to leave a home in which she is the victim of violence requires not only enormous courage but also substantial assistance.

She needs to find employment, shelter and, possibly, childcare. All of these are extremely scarce.

On a very small scale, some autonomous organizations try to provide both courage and resources. Bombay's Women's Centre and Delhi's Saheli, philosophically and operationally quite similar, provide good examples.[77] In their day-to-day operations, both groups counsel and offer limited material resources to women who are the victims of domestic violence. Their first service is to listen sympathetically, to let the woman know that she is not alone in her troubles and, by so doing, to begin to have her see that her problems are systemic rather than personal or unique to her. Saheli and the Women's Centre also sponsor discussion groups for women with similar problems, designed to raise feminist consciousness and political awareness, provide mutual support, and help the women to decide what action they want to take. Volunteers in both organizations are conscious of the need to empower the woman who has been battered, to help her psychologically and financially to stand on her own feet, and to prevent her from merely transferring her dependency on her family to dependency on the volunteers.

By way of immediate practical assistance, the groups help women file police reports, establish contacts with sympathetic lawyers and physicians, and try to find them jobs and housing. The last is by far the most difficult. Members of both organizations frequently provide temporary shelter in their own homes; Saheli, with some government funding, also has two rented rooms available. Both organizations lament their limited capabilities in this area, and they have called on the state to provide safe temporary as well as affordable permanent housing for women.

Each organization developed out of agitational activity, and each remains active in efforts to move the state. Saheli is a regular participant in Delhi-based demonstrations and petitions; volunteers and staff of the Women's Centre are often members, too, of the Forum Against the Oppression of Women, which generates publicity and organizes demonstrations around women's issues. They are acutely aware that their efforts to empower individual women can have only a very small impact in the absence of greater social and political change.

Indeed, it is the limits of private efforts to help the individual victims of violence that point up the need for broad social and political action. There must be greater societal acceptance of independent women; and so broad ideological transformation is necessary. It is the state that has the resources to create housing and employment training, and the state that has the power to change the laws that deprive women of community property and equal inheritance rights. Again, a widespread change in consciousness is needed to move government to act, and that change will not come without the pressure of movement activity.

To be sure, efforts to change law have thus far been far from successful in altering behavior. Small-scale efforts to empower women to escape violence, while of critical importance to the few women they touch, presently exist on too small a scale to have broad effect. Still, both efforts are necessary, for both are means of struggling against deeply imbedded sexism in ideas and in law that deprive women of equal political rights and economic opportunity. The first task of the rights wing of the movement is to shake up the status quo, to raise questions, to challenge. Both agitations aiming directly at government and efforts to empower at the grass roots are means of accomplishing this; they are complementary efforts.

But the battle will not be easily won. The state has shown itself to be fundamentally conservative in relation to rape and domestic violence; the new laws are but slight improvements over the old. The victory, if there has been one, must be seen as resting in the struggle itself, and the debate that has been initiated; new ideas have become thinkable, but significant structural changes will still be a long time coming.

The situation is even more grim with respect to the rights the state is willing to guarantee women through "personal" or family law. Here we find active opposition coming from politically powerful forces; the struggle for a heightened feminist consciousness and state-sponsored equality for women comes into a direct conflict with religious sensibilities and communal tensions. It is to this topic that we now turn.

Notes

1. Joseph Gusfield, "Social Movement and Social Change: Perspectives of Linearity and Fluidity," in *Research in Social Movements, Conflicts and Change*, 4 (1981), p. 324, emphasis added. Gusfield gives as an example the success of the U.S. temperance movement in passing the prohibition amendment. If, however, we judge this movement by its effect on drinking *behavior*, it was a dismal failure.

2. C.P. Sujaya, Joint Secretary of the Department of Women and Child Development, speaking of the Equal Remuneration Act and the Minimum Wages Act (Interview, New Delhi, 23 June 1986).

3. Cited in "Such Lofty Sympathy for a Rapist!" *Manushi* no. 5 (1980), p. 35.

4. The case and decision are detailed in "The New Rape Bill," *Manushi* no. 7 (1981), pp. 38–45.

5. The woman and her companion considered themselves married; they had been married by an exchange of garlands. However, she was the man's *second* wife; the High Court therefore considered her to be his concubine.

6. For analyses and critiques of the Criminal Law (Amendment) Act, 1983, see: Lawyers Collective, *Recent Changes in Laws Relating to Women* (Bombay: Lawyers Collective, 1985), pp. 2–8; Ruth Vanita, "The Bills to Amend the Rape and Dowry

Laws—Mending or Marring?" *Manushi* no.16 (1983), pp. 27–30; "The New Rape Bill," *Manushi* no. 7 (1981), pp. 38–45; "Rape: Loopholes in Law," several articles in *How* 4:2-3 (1981), pp. 24–30; Kalpana Sharma, "Cosmetic Changes in Rape Law," *Indian Express*, 31 Dec. 1983; "The New Law on Rape," *CWDS Bulletin* 2:1 (1984), pp. 8–9; and "A Watered Down Amendment," *Eve's Weekly*, 7–13 Jan. 1984, p. 19.

7. See, for example, "Police and Women," *Economic and Political Weekly*, 22 Jan. 1983, pp. 99–100; "Custodial Rape," *Indian Express*, 7 April 1984; "Exploitation of Women," *Economic Times*, 23 June 1985; "Rape in Police Custody," *Sunday*, 14–20 April 1985, p. 48; "Cover Up of Gang Rape by Policemen," *EPW*, 22 Feb. 1986; "Grave Charges," *India Today*, 15 Dec. 1986; "Rapists in Uniform," *The Times of India*, 31 March 1986; "Crimes Against Women: Government Indifference," *EPW*, 2–9 Jan. 1988, pp. 5–6.

8. "Interview of the Week: Geeta Mukherjee," *Sunday Observer*, 11 Dec. 1983. A study by the Bureau of Police Research and Development in 1983 found that accused rapists in rural areas "were mostly those holding women in positions of economic subordination." (Reported in "Rape: Controversial Code," *India Today*, 31 Dec. 1983, p. 134.) In addition, some local studies bear out the contention that women of scheduled castes and tribes are the most frequent victims. See "He's Probably Someone You Know," *The Times of India*, 27 May 1984. There are also ample examples of massive, systematic rapes that occur during social and labor unrest by hired thugs of landlords or by the police against agricultural laborers or industrial strikers. See Shahnaz Anklesaria, "Women and Rape: Defenceless Before Laws and Man," *Himmat*, 7 March 1980, pp. 13-18; and Uma Chakravarti, "Rape, Class and the State," *PUCL Bulletin* [People's Union for Civil Liberties] 2:9 (1982), pp. 16–17.

9. Subhadra Butalia, "Karmika Demands Abolish Humiliating Cross Examination, Place the Onus of Consent on Accused," *How* 4:2–3 (1981), p. 30.

10. *How* 4:2–3 (1981), p. 27 published a statement by five Delhi women's organizations—Delhi Women Lawyers Federation, Karmika, Manushi, Stri Sangharsh, and Action India—which made these recommendations.

11. "Bill on rape passed after walkout," *Hindustan Times*, 7 Dec. 1983.

12. See Kalpana Sharma, "Cosmetic changes in rape law," and Ruth Vanita, "The Bill to Amend."

13. Madhu Kishwar, "Introduction," in *In Search of Answers*, ed. Madhu Kishwar and Ruth Vanita (London: Zed Press, 1984), p. 16.

14. Maria Mies, *Indian Women and Patriarchy* (New Delhi: Concept Publishing, 1980), p. 98.

15. See Govind Kelkar, "Women and Structural Violence in India," *Women's Studies Quarterly* 12:3–4 (1985), pp. 16–18.

16. Dorothy Stein makes the excellent point that marriages among the more urbanized are "frequently contracted with families hitherto unknown, sometimes through newspaper advertisements. . . . The families of the prospective mates are checked and assessed by respected third parties and acquaintances, but such judgments can hardly be expected to have the thoroughness of many years of local rep-

utation." "Burning Widows, Burning Brides: The Perils of Daughterhood in India," *Pacific Affairs* 61:3 (1988), p. 477.

17. "Equality for Women," 12 June 1986.

18. Ruth Vanita, "Can Police Reform Husbands?: The Crimes Against Women Cell, New Delhi," *Manushi* no. 40 (1987), p. 14.

19. Stein, "Burning Widows," p. 478.

20. These examples are taken from the 22 June 1986 editions of *The Times of India* and *The Hindustan Times Weekly*; there are pages and pages of such ads each week.

21. See J. Goody, *Production and Reproduction: A Comparative Study of the Domestic Domain* (Cambridge: Cambridge Univ. Press, 1976).

22. "Beginning With Our Own Lives," *Manushi* no. 5 (1980), p. 3; and Kishwar, "Rethinking Dowry Boycott," *Manushi*, no. 48 (1988), p. 10.

23. Ursula Sharma, *Women, Work and Property in North-West India* (London: Tavistock Publishers, 1980), pp. 47–48. See also Kelkar, "Women and Structural Violence," p. 17.

24. "Born To Die," *India Today*, 15 June 1986, pp. 10–17.

25. Shahnaz Anklesaria states, "The Hindu Marriage Act, 1955 made bigamy a criminal offence in most states. . . . After this Act came into force, killing a wife has become one of the easiest ways of circumventing it." "Women in Gujarat: Behind the Facade," *Eve's Weekly*, 26 Feb. 1981, p. 14.

26. "The Horror Spreads," *India Today*, 30 June 1988 and *Indian Express*, 10 Dec. 1987.

27. *Indian Express*, 3 Dec. 1983.

28. Rajashri Das Gupta, "Reaching Out Towards Brave New World," *Business Standard*, 10 March 1985.

29. Neerja Chowdhury, "Some Haunting Question Marks," *The Statesman*, 6 July 1985.

30. Malini Karkal, "How The Other Half Dies in Bombay," *EPW*, 24 August 1985.

31. Neerja Chowdhury, "Where Parents of Murdered Bride Slip Up," *The Statesman*, 23 Dec. 1985.

32. "Feeble Efforts," *The Hindu*, 1 May 1985.

33. "The Horror Spreads," *India Today*, 30 June 1988; "Public Outcry," *India Today*, 31 Dec. 1987; Shahnaz Anklesaria, "Women in Gujarat," pp. 13–15; and dowry files in the Center for Education and Documentation, Bombay.

34. Interview, C. P. Sujaya, New Delhi, 23 June 1986. See also Sevanti Ninan and Sanjay Suri, "Most deaths in lower middle class," *Indian Express*, 5 August 1983; and Sonal Shukla, *Dowry in Bombay: Some Observations* (Bombay: Women's Center, 1985), p. 20, who says that the practice of dowry seems to be spreading among the working class of Bombay.

35. Interview, Govind Kelkar, scholar at the Center for Women's Development Studies, New Delhi, 9 June 1986.

36. "The Horror Spreads," p. 59.

37. Ibid. See also Runu Chakravarty, "Dowry among Muslims—A Case His-

tory," *HOW* 6:3 (1983), p. 9; Sonal Shukla, *Dowry in Bombay* pp. 22–23; and "Dowry: Spreading Among More Communities," *Manushi* no. 16 (1983), pp. 31–32.

38. *Hindustan Times,* 2 July 1982; *The Statesman* 18 March 1983.

39. "Anti-Dowry March to Parliament," *The Voice of Working Women* (1982), p. 12.

40. *Times of India,* 1 March 1983.

41. *The Statesman,* 18 March 1983.

42. *Indian Express,* 10 July 1983 and 14 July 1983; *The Statesman,* 9 August 1983.

43. *Indian Express,* 27 August 1983.

44. For report of DVCM press conference, see for example, *The Statesman,* 26 April 1984.

45. Suseela Gopalan, CPM; Pramilla Dandavate, Janata; and Geeta Mukherjee, CPI, all immediately denounced the bill from the floor as a "mockery" and "useless." *Hindu,* 10 May 1984.

46. See *The Statesman,* 8 Nov. 1983; *Indian Express,* 3 Dec.1983; and *The Daily,* 1 August 1984.

47. "Bangalore: Anti Dowry Actions," *Manushi* no. 15 (1983), p. 30.

48. "Maharashtra: People Pressurize for Justice," *Manushi* no. 9 (1981), pp. 21, 25.

49. "Mobilizing Against Dowry Murders," *Manushi* no. 13 (1982), p. 41.

50. "Protest Against Bride's Death," *Manushi* no. 36 (1986), p. 21. For some more recent cases of public demands for police action see "Who Can Stop a Man," *Manushi* no. 46 (1988), pp. 11–13; and "Public Outcry," *India Today,* 31 Dec. 1987, p. 21.

51. Interview, C. P. Sujaya, New Delhi, 23 June 1986.

52. For some commentary of this Act, see Lawyers Collective, *Recent Changes in Laws Relating to Women* (Bombay: Lawyers Collective, 1985), pp. 9–11 (and text of the Act, pp. 36–40); and Pinky Anand, "Positive Potential," *Manushi* no. 24 (1984), p. 28.

53. This law also expands the definition of abetment to suicide, a crime since 1860 under Penal Code section 306. Section 306 was designed to prosecute only those who forced or encouraged a woman to commit *sati* (widow self-immolation). In response to local public pressure, police had occasionally called on section 306 to arrest family members who had apparently driven a woman to suicide. However, until 1983 there had been only two convictions throughout India under section 306 relating to a dowry death. Neerja Chowdhury, "Tears Can't Be Measured," *The Statesman,* 9 July 1983.

54. *CWDS Bulletin* 1:2 (1983), p. 8.

55. Shahnaz Anklesaria, "No Effort to Amend Rape Law," *The Statesman,* 29 August 1983.

56. *Smt. Harvinder Kaur v. Harmander Singh Choudhary* A.I.R. (1984) Delhi 66, discussed in Nandita Haksar, *Demystification of Law for Women* (New Delhi: Lancer Press, 1986), pp. 98–99.

57. "No Effort to Amend Rape Law," 29 August 1983.

58. The 1976 Orissa Dowry Prohibition (Amendment) Act.

59. A summary of the Committee's recommendations is available in "Curbing the Evils of Dowry System," *Yojana,* 1–15 November 1983, pp.10–14.

60. For criticism by women's groups, feminists and the press of the 1984 Act, see Lawyers Collective, *Recent Changes in Laws Relating to Women;* "The Dowry Prohibition Act, 1961: the Struggle for an Amendment," *Samya Shakti* 1:2 (1984), pp. 131–134 (this records a memorandum prepared by ten women's and civil liberties organizations in response to the Act); Ruth Vanita, "Nominal Changes," *Manushi* no. 24 (1984), pp. 29–31. Editorials in *Times of India,* 26 March 1985; *The Hindu,* 1 May 1985; *Hindustan Times,* 14 May 1985; and *Deccan Herald,* 16 May 1985.

61. Lawyers Collective, *Recent Changes in Laws Relating to Women,* p. 14.

62. Shahnaz Anklesaria, "Dowry Amendment Bill Likely to Raise Furor," *The Statesman,* 12 May 1984.

63. "The Dowry Prohibition Act, 1961," p. 133.

64. Gayatri Singh "Dowry Prohibition Law," *The Lawyers Collective,* Jan. 1986, p. 1.

65. "Mrs. Margaret Alwa on Indian Women and Changing Society," *Choice India* 2:12 (1985), p. 6.

66. Harish Chandra, "Dowry Prohibition," *Hindustan Times,* 16 Oct. 1985.

67. Dowry death is defined as the death of a woman "caused by any burns or bodily injury or [which] occurs otherwise than under normal circumstances within seven years of her marriage and it is shown that soon before her death she was subjected to cruelty or harassment by her husband or any relative of her husband for, or in connection with, any demand for dowry." The penalty ranges from seven years to life imprisonment. *Times of India,* 22 August 1986.

68. The conviction of her husband, mother-in-law, and brother-in-law was widely hailed as just, as a victory for the women's movement, and as a possible deterrent to crimes against women. See "A Welcome Reversal," *Times of India,* 30 Sept. 1985; and "Deterrent Judgment," *Indian Express,* 27 Sept. 1985. However, the *Indian Express* of 23 Jan. 1988 indicated that the murderers, sentenced to life imprisonment on 23 Sep 1985, had not yet been arrested!

69. A Saheli volunteer says that landlords think two women together seeking an apartment may be prostitutes; at best, if they rent to women, they will keep a close, often harassing, eye on them. "At the New Delhi Women's Center," *Off Our Backs,* Jan. 1985, p. 5.

70. An activist in the Women's Centre reports that living alone is somewhat more possible in Bombay. (Interview, Susie Methai, 14 July 1986.)

71. According to Ruth Vanita and Madhu Kishwar, "women's hostels . . . are like prisons. These women are to be guarded until they marry or otherwise return to the custody of the male-headed family." ("A Woman's Home is Not Her Own," *Indian Express,* Bombay, 8 June 1986.)

72. Ibid.

73. Shahnaz Anklesaria, "Divorce Can Leave Her Homeless," *The Statesman,* 10 Jan. 1984.

74. Interview, C.P. Sujaya, New Delhi, 23 June 1986.

75. "Shelter Home for Women from Nov. 19" *Hindustan Times,* 13 Oct. 1985.

76. Interview, Susie Methai, 14 July 1986.

77. See Saheli, "Relationship Between Consciousness Raising and Helping Individual Women," unpublished paper; *The Saheli Newsletter,* which began publication in 1984; "A Woman's Best Friend," *Free Press Journal,* 3 Feb. 1983; Savia Veigas and Shrabani Basu, "Like a Bridge Over Troubled Waters," *Femina,* 8–22 Sept. 1984; Women's Centre, "The Last Five Years," mimeographed report, Dec. 1985; Women's Centre, "Helping Women in Distress . . . Answers to Some Questions," leaflet, 1985. The following is also drawn from an interview with several members of Saheli, New Delhi, 11 June 1986, and one with Susie Methai of the Women's Centre, Bombay, 14 July 1986.

6

The Uniform Civil Code

Of obvious concern to a movement dedicated to the rights and empowerment of women is their status in laws pertaining to family life. In India, there is much to stimulate protest. The position of women vis-à-vis men is distinctly inferior in much of the law regulating marriage, divorce, inheritance, and the guardianship of children.

However, for a movement to challenge these laws is to take on more than the state: although the preamble to the Indian Constitution proclaims India a secular state, and although the Constitution delegates to the government the right to legislate with regard to family matters, in practice, the state has been reluctant to interfere with the religious laws that govern family relations, particularly as they are observed within minority communities. There is no set of family and personal laws—no uniform civil code–that is applied consistently to all Indian citizens without reference to their religious community. The struggle for equality for women, then, must be fought in several arenas, as the laws governing Hindus, Muslims, Christians, Parsis and tribals are all distinct.

It is not only the multiplicity of the battles that is daunting. Of still greater moment is the fact that the ability to control the governance of personal law is integral to the various communities' sense of identity. And for the minority communities—particularly for the Muslims—the continuance of religiously based personal law is key to the sense of autonomy they claim from the Hindu majority. To suggest that the state impose a uniformity which would erase the differences among family practices is to simultaneously challenge the freedom of the religious communities to practice their religions, the relationship of the different religious communities to each other, and their relationship to the Indian state.

The issues that in personal law pertain to women, then, cannot in practical terms be separated from those issues that demarcate communal differences. Consequently, for women to suggest the altering or reinterpretation of personal laws, particularly those of the minority communities, is to enter into a minefield of communal tensions and to risk sparking their explosion. Indeed, although virtually every call by prominent women's activists for the creation of a uniform civil code is accompanied by the statement that *all* of the religious codes recognized by Indian courts fall short of providing gender justice, still the prospect of a uniform code is generally believed to—and probably would—portend a greater change for the Muslim community than for the Hindu.

Consequently, in recent years, as communal violence and the threat of violence have increased throughout India, the rights wing of the women's movement has elected to back away from its previously asserted demand for a uniform civil code that would both govern all Indian women and enhance their rights. That it has done so is not an indication of a weakening of resolve that personal laws must be transformed, but rather marks a recognition that pressing for a uniform code may give the appearance of pressing for majority—i.e. Hindu—sentiments and power at the expense of beleaguered minorities. As a result of the desire to avoid giving aid and comfort to the forces of Hindu chauvinism, and to avoid fueling communal violence, the rights wing of the women's movement has deferred its demand for a uniform civil code and instead is making its demands for female equality under the law in more piecemeal fashion. This chapter explores that point at which the demand for gender justice confronts the assertion of religious and communal rights, and shows why activists for women's rights have elected to alter their strategy.

Unfortunately, while the ethic of human rights embraced by the women's movement causes its adherents to support the rights of minorities, the sense of mutual need is not shared by religious fundamentalists. Events of the mid-1980s pitted fundamentalist Muslims and the politicians who benefit from their support against women's rights activists; and women's rights suffered a resounding defeat. This chapter is also, then, a demonstration of the limits of a movement politics that relies too heavily on movement elites and media support to influence parliamentary politics. It shows the need for a much vaster mobilization of women, particularly Muslim women, and for the empowerment of women that would make that possible. To achieve its ends, a movement that seeks rights must also embrace the quest for empowerment.

The Development of Personal Law in British India

That personal law in a theoretically secular democracy is still governed by religious rather than by civil law is a product both of the legacy of British rule in India and of the communal violence that came to a head with independence. The result has been not only a blow to secularism and national unity but a stagnation in the evolution of law that has perpetuated enormous inequality between the sexes.

When in the sixteenth century Moghul invaders established their rule in the Indian subcontinent, they applied Muslim law to their own community, while allowing Hindu law to govern Hindus. This practice continued under British rule. Given their desire to maintain public order and to create uniformity and predictability in the transaction of business, the British did not hesitate to create a common criminal law that applied equally to all citizens as individuals, as well as a uniform code of civil procedures.[1] However, the British felt it prudent to interfere as little as possible with the operation of existing social structures; thus the corporately based personal laws were allowed to remain.

But, although it may have been the intention of the British to leave religion-based personal law untouched in substance, they did feel it necessary to rationalize the law so that it could be understood and adjudicated by Western-educated jurists. In the case of Hindu law, the British were disturbed by the elasticity with which law was interpreted and applied by Hindu Pandits, and sought to impose greater uniformity and predictability.

In 1772 Governor Warren Hastings designated written Hindu texts as the exclusive source of Hindu law. This had two repercussions. First, "high culture" Brahmanical laws were now imposed on lowercaste Hindus who had heretofore not been governed by them. This was a step harmful to women, since local custom was often more favorable to women (for instance, in their freedom of movement and in widow remarriage) than the orthodox Brahmanical law.[2] It meant, too, that with the exception of a few laws the British created on behalf of women's rights,[3] the evolution of law stagnated; as Lotika Sarkar notes, "there was no way by which . . . socio-economic changes could be reflected in the prevailing legal system."[4] While formerly it was possible for the Pandits or local *panchayats* (councils) to react flexibly to local conditions and needs, the British courts—and the British government—felt that their only job was to interpret existing law. There was thus no body empowered to create new Hindu law pertaining to women or family life.

Instead of the non-interference to which the British aspired, their promotion of the ancient texts from sources of guidance into unyielding legal precedent, and their consequent failure to allow law to evolve, led to a legal system that grew increasingly conservative and incapable of responding to social change. For women, the result was the promotion of a rigid, outmoded religious orthodoxy.

In 1772, Hastings had also declared that the British courts were to apply "the laws of the Koran" to Indian Muslims. However, in practice, the courts often took into account local circumstances—including the customs of the Hindus. Muslim reform movements of the late nineteenth and early twentieth centuries, including those groups dedicated to the advancement of Muslim women,[5] called upon the British to reaffirm that Koranic law—which, compared to Hindu practice, was relatively advanced in the areas of property, inheritance, and choice in marriage—was to govern Muslim personal relations. The British responded in 1937 with the Shariat Act and in 1939 with the Muslim Marriages Act.

The British believed that the formal substitution of Shariat for customary law would not only be beneficial for women, but would rationalize the law. The Shariat Act states, "Muslim Personal Law (Shariat) exists in the form of a veritable code and is too well known to admit any doubt."[6] That there would be perpetual agreement on the interpretation of Shariat was of course a naively over-optimistic viewpoint, as has been evidenced most recently in the controversy over the 1985 Shah Bano case, discussed below. And, particularly in light of the passage in post-independence India of a new Hindu code that gave greater rights to Hindu women, Shariat has become increasingly conservative. Because amending Muslim personal law has been politically impossible, the legal position of Muslim women has fallen further behind that of Hindu women in India and of Muslim women in many other countries where Muslim law has evolved.

The Omission of a Uniform Civil Code in the Indian Constitution

The practice of maintaining distinct personal law systems for the different Indian religious communities has continued into the post-independence period, and the wishes of the leadership of the minority communities to continue this practice have carried far greater political clout than have the wishes of women's rights activists.

The Indian Constitution contains two separate sections of great importance to outlining the type of society the writers of the constitution wished it to become. The Fundamental Rights section declares rights which the state confers and which can be adjudicated. The section entitled Directive Principles of State Policy is the wish list of the Constituent Assembly, outlining goals toward which the government should strive; nothing contained in this section has legal force. It is here, in Article 44, that the Constitution's framers placed the goal of a uniform civil code.

This deferral of a secular code into the indeterminate future must be understood in the context of the partition of British India into the predominantly Hindu India and Muslim Pakistan at the time of independence. The Congress leadership which dominated the Constituent Assembly had long espoused the creation of a secular India; many were devastated at the religious division of the country and at the brutal violence which accompanied it. In light of these events, they were more determined than ever to create a state in which India's religious minorities could live in harmony with the Hindu majority.

One of the results was an unwillingness to create a uniform civil code that would apply to all citizens. While some of the Constitution's framers thought imposing uniformity would create a more closely knit Indian nation, others, including Nehru, were sensitive to the fears of Muslims and Sikhs that their customs would be destroyed by Hindu-controlled legislatures and courts.[7] In the wake of Partition, their viewpoint triumphed. However, in deferring to the wishes of religious minorities at the time the Constitution was written, a critical opportunity for advancing the position of women in law was lost and, from the perspective of women's rights advocates, a devastating precedent set.

There were good intentions among the Constitution's authors. Article 14 of the Constitution guarantees all persons the equal protection of the law. Article 15 explicitly prohibits discrimination on the grounds of sex[8] and mandates that the state may not be prohibited from "making any special provision for women and children": in other words, the state may, in reality, discriminate *in favor of* women.

Article 25 of the Constitution guarantees freedom of religion:

> Subject to public order, morality and health *and to the other provisions of this Part,* all persons are equally entitled to freedom of conscience and the right freely to profess, practise and propagate religion. (emphasis added)

The italicized language indicates that freedom of religion cannot interfere with the other rights listed in the Fundamental Rights section of the Constitution—including women's right to equality under the law. But in practice, the maintenance of different codes of personal law has meant that women of different religions are governed by dramatically different laws; there is, then, discrimination among women. In addition, gross discrimination against women vis-à-vis men exists in virtually all the religiously based personal law codes.

A few examples will suffice here to indicate the depth and breadth of the problem. In the mid-1950s, after a campaign of over thirty years by the All India Women's Conference, and with the crucial support of Jawaharlal Nehru, parliament passed a series of laws effectively creating a new Hindu personal code.[9] In so doing, the proponents of the new laws had to overcome opposition arguments that the reforms violated sacred, eternal truths of Hinduism; that their advocacy was Western-inspired and un-Indian; that allowing women to inherit property would destroy the structure of Hindu society by, among other things, encouraging women not to marry; and that the majority of citizens would not approve of change. However, Congress won an overwhelming legislative victory in the first parliamentary elections and, since the removal of women's legal disadvantages had been part of its platform, Nehru proceeded to push through the new Acts.[10]

Some of the reforms created as a result of these Acts were an option for civil marriage; divorce by mutual consent; a minimum age for marriage of 18 for women and 21 for men; the abolition of polygamy; and an entitlement for daughters in inheritance—except of coparcenary properties (land owned by the joint family)—equal to that of sons.

But the Acts have had little effect. Bigamous marriages are still rampant among Hindus; the age of consent for marriage is ignored; divorce is not a socially accepted norm among most Hindus; and there is continuing inequality in inheritance.[11] The legal exclusion of women from inheritance of coparcenary properties continues to rankle. Moreover, a number of states have passed laws which deprive women of their inheritance rights to land.[12] Under Hindu law, as under India's other personal laws, a husband may write a will depriving his wife of everything; the law does not recognize the wife's economic contribution to the household, and marital property is not held jointly. She may also be excluded from a share of all property acquired during the marriage in the event of divorce.[13]

Although there are thus serious problems in Hindu law, still it is significantly more equitable than either Muslim or Christian law.[14] Bigamy, for instance, is outlawed under Hindu (and Christian) law; but under Muslim law, a man is entitled to have as many as four wives. The most common reason for polygamy is a man's abandonment of his first wife (and often children); rather than divorce her and repay her the *mehr* (or brideprice) and three months' maintenance that are her due, he simply beomes a polygamist. Alternatively, a woman may consent to her husband's marrying again because she is economically dependent upon him and has little choice.[15]

Divorce is available to the Muslim woman. Under the Dissolution of Muslim Marriages Act of 1939, she may divorce for several reasons, including her husband's absence over a four-year period, his failure to provide for her maintenance over a period of two years; his imprisonment for seven years or more; his impotence or failure to perform his "marital obligations" for three years; or for cruelty. Her husband, however, has an "absolute and unlimited" right to divorce,[16] known as *talaq*. He has only to declare himself divorced for it to be so; the courts need not be involved, and she has no recourse whatsoever.

Divorce is available, too, to Christians.[17] A husband may obtain a divorce if he can prove his wife has committed adultery. A husband's adultery, however, is not sufficient grounds for a wife to seek divorce. The Christian husband must have committed *incestuous* or *bigamous* adultery; combined adultery with cruelty or with desertion; committed rape, sodomy or bestiality; or converted from Christianity and then committed bigamy. None of these alone is sufficient to win his wife a divorce decree; he must have committed at least *two* of the above offenses.

Inheritance is another area in which Muslim and Christian women fare badly. Under Muslim law, women do not inherit equally with men; if there are male heirs and female heirs of the same relationship to the deceased (such as daughters and sons), the share of the female relation is just half that of the male. And if a Muslim dies leaving a daughter as his only close relative, she is not be allowed to take more than half of his estate; the other half goes to some distant agnatic relative.[18]

Christian women have been particularly discriminated against in the matter of inheritance. The Travancore Christian Succession Act of 1916 provides that if a father dies intestate, a daughter is entitled to only one-quarter of the share of a son, or five thousand rupees (about four hundred dollars)—whichever is *less*. Although a more equitable Indian Succession Act was passed in 1925 (and revised in 1951) under which daughters and sons were to receive equal shares, and although that Act was intended to govern all Indians who were neither Hindu nor Muslim, in practice the Courts refused to apply it, relying instead on a loophole in the Act which defers to "any other law for the time being in force."[19] Not until 1986 was this practice overthrown by the Supreme Court, which ruled in a case brought by Mary Roy that the Travancore Act was superseded by the Indian Succession Act. In so ruling, the Court did not address the question of the inequality of women imposed by the Christian Succession Act, which would seem violative of the constitution, but ruled instead solely on the basis of the applicability of the Indian Succession Act.[20]

The aspect of personal law that in recent years has sparked the most controversy is that dealing with the maintenance (alimony) to be paid to a wife in the event of divorce. The Hindu Marriage Act of 1955 and the Hindu Adoption and Maintenance Act of 1956 provide that in judging a divorce suit the court may award maintenance to either spouse, depending on their respective financial capacities, and that the maintenance awarded should be real and not merely symbolic. Christian women are also entitled to maintenance: under the Indian Divorce Act, 1869, a divorced Christian wife is entitled to as much as one-fifth of her husband's net income.[21]

Muslim law, however, does not provide permanent maintenance in the event of divorce. A Muslim wife is entitled to maintenance for as long as the marriage lasts, but upon divorce, she is entitled to only three months' payment of money to maintain her (the period of *iddat*).[22] After that, the husband has absolutely no obligation to her. In theory, she is to be cared for by her male relatives: father, uncles, brothers, even sons.

In an attempt to prevent the vagrancy and starvation of people who were being abandoned by their families (including elderly parents and minor children) the British in 1898 enacted a provision in the Criminal

Procedure Code (CPC) that made it a crime for any man of "sufficient means" to refuse to maintain a child, parent or wife.[23] By incorporating this obligation to maintain dependents into the *criminal* code, the British, in this instance, circumvented the personal laws of the various communities, for the criminal code is applicable to everyone, of every community.

Wives were included in the provision. It was not until 1974, however, that an amended CPC expanded the scope of those who should receive maintenance to include *divorced* wives who have not remarried.[24] This made it possible for divorced Muslim women to apply to the courts, not under their community's personal laws, but under Section 125 of the criminal code, for a decree of maintenance from their ex-husbands. And, in the years since 1974, some Muslim women have done precisely that, and with success.[25]

In 1985, however, a case came before the Supreme Court that rocked Muslim/Hindu relations in India, prompted the Congress government to act dramatically to defeat the goal of equality for women, and ultimately dealt a severe blow to feminist hopes for a uniform civil code. We turn now to the Shah Bano decision and its aftermath.

The Shah Bano Judgment

In April 1985 the Supreme Court of India upheld the judgment of the High Court of Madhya Pradesh which had ruled in favor of a divorced Muslim woman's suit for maintenance. In so doing the Court confirmed the validity of Section 125 of the CPC and its applicability to Indian Muslims. In the manner of its decision, the Court also inflamed Muslim public opinion, creating what *India Today* called "trauma, fear and indignation" among the Muslim community.[26]

Shah Bano and Mohammad Ahmed Khan had married in 1932. Together they had three sons and two daughters. In 1975, after forty-three years of marriage, Mr. Khan drove his wife from the house; in 1978 he proclaimed a divorce. She petitioned the courts for maintenance under Section 125 of the CPC, asking for 500 rupees (about forty dollars) per month; she alleged that he, an advocate by profession, earned 60,000 rupees per year. Her husband argued that he had paid her 200 rupees a month during the three month period of *iddat* and had further deposited for her 3000 rupees as *mehr*, and that he had thus met his obligations under Muslim personal law. The local magistrate ordered Mr. Khan to pay his seventy-three-year-old ex-wife what the Supreme Court later derisively labeled the "princely sum" of 25 rupees a month (about two dollars). She submitted an application for increased maintenance to the High Court, which ordered Mr. Khan to pay her 179 rupees (about $14) per month. It was this decision that he appealed to the Supreme Court, which upheld it.[27]

The Court's judgment made three critical points: first, that despite the applicability to Mr. Khan of Muslim personal law, he was also subject to Section 125 of the Criminal Procedure Code. It declared that Section 125 is "truly secular in character," cutting across "the barriers of religion"; and that the payments Khan had made were insufficient to meet the law's goal of enforcing the "individual's obligation to the society to prevent vagrancy and destitution."[28]

Secondly, the Court ruled that Section 125 does not contradict Muslim law with regard to the question of the liability of the husband to provide maintenance to the divorced wife. In order to reach this conclusion, the Court consulted the Koran. It found that the common interpretation of Muslim law limiting the payment of maintenance to the three-month period of *iddat* "must be restricted to . . . cases in which there is no possibility of vagrancy or destitution arising out of the indigence of the divorced wife." The correct Koranic interpretation, according to the Court, is that *"if the divorced wife is able to maintain herself,* the husband's liability to provide maintenance for her ceases with the expiration of the period of iddat" (emphasis added). Thus,

> If she is unable to maintain herself, she is entitled to take recourse to section 125 of the Code. . . . [There] is no conflict between the provisions of section 125 and those of the Muslim Personal Law on the question of the Muslim husband's obligation to provide maintenance for a divorced wife who is unable to maintain herself.[29]

It was not only the Court's decision, but also the fact of its having reached its decision through an interpretation of the Koran, that enraged portions of the Muslim community. While there was considerable Muslim opinion expressed (especially in the English-language press) by those who acknowledged the right of the courts to interpret Islamic law, others argued angrily that, at best, the courts had no expertise in this area, and, at worst, their intrusion would mean the end of a distinct Muslim personal law and thus gravely endanger the very existence of the community in India.[30]

Thirdly, the Court ruled that just as payments during *iddat* did not absolve the husband of the responsibility to pay maintenance, neither did his payment to the divorced wife of *mehr*. This decision in effect nullified what was thought by many Muslims to be the meaning of Section 127(3)(b) of the CPC, a section that had been put in place in 1974 in response to lobbying by members of the Muslim community. Section 127(3)(b) states that a Magistrate may cancel an order to pay maintenance to a divorced wife issued under Section 125 if he is satisfied that she has received "the whole of the sum which, under any customary or personal law applicable to the parties, was payable on such divorce." This language apparently refers to the *mehr*, which in Muslim custom is "a sort of bride price, but a price to be paid to the bride herself and not to her parents." In practice, the amount of the *mehr* is very small and "never likely to be claimed";[31] a sum is, however, agreed to at the time of marriage.

Citing a number of authorities in Muslim law, the Supreme Court concluded that the *mehr* is a mark of respect of the husband for the wife, and that it is agreed to in consideration of marriage; it is *not* an amount payable to the wife by the husband upon divorce.[32] Consequently, the payment of *mehr* does not exempt a husband from the injunction of Section 125 to pay maintenance. This decision, too, led to great protest.

In addition to the content of its decision, and its willingness to reach it through Koranic interpretation, two other aspects of the Court's judgment rankled with certain sections of the Muslim public. Several remarks about Islam contained in the decision written by Chief Justice Chandrachud were interpreted, with reason, as gratuitously insulting. Among them are these:

> . . . it is alleged that "*the fatal point in Islam* is the degradation of woman." To the Prophet is ascribed the statement, *hopefully wrongly* that "Woman was made from a crooked rib, and if you try to bend it straight, it will break; therefore treat your wives kindly."
>
> *It is too well known* that "A Mahomedan may have as many as four wives at the same time but not more."

The Chief Justice also declared that Section 125 is a moral edict and that "morality cannot be clubbed with religion"—apparently implying that Islam and morality are distinct.[33] This judgment was not the first by the Supreme Court awarding maintenance to a Muslim divorced wife; two earlier ones, with the decisions written by Justice Krishna Iyer, had sparked little controversy.[34] The disdainful tone of Justice Chandrachud's decision is in substantial part to blame for the outrage that greeted it.

Finally, the judgment despaired of the lack of political courage demonstrated by the state and explicitly called for the creation of a uniform civil code, a suggestion that has long been anathema to powerful forces in the Muslim community. Fundamentalist Muslim leaders and those who hoped to build political power from the crisis made a populist appeal that Islam was in danger from the threat of a uniform civil code—despite the fact that the government showed not the slightest sign that it intended to introduce such a measure.

In the weeks and months following the judgment, Muslim religious and political leaders issued statements condemning it; articulated fears that forces "inimical to the Muslim community shall use the judgement to secure the extinction of Islamic law and the promulgation of common civil code";[35] called for the deletion of Article 44 of the Constitution and the amendment of the CPC;[36] and organized massive demonstrations throughout India. In Bombay, half a million people turned out to "save Shariat."[37]

Voices were also raised in defense of the Supreme Court decision, but they were fewer and weaker. Only one Muslim leader in the Congress(I), the Minister of State for Energy, Arif Mohammad Khan, spoke up in favor of the grant of maintenance to Shah Bano, while the others, including prominent Muslim Congresswomen, protested it.[38] The Janata Party found itself divided. The women's wing passed a resolution which welcomed the judgment and appealed to members to educate Muslim women about its importance and to "bring them into the mainstream of the movement for the emancipation of women"; it further called for a uniform civil code. Muslim leaders of the party in turn issued a statement angrily denouncing the women's wing.[39]

Two sets of organizations were most active in defense of the decision. First were the various types of women's organizations which consistently had expressed concern for women's legal rights. Women's groups tried to define the issues raised by the decision as *women's* issues—of equality under the law, of the right to marital property—rather than as Muslim or communal issues. They urged Rajiv Gandhi not to amend the CPC in response to Muslim fundamentalist pressure.[40] To these ends, women's rights groups held numerous demonstrations;[41] but, compared to the hundreds of thousands of Muslims who paraded in the streets, their numbers were tiny.

In addition, progressive Muslim intellectuals, both male and female, came together in newly formed organizations to proclaim their support for the Court decision, to denounce Muslim communalist forces, and to urge change beneficial to women from within the Muslim community.[42] While there was thus a progressive Muslim voice being heard, it was the voice of an undeniably small sector of Muslim opinion; press reports almost invariably described the pro-Shah Bano Muslims as "educated" or of "the intelligentsia." Like the members of the national women's rights groups, they were predominantly urban and at least middle class. And while those of more fundamentalist motivations had at their disposal numerous preexisting and community-based organizations (some of which became revitalized in the wake of the Shah Bano judgment),[43] those of more secular and reformist beliefs tended to wage most of their campaign through newspaper articles, letters to the editor, or petitions directed at the Prime Minister.[44] The visible *mass* Muslim response was opposed to the decision.

It is evident that no one truly spoke on behalf of Muslim women. Indeed, Muslim religious and political leaders always claimed to speak on behalf of *the* Muslim community; and Rajiv Gandhi and the Congress(I) worried about the sensibilities of *the* Muslim community; but neither these nor the press ever appeared to entertain a thought that the Muslim community might itself be divided not only between those of more fundamentalist and those of more reformist attitudes toward Islamic law, but also between women and men.

There were scattered accounts that claimed that the silent majority of Muslim women welcomed the Supreme Court decision, but that their voices were "muffled by their fathers, husbands, and the mullahs."[45] It appears likely that Muslim women would not have agreed as readily as did Muslim men that the acceptance of maintenance after divorce would be beneath their dignity. But the reality is that the opinion of Muslim women is unknown: there are no reliable survey data that record in a systematic way the opinions of Muslim women.[46] Nonetheless, politicians took to heart the vocal exhortations of the fundamentalists who claimed to speak for the community as a whole.

Their willingness to do so was prompted in large part not merely by the silence of Muslim women's voices but by the political implications of offending those who showed evidence of the ability to organize Muslim voters. (It is of no little importance that Muslim women vote with much less frequency than Muslim men.)[47] Rajiv Gandhi quickly became persuaded of the desirability of appeasing this sector of the Muslim community in order to maintain Muslim electoral support for Congress. That there was reason for him to be worried was made apparent by a number of events around the time of and just after the Supreme Court judgment.

Muslim Agitation and Communal Tensions Lead to the Muslim Women (Protection of Rights on Divorce) Bill 1986

Muslims make up less than twelve percent of India's population, but they are not equally distributed throughout the country. In selected districts, they constitute a majority of the electorate, and in others, their numbers are sufficiently concentrated that they can swing an election. Since independence, the "Muslim vote" has most often gone to Congress candidates and has been a critical component in Congress success. However, in the wake of the Shah Bano decision and the communal turmoil that accompanied it, Muslim voters began turning toward opposition parties. In the December 1985 by-election, a district in North Bihar which a year earlier had elected a Congress candidate to the Lok Sabha by a margin of over 130,000 votes now elected a known proponent of Muslim conservatism, Syed Shahabuddin of the Janata party, by a margin of 70,000.[48] "It was not a vote for Shahabuddin," said one observer, "it was a vote for

Shariat."[49] In Assam, campaigning on a platform that cited the threat to Muslim identity from the Shah Bano decision, a newly constituted United Minorities Front garnered eighteen Assembly seats in constituencies with Muslim majorities. In Gujarat, in Orissa, in West Bengal the story was the same: Congress candidates lost, or won by significantly smaller margins, as Muslim voters deserted the party.[50]

In addition, there were several incidents of communal tension and violence that left the Muslims feeling vulnerable; this added fuel to the anti-Congress flames and increased Congress' desire to appease the Muslim community. The most urgent conflict began in Ayodhya, Uttar Pradesh, in February 1986. In a dispute over whether a particular site should remain a Muslim mosque, the Babari Masjid, or whether, instead, it had originally been and should once again be a Hindu temple, the Faizabad court ruled in favor of the Hindus. Throughout northern India, Hindus and Muslims exploded in communal demonstrations and violence, with dozens killed. The decision, said one commentator, "reinforced the siege mentality among the Muslims, giving greater credibility to the section of the community's leadership that has been arguing that the Congress(I) government is only paying lip service to . . . secularism."[51]

In the meantime, large Muslim demonstrations protesting the Shah Bano judgement continued; in early January more than 300,000 marched in Dhanbad, Bihar. Women's organizations and progressive Muslims also organized rallies, such as the one sponsored by fifteen women's organizations in New Delhi,[52] but they attracted hundreds or thousands of demonstrators, not hundreds of thousands. The agitation in favor of Muslim women's rights was essentially elitist and marked by the absence of strong protest from Muslim women specifically. While this is hardly surprising given the Muslim social order that limits women's access to the public world, still it stood in striking contrast to the enormous outcry and electoral backlash organized by Muslim traditionalist men.

By late January or early February, Rajiv Gandhi had decided to introduce a bill that would undo the impact of the Shah Bano decision by negating the applicability of Section 125 to Muslims.[53] His response in April to a deputation of women's organizations which pleaded with him to support equal rights for women and maintenance for divorcees was to dismiss their demands on the grounds that these were "Western" and "not Indian" concepts.[54] He shamelessly expounded the proposition that Muslim women would in fact be better protected under the new bill, and, in so doing, attempted to mask the fact that in order to retain the votes of Muslim men he was selling out the rights of Muslim women. This ostensibly forward-looking prime minister, the one who had promised to bring India into the twenty-first century, in fact condemned Muslim women in India to a reactionary law that newly engaged the state as an actor in their victimization.

The cynically titled Muslim Women (Protection of Rights on Divorce) Bill 1986 removes the Muslim husband's responsibility to pay maintenance to his divorced wife; for Muslims (and not, of course, for other Indian citizens) it nullifies Section 125 of the Criminal Procedure Code. This marks a significant departure from the standard by which all Indians were held to the same, secularly based, criminal law, and thus has the effect of moving India further away from secularism. The bill also appears to be in violation of Article 15 of the Constitution, which prohibits discrimination on the grounds of both religion and sex.

Under the provisions of the bill, a Muslim man must pay the woman he divorces the *mehr* that was agreed to at the time of marriage; pay her "a reasonable and fair" maintenance for the three months of the *iddat* period; and, if she is to care for their children, he must pay her maintenance until their youngest child is two years old. (Ordinarily, the Muslim father retains custody of children.) That is the sum of his responsibility to a woman he has, in all likelihood, divorced unilaterally and with no demonstration of just cause.

If, after these payments, a divorced wife has not remarried and is unable to support herself, a magistrate may order her "relatives who would be entitled to inherit her property on her death" (i.e. father, uncles, brothers, sons), and who are financially able to do so, to pay maintenance. In the event that no such relatives can be located, the magistrate is empowered to order a *wakf* board to pay maintenance to the woman.

The *wakf* boards are private Muslim organizations that give money for "pious, religious, or charitable" purposes; most of their funds come from private sources or the income generated by properties, but the central government has also funneled welfare funds through the *wakf* boards, in keeping with the 1954 Wakf Act.[55] Immediately after passage of the bill, dozens of articles appeared in the press analyzing the existing status of the *wakf* boards. The typical conclusion was that the boards had nothing approaching the financial capacities that would be demanded of them by the bill: "To expect the *wakf* boards to undertake to pay maintenance in the not unlikely event of the divorcee's family pleading inability is absurd and unrealistic."[56] In short, the bill is a prescription for the destitution of divorced Muslim women.

In addition to the protests of women's groups and of prominent Muslim intellectuals, and scathing editorials and commentary in the national press, the national opposition parties—including communist parties, the Janata party, and the Bharatiya Janata party—opposed the bill; the West Bengal Assembly passed a resolution declaring that the bill was contrary to human rights and "humiliating to Muslim women."[57] There were protests, too, within Congress ranks: the Minister of State for Energy Arif Mohammad Khan, who had earlier defended the Shah Bano decision, resigned, and there were numerous internal party complaints that Gandhi was attempting to ram the bill through without adequate consultation.[58] After some agitation for Congress(I) MPs to be allowed to vote their conscience, the party issued a whip on the bill, forcing them to vote as the party directed. The bill became law in May 1986.

The Uniform Civil Code Deferred

Women's rights groups in India have long demanded that the state create a uniform civil code in compliance with Article 44 of the Constitution. The All India Women's Conference first called for a uniform code in 1936, and has done so ever since. It has been joined at various times by NFIW, the Indian Federation of Women Lawyers, the YWCA, CPM-affiliated women's groups, Mahila Dakshata Samiti, and a host of autonomous women's organizations.[59] The Committee on the Status of Women in India added its weight to the demand, and so, too, have the National Conference on Women's Studies[60] and India's major human rights organizations: the People's Union for Democratic Rights and the People's Union for Civil Liberties.[61] All explicitly deny any intention of imposing a *Hindu* code on others; their goal is a civil code that eliminates the inequities women face in each of the religious codes.

The passage of the Muslim Women (Protection of Rights on Divorce) Bill is directly counter to this goal of equality. It is undeniably a step away from the equal treatment of women under the law, preventing both the equality of women to one another, and the equality of women to men. It reaffirms the authority of conservative male religious leaders, rather than elected officials, to determine law for women, and thus denies women a voice in the creation of the law that governs them. It is undemocratic, it is contrary to secularism, and it is sexist.

Nonetheless, although outraged at Congress for succumbing to fundamentalist pressure, most women's rights advocates have deferred their quest for a uniform civil code. Most people who are supporters of women's rights are sympathetic, too, to the rights of ethnic and religious minorities, including Muslims. This does not make them allies of Muslim men in their quest to retain power over Muslim women. But it does put them at odds with the other political movement that actively supports a uniform civil code: Hindu communalism. Women's rights advocates are caught between their desire to advance equality for women and their determination not to intensify communal hatred and violence.

The tensions between Hindus and Muslim that existed just after partition have not abated over the years. Although Muslims are an economically and educationally underprivileged group in Indian life, Hindu communalism has been on the rise since the 1980s, and it has become more common for what one observer calls "'cultural' Hindu organizations of a militant messianic kind"[62] to preach a gospel of Hindu superiority and to decry what they perceive to be state favoritism toward religious and cultural minorities—Muslims, untouchables, and tribals.

The support of these organizations—including the Rashtriya Swayamsewak Sangh, the Vishwa Hindu Parishad, and the Shiv Sena—for the uniform civil code has nothing to do with a desire to improve the status of women, which is far from their minds. Their goal is to force religious minorities to accept the laws and practices of the majority community. For example, one of the practices Hindu communalists believe a common civil code should outlaw is polygamy. Their argument against polygamy is not that it is detrimental to women, but rather that Muslim polygamists produce innumerable children and thus Muslims multiply more rapidly than Hindus; they propagandize about the danger of Muslims (currently less than twelve percent of the population) rapidly overtaking the Hindus in numbers. They say virtually nothing about the polygamy which, while illegal, is known to flourish also among Hindus.[63]

The women's movement has been at the same time a movement for secularism, democracy and human rights: it cannot support organizations that preach bigotry and foster an atmosphere of violence. In order to avoid seeming to condone Hindu communalism, women's groups have by and large shelved their campaign for a uniform civil code.

Thus, the women's movement has been bested by not one but by two communal movements. The willingness of the Congress government to pass the Muslim Women (Protection of Rights on Divorce) Bill underscores the relative weakness of the women's movement and its inability to mobilize mass support, as compared with the strength of Muslim communalism. That women's rights organizations are afraid that their clear moral message about the need for legal equality for women will be subsumed into a campaign of hatred for minorities demonstrates the greater power of Hindu communalism.

The feminist defeat represented by the Muslim Women Bill points up the limits of organizing for women's rights in the absence of mass outreach. The struggle for improved legislation with regard to violence against women and to dowry that was discussed in Chapter 5 meets with a pervasively conservative, gender-biased reaction; but it does not confront a well-organized mass constituency that directly opposes its goals. Thus, there is little cost to a political party for supporting laws against violence against women. The elite politics of influencing decision makers in the capital through moral arguments and public embarrassment can take the place of mass organization only in those instances in which there is no large, well-organized constituency in opposition.

Feminist organizing for women's rights in the absence of a mass base, then, has its limits. Access to decision makers, the sympathetic support of influential journalists, financial resources: all these, we have seen, can help to stir debate, raise consciousness and bring a secular, rights perspective to the forefront of discussion. But such an elite approach does not guarantee success in changing law (and certainly not in changing behavior). To build up a more mass-based movement among women that would lend more clout to the legislative and judicial maneuverings of movement elites requires the increased autonomy and empowerment of women. The silence of Muslim women with regard to Shah Bano and the Muslim Women Bill is eloquent confirmation of this necessity. The growth of the movement for women's rights thus ultimately hinges on the greater empowerment of more women.

Notes

1. For further discussion of the British impact, see Lloyd I. Rudolph and Susanne Hoeber Rudolph, *The Modernity of Tradition* (Chicago: Univ. of Chicago Press, 1967), Part 3; and Indira Jaising, "The Politics of Personal Law," *The Lawyers,* February 1986, pp. 6–8.

2. See Jana Everett, *Women and Social Change in India* (New Delhi: Heritage, 1981), pp. 140–145.

3. Notably the prohibition of female infanticide in 1795; the abolition of suttee, or widow self-immolation, in 1829; the legalization of widow remarriage in 1856; and the Age of Consent [for marriage] Act, 1891.

4. Lotika Sarkar, "Jawaharlal Nehru and the Hindu Code Bill," in *Indian Women From Purdah to Modernity,* ed. B.R. Nanda (New Delhi: Vikas, 1976), p. 88.

5. See Gail Minault, "Sisterhood or Separatism? The All-India Muslim Ladies' Conference and the Nationalist Movement," in *The Extended Family,* ed. Gail Minault (Columbia, MO: South Asia Books, 1981), pp. 83–108.

6. Cited in Jaising, "The Politics," p. 7.

7. See Granville Austin, *The Indian Constitution: Cornerstone of a Nation* (Bombay: Oxford Univ. Press, 1966), pp. 80–81.

8. It also prohibits discrimination on the grounds of religion, race, caste or place of birth.

9. They are: the Special Marriage Act 1954, the Hindu Marriage Act 1955, the Hindu Succession Act 1955, the Hindu Minority and Guardianship Act 1956 and the Hindu Adoption and Maintenance Act 1956. See Everett, *Women and Social Change in India,* chapter 7; and Sarkar, "Jawaharlal Nehru and the Hindu Code Bill."

10. Everett, pp. 175–189.

11. See CSWI, *Towards Equality,* pp. 108, 111, 117 and 135.

12. M.J. Anthony, *Women's Rights* (New Delhi: Dialogue Publications, 1985), pp. 171–172.

13. *Towards Equality,* p. 140.

14. A valuable source is T.N. Srivastava, *Woman and the Law* (New Delhi: Intellectual Publishing House, 1985).

15. *Towards Equality*, p. 107.

16. Ibid., p. 119.

17. Under the Indian Divorce Act 1869, and the Indian Christian Marriage Act 1872.

18. *Towards Equality*, p. 139.

19. Section 29 (2). See discussion in WINA [Women's Institute for New Awakening], *On Legal Bondage: Women's Struggle for Justice* (Bangalore: pamphlet, 1985), pp. 7–8.

20. "One Woman's Crusade," *The Week*, 9–15 March 1986, pp. 26–27. See also "Women's Victory," *India Today*, 31 March 1986, p. 78; and *The Times of India*, 5 August 1986.

21. *Towards Equality*, pp. 128–131; Srivastava, *Woman and the Law*, pp. 103–110.

22. The period of *iddat* is three months long so as to determine that the wife is not pregnant.

23. See Judgement, Criminal Appeal No. 103 of 1981, the Supreme Court of India, Criminal Appellate Jurisdiction [hereafter referred to as Judgement; page numbers will refer to the reprint in *The Shah Bano Controversy*, ed. Ashgar Ali Engineer (Bombay: Orient Longman, 1987)].

24. Section 125, replacing Section 488 of the 1898 Code. In the Judgement, Chief Justice Chandrachud described the prevention of "vagrancy and destitution" as the goal of Section 125.

25. See two Supreme Court decisions: *Bai Tahira v. Ali Hussain Fidaalli Chothia* [1979 (2) SCR75] and *Fazlunbi v. K. Khader Vali* [1980 (3) SCR 1127].

26. Shekhar Gupta, "The Muslims: A Community in Turmoil," *India Today*, 31 Jan. 1986, p. 50.

27. The details of the case are presented in Judgement, p. 23.

28. Judgement, pp. 25–26.

29. Judgement, p. 28.

30. See Nawaz Mody, "The Press in India: The Shah Bano Judgement and Its Aftermath," *Asian Survey* 27:8 (1987), pp. 940–941.

31. Jamila Brijbhushan, *Muslim Women: In Purdah and Out of It* (New Delhi: Vikas, 1980), p. 45. Many Indian Muslims have adopted the Hindu practice of the bride's family paying large sums of money to the groom's. Still, the custom of *mehr* remains.

32. Judgement, p. 30.

33. Judgement, pp. 23, 26.

34. See note 25 above.

35. Statement issued by fourteen Muslim leaders reported in *Indian Express*, 6 May 1985.

36. *The Statesman*, 13 June 1985. Article 44 is the Directive Principle that urges the state to adopt a uniform civil code.

37. Gupta, "The Muslims," p. 51.

38. "Muslim Personal Law: Evading the Issue," *Economic and Political Weekly*, 30 Nov. 1985, p. 2096.

39. *The Hindu*, 14 Oct. 1985.

40. For instance, in December 1985, representatives of AIDWA, NFIW, MDS and the All-India Lawyers Association met with Rajiv Gandhi to press these points (*The Statesman*, 18 Dec. 1985).

41. "Events" in Engineer, pp. 237–242, is a chronology of major events surrounding the Shah Bano decision and the Muslim Women (Protection of Rights on Divorce) Bill.

42. For example, the *Indian Express* of 25 August 1985 reported a meeting of 200 Muslim women from Jamia Millia University in Delhi; on 13 October the same paper described a letter addressed to the prime minister from 200 women in Madras protesting any move to amend the Constitution or the CPC. The Hindustani Muslim Forum was inaugurated in Bombay on 19 October 1985, and the Committee for the Protection of the Rights of Muslim Women was formed in New Delhi. The latter's memoranda to the prime minister are reprinted in *Mainstream* 8 March 1986.

43. *The Hindustan Times*, 31 March 1986, reported an upsurge in the popularity of the Muslim Majlis Mushawarat (an umbrella group of political and religous parties that had been recently inactive); the Muslim Personal Law Board; the Muslim League (which had been active primarily in the south but was now able to expand in the north); and the Jamat Islami.

44. Shahida Lateef, "Indian Women Caught in a Time Warp," *Indian Express Sunday Magazine*, 30 March 1986.

45. Hasan Furoor, "Most Muslims in U.P. Opposed to Bill," *The Statesman*, 7 March 1986. See also Sakina Hassan, "Judgement a Welcome Decision," *Indian Express*, 10 August 1985; and Gupta, "The Muslims," p. 57, who claims that *India Today* correspondents who traveled throughout Muslim regions of the country found "plenty of silent support for Shah Bano but only an occasional open expression [of it]."

46. *The Times of India*, 13 Jan. 1986, did report on one survey conducted by the post-graduate department of law at the Sri Venkateswara University, in which 234 Muslim men and 188 Muslim women were interviewed. Once made aware of the provisions of the Shah Bano decision (only 51% of the men and 22% of the women were familiar with it), 60% of the men and 94% of the women supported the decision. While suggestive, the survey was much too limited in scope to support any all-India conclusion.

47. *Towards Equality*, p. 290.

48. Seema Mustafa, "Behind the Veil," *Telegraph*, 2 March 1986.

49. Gupta, "The Muslims," p. 55.

50. Ibid., p. 55.

51. Ajay Kumar, "The Muslims: Anger and Hurt," *India Today*, 15 March 1986.

52. *Times of India*, 8 March 1986. See also "Events," in Engineer, pp. 237–242.

53. *Times of India*, 6 March 1986.

54. The delegation countered the prime minister's stand by pointing out that even parliamentary democracy was a Western concept. The group included members of AIDWA, NFIW, the Committee for the Protection of Rights of Muslim Women (Delhi and West Bengal), Muslim Satyasodhak Mandal (Pune), and Muslim Women's Rights Protection Committee (*Telegraph*, 19 April 1986).

55. Neerja Chowdhury, "Wakf Boards in No Shape to Help Out," *The Statesman,* 12 March 1986; and "Subsidizing Divorce," *The Statesman,* editorial, 20 March 1986.

56. "Muslim Women Bill: Ill-Considered, Anti-Woman," *Economic and Political Weekly,* 1 March 1986, p. 362. See also "Wakf Funds to Belie Government Hopes," *Indian Express* 13 March 1986.

57. "Anti-Women Law," *Economic and Political Weekly,* 10 May 1986, p. 801. See also Ajay Kumar, "Muslim Women Bill: the Gathering Storm," *India Today,* 31 March 1986, pp. 14–17. The CPM had the majority in the West Bengal Assembly.

58. See Kumar, "Muslim Women Bill," and Mustafa, "Behind the Veil."

59. Jessica Jacob, "A Growing Awareness," *Hindustan Times,* 9 March 1986; Interview, Ivy Khan, New Delhi, 4 August 1986.

60. At its second meeting, the Conference passed a resolution in favor of a uniform civil code. Research Unit on Women's Studies, SNDT University, *Newsletter,* May 1984, p. 1.

61. See *Indian Express,* 2 September 1983.

62. Rajni Kothari, "Communalism in India: The New Face of Democracy," *Lokayan Bulletin,* 3:3 (1985), p. 14.

63. Asghar Ali Engineer, "Does the Quran Discriminate Against Women?" *Onlooker,* 8–22 September 1985, pp. 41–42; Mody, "The Press," pp. 945–947; Vibhuti Patel, "Shah Bano's Case and its Aftermath," *Women News,* 16 April 1986.

7

Actions for Empowerment

Indian women's movement organizations that are structured so as to maximize participation in group decision making provide psychological empowerment and a sense of political efficacy to those who have felt powerless to influence public decisions that affect them. Within the parameters of movement activity, women learn new skills, gain self-confidence, achieve greater autonomy as individuals and feel a sense of unity with a group. They may question existing ideologies that prescribe their subservience, and develop new consciousness. Each of these developments has its own value apart from any efforts to influence the state. Yet none is antithetical to expanded participation in the institutions of parliamentary democracy.

The political empowerment of women calls, additionally, for an attack on material problems that limit their participation: the poverty, malnutrition, ill health and illiteracy that plague Indian women also keep them politically negligible. These are problems that women's movement organizations, acting at the local level, have also begun to tackle.

Movements for empowerment may thus be the best vehicles for bringing women into the mainstream of Indian political life. For women to be able to press a political agenda, to engage in public life, they must first be empowered privately: they must have some control over their own lives. To the extent that their personal autonomy is limited by social, cultural, and religious structures that confine women—whether they dictate a customary social subservience to men or impose a more immediate threat of violence—these structures must be defied. When women lack a sense of personal efficacy, when they have no confidence in their ability to participate, and thus fail to act politically, building their confidence and giving them a forum in which to learn participation are political acts. These are tasks that movements, not parties or interest groups, legislators or judges, can best accomplish.

Movement organizations may also provide a channel through which the state may reach out to citizens. A point of contention among women's groups is the extent to which they should accept aid from international donors, and particularly from the government of India. At stake is their ability to reach more women; but also at stake is the ability of movement participants to fully control decision making. The growth of personal and community autonomy is a key to empowerment. Will the intervention of government destroy that?

This chapter examines the accomplishments and limitations of particular movement organizations that seek to empower women. Of particular interest here and in the conclusion that follows are the effects of the internal structure of the organizations and of their relationship to the state.

Rural Movements

In both rural and urban areas, women's organizations anxious to empower women attempt to alter the material conditions to which women are subject. They may seek ownership of land, strike to raise wages, or create new local industries with the support of bank loans or credit unions. They also recognize that lessening physical violence is necessary for women's empowerment. But setting these goals is just a part of their agenda; empowerment organizations also try to create mechanisms which allow for the direct participation of poor women in making and acting upon group decisions that affect them.

As described in Chapter 4, several groups of organized tribals in the state of Maharashtra have provided models for mobilization and action. All of them make "conscientization" central to their organizing; activists believe that empowerment develops from the process of collective reflection. The first step is to name and analyze problems (of landless men and women, of poorly paid workers, of women specifically) and then collectively to seek solutions. The agenda for action, for participation, flows from the groups' own understanding of a given situation.

Many groups throughout India have adopted a similar method.[1] The most common vehicle for facilitating group reflection among women has been the *shibir,* or meeting. When possible, a *shibir* lasts for several days and takes place in the absence of male participants. This enables women to speak who are reluctant to do so while in the presence of men, or whose ideas are ignored by the men, who tend to dominate integrated meetings.

The discussions may be about economic matters, and the activism planned aimed at landlords or government bureaucrats. The women-only meetings also allow women to discuss problems of sexual harassment and violence against women. In this setting, they have uncovered and discussed common experiences of harassment and rape at the hands of landlords, rich peasants, and moneylenders.[2] They also have aired their rage at the men in their own families. Common to many women's *shibir*s is a sharing of anger at the frequent abuse to which women are subjected by intoxicated husbands. While the women generally express sympathy for the difficulties of their husbands' lives, characterized by chronic underemployment and persistent economic exploitation, they resolve not to be victimized by their misplaced aggression. Actions that have evolved out of these meetings have included smashing local stills and liquor storage pots; public (verbal) confrontations with wife beaters; the collective beating of drunken husbands who have beaten their wives; and, in one instance, a march of 65 kilometers to the state capital to demand that the government shut down local liquor shops.[3]

Not only the occasional meeting is reserved for women only. Organizers in rural areas often begin with a focus on men, thinking that they will organize women only "as a part of the [economic] class."[4] They may find, though, that the women become more active and more militant than the men.[5] In other cases, a movement sets out to organize both men and women together. In each circumstance, women's organizations frequently develop within the context of the overall structure. These groups provide a greater latitude for the development of women's confidence and power, and for work around gender-specific issues.

CROSS organizers, for example, found that women came infrequently to evening meetings or classes, and never became office holders in the village associations. They learned that women were not able to attend meetings at night because they had to do their housework and cooking then.[6] By creating women's associations, CROSS has enabled women to participate and to take leadership positions; meeting times and group activities, including literacy and health-care classes, have become geared to women's needs and women's issues.

Over time, investigators for the ILO have found, women in CROSS have gained a "sense of collective power" from their association. As a result, they have successfully acted to gain better wages and to combat wifebeating.[7]

Sometimes, then, organizers find that to involve women they must create women's groups. In other cases, women's associations have been started by women with their own experience of organization, who wish to develop gender issues further. In August 1980, women who were members of Shramik Sanghatana developed a new organization for women only, the Stri Mukti Sanghatana. The (mostly tribal) women had long been organized; Shramik Sanghatana began in 1971, and has worked on issues of landlessness, underemployment and poor wages. The concerns of the new organization, however, are gender specific, and try to cut across class, caste and religion. The group's founding was prompted by the beating of a Muslim maidservant in a nearby town. At the rally marking the formation of the group, the women declared that "all women are oppressed and should unite and fight as women"; they vowed to assist the wife of a rich farmer or an upper-caste woman if she requested it.[8]

This is not to suggest that the going is always easy: far from it. In addition to struggling against landlords, government officials, money-lenders, and the religious or caste prejudice that keeps women divided, rural women in the process of organizing also come up against considerable resistance from their husbands and fathers. To some extent, they are dependent on these men for support: someone has to look after the children and cook the food while the women are at a *shibir*, and if women have to constantly fight with men over their attendance at meetings, it drains valuable energy. Successful organizers of women thus have to struggle to persuade men not to be obstructionist. This generally works best when the men can be convinced that the economic gains the women can make will benefit their families, or that advances in the collective power of women can be used against vested interests or the government for the good of the community as a whole.[9]

Overall, the participation of women in separate women's associations has allowed for the growth of consciousness and confidence. Their ideas are listened to, their creativity and skills given room to develop.[10] In the best of circumstances they themselves, collectively, evolve the strategies for the struggles in which they subsequently engage. As a result, as the observers of an organization in Himalchal Pradesh note, "the women's awareness that they can make changes in their lives is growing."[11] In identifying problems and generating strategies to confront the problems, they come to realize that neither the poverty of their class and community nor the violence and discrimination to which they are subjected as women are justifiable or inevitable. They gain a broader perspective concerning the cause of their economic, caste and gender position; they gain self-confidence; they become available for participation in organized political activities: they begin to become empowered.

While this psychological empowerment is of critical importance, organizations among rural women do more: they also provide a means to pursue economic empowerment in cooperation with other women. The strategies and tactics for gaining economic empowerment vary from group to group. The major differences rest with the organizations' attitudes toward the state and toward hierarchical or decentralized modes of organization.

On the one hand are organizations, such as Shramik Sanghatana, that hold to a Marxist perspective in which the state is viewed as the representative of the propertied classes and the enemy of the poor. (This antipathy to the state is also characteristic of a variety of groups that identify themselves as Gandhian or share J.P. Narayan's commitment to "total revolution."[12]) Although in day-to-day activities such groups are primarily interested in the process of transforming and empowering the grass roots, they would not be averse to an eventual overthrow (perhaps through non-violent actions) of the state. Groups sharing this radical philosophy generally remain localized and small; their financial resources may come from individual urban supporters,[13] but they do not seek government or foundation support. In part, the rejection of such support reflects their commitment to decentralization and the exercise of complete control from below. It is also a specific rejection of the state and of any state supervision: to be eligible to receive international funds, organizations must register with the Ministry of Home Affairs and must report their funding in detail.[14] Registration subjects them to a number of government regulations, including government censorship of the publications of any nongovernmental agency receiving foreign assistance.[15] Obviously, accepting funds from the government of India itself means an organization must to some degree conform to the government's dictates and expectations.

Groups of women, or of women and men, that organize under this ethic generally aim their protests at local power structures. These may be private individuals or groups of private individuals, including landlords and the *goonda*s (armed thugs) who work for landlords, moneylenders, and employers. But actions are also aimed at government and are usually intended to get the government to do what it is already committed to doing in principle and, often, in law, but what it has failed to do in practice.

Goals common to rural empowerment movements have included gaining land for the landless, retaining control of the forests by resisting the forest encroachments of private developers and the government; freeing bonded laborers (those who because of indebtedness are virtually enslaved to those to whom they owe money); and improving the wages of agricultural workers.

The demand for the return to the cultivators of land that has been illegally taken from them by wealthier landlords is generally addressed to government officials. Pressure is applied to the local government to implement the land ceiling laws that limit how much land may be owned by one individual or institution, and/or laws that outlaw the alienation of land owned by tribals. In all manner of direct action techniques— marches, *gherao*s of public officials,[16] confrontations with landlords' goondas—women have been active planners and participants.

In the case of the Chhatra Yuva Sangharsh Vahini women have gone further, demanding that lands illegally held by a Hindu monastery in Bodhgaya not only be returned to the tillers, but that ownership be given directly to women cultivators. After years of struggle within the movement, the women gained a consensus among their male colleagues that women should have land registered in their own names; they argued that women had participated fully in the struggle, and that an end to women's oppression required that they have access to basic economic resources. When the movement did succeed in wresting 1500 acres of land back from the monastery, district officials at first refused to give it to women, insisting that ownership must go to the heads of households, that is, to men. However, continuing agitation by the Chhatra Yuva Sangharsh Vahini persuaded the authorities to turn some of the land over to women; ten percent of the acres redistributed to the laborers have been registered in women's names.[17]

Another common demand is for increased wages for agricultural workers, both men and women. Tactics for obtaining better wages include strikes against employers; or the target may be the local government, when workers demand that the government apply pressure to local employers to obey the minimum wage laws that exist but are rarely enforced. Ultimately, though, it is only the organized pressure of the workers that can ensure that wage laws are implemented. The Minimum Wages Act passed in Maharashtra in 1974, for example, does not allow local government officials to arrest or fine employers for failing to pay the state-prescribed minimum wage; only the workers themselves can bring employers to court. The process of adjudication can take many years. In the meantime, the workers may strike, and, because the minimum wage law is on their side, even those local government officials who are supportive of the landlords are to some extent neutralized. It is readily acknowledged by some government officials at the national level that only through the pressure of organized groups can workers, and particularly women, get what is due them under the labor laws of India.[18]

Organization is also necessary to obtain resources for women that may be available from the government or from foundations but are only delivered when there is organized demand. Not all who set out to mobilize and empower women share the radical perspective of the groups discussed above either with reference to the need to erode the state, or with regard to the value of completely nonbureaucratized movements. Instead, some movement organizations working in rural areas, including the rural branches of Working Women's Forum and SEWA, and local groups including CROSS, take a much more benign view of the state, viewing it as a repository for resources that can be acquired by the organized poor.

CROSS has successfully funnelled state and international resources to poor rural women. CROSS activists do express some ambivalence about using these funds to promote capitalist development among the land-poor people of the Telengana region of Andhra Pradesh with whom they work; they believe that the present economic structure limits how far the poor can advance. Still, they acknowledge that the poor themselves are intent on economic development and that existing poverty is so deep that "economic projects, even relief work, cannot be neglected or postponed because of ideological reasons."[19]

So, although CROSS activists emphasize the long-term importance of ideological transformation and politicization, they also facilitate the utilization of private funds and government bank loans to improve farming and to create income-generating projects, such as dairies and village industries. Surely, generating added income is nothing to belittle. But whether this creates *empowerment* depends on how active women are in making the decisions and planning the actions that affect them and how much autonomy the additional income creates. The goal of CROSS organizers to promote empowerment is met in the process of determining how the funds are to be used. Decisions are made together after considerable group study at meetings of the women's associations. Probably more important than the small economic gains which have derived from the use of outside funds are the skills in management and democratic decision making the women have gained and the sense of collective power that has developed in the process of organizing, discussing, and acting upon their common circumstances.

Urban Movements in Rural Areas

Two large urban-based organizations, SEWA and Working Women's Forum, have expanded their work into rural areas. As discussed in Chapter 4, both are quite at ease ideologically with their role of channeling bank loans and other government, private, and international funds to poor women to generate new income-producing schemes or to help them expand existing ones. Although their cooperation with government opens them up to criticism from more radical grass-roots organizations, SEWA and WWF show a similar concern with, and some marked success in achieving, the empowerment of women. Their utilization of government resources allows them to reach tens of thousands of women, and they do so while remaining committed to a continual expansion of participation at the grass roots. Both intend not to "deliver" economic benefits from above, but instead to create the opportunity for poor women to make decisions collectively, to gain access to new skills, and to become politically engaged while improving their economic status.

SEWA's expansion from its base in Ahmedabad into the rural area of Dholka taluka, Gujarat, was prompted by the failure of a campaign by organized agricultural laborers to obtain the legal minimum wage.[20] Together with the rural wing of the Textile Labour Association, with which SEWA was then associated, SEWA organized over 1800 agricultural workers—more than half of them women—to demand payment of the minimum wage. However, since they had no alternative sources of employment, they had little capacity to strike or to bargain and were largely unsuccessful in moving their employers to pay the legal rate.

Since there was so much unemployment in the area, men often migrated to Ahmedabad or other nearby towns to seek work; the women remained to eke out a living. In the late 1970s, SEWA began to organize village-level women's associations, which have come to perform a number of functions. Through them, SEWA has created income-generating projects and economic cooperatives, coordinated bank loans and government grants, and organized services necessary for women's self-advancement, including training in employment skills, the provision of child care, and classes in health-care (particularly maternal and infant health). All these are seen as important in their own right, but also as necessary to political organization and to the development of leadership.

The importance SEWA leaders place on improving women's consciousness and expanding their growth socially and educationally as well as economically is symbolized by the title they gave to their coordinated rural programs in 1981: SEWA-Jaago. *Jaago* means "awakening" in Gujarati, and the awakening of consciousness about women's capacities in government officials, in the local community, and among women themselves in part defines SEWA's goals.

Two types of income-generating ventures have been introduced among the women of Dholka taluka. The first, in keeping with SEWA's Gandhian roots, was a *khadi* producing project. Since the time of the independence movement, the spinning and weaving of cotton cloth on simple hand-operated machines has been promoted as a way to create employment. Working with the government's Khadi and Village Industries Board, SEWA was able to bring spinning machines to the villages. SEWA provided the women with training in their use and maintenance, and the government provided raw materials and a market for the finished product. As a result, the households involved in the project have come to earn an average of one hundred fifty rupees per month during the agricultural off-season, compared to the twenty rupees per month they had earned previously.[21]

SEWA has also helped develop dairying in Dholka. In the late 1970s, SEWA convinced the government's National Dairy Development Board that it should train women for dairying, as well as provide for them the same kind of services it did for men in the form of loans and assistance in the establishment and management of milk cooperatives. Since then, working with additional government agencies, including the Gujarat Dairy Development Board, the district dairy, the Integrated Rural Development Programme and the nationalized banks, SEWA has trained hundreds of women in dairying, organized the receipt and repayment of bank

loans for the purchase of cattle, and established four successful cooperatives.

The women were not the only ones who required training. Raising the
consciousness of the bankers was no small task:

> . . . just a few days before we all were to sign the papers [for the loans] we
> found out they planned to give the loans to the women in their husbands'
> names. We said nothing doing. They tried to tell us that the women did not
> have property and had no steady income, while the men did. We told them
> that the cows would be property, the milk would give the women income,
> and after all that's the whole purpose of the loan! We said we would only
> take the loans if they were given to the women in their own names. They fi-
> nally agreed.
>
> With the first batch of loans we arranged payment directly through the
> co-ops. The women's installments have been absolutely on time. . . . Now
> the banks are quite willing to advance loans to women in other milk co-ops
> on the same basis.[22]

The creation of the cooperatives has been rife with difficulties. The project encountered tremendous resistance from local officials and private
dairy owners, who were successful in several instances in destroying
cooperatives. In addition, there was an internal problem of administration: the management of a cooperative requires literacy and mathematical
skills, and initially SEWA was unable to find local women with these at-
tributes. As a result, men were hired to manage the cooperatives, a move
that seemed to contradict SEWA's stated commitment to developing the
leadership abilities of women. To make matters worse, a number of these
men proved to be corrupt. By 1983, the men had been replaced by literate
SEWA organizers, some of whom have taken up residence in the villages,
and by local women who serve as assistants. As a result, the cooperatives
have been operating more efficiently and at a greater profit.

The administration of the cooperatives is thus hierarchical and not
democratic. Still, the meetings of cooperative members do provide a forum for women's public participation that is for them unique. In addition,
as a result of their involvement in the cooperatives, their political
horizons are expanded; they must interact with agencies far beyond their
villages. The training they all receive, and the local recruitment of assistants, allows some women to significantly gain in skills and public
responsibilities. While this model still has a long way to go toward
democratization, at least the women's opinions and experiences are taken
into account; as one organizer says, the village women who are dominated by men in their homes do speak out in meetings organized by
SEWA. And while initially "the ideas for SEWA's activities may not be
their own . . . the decisions taken by the leaders and organizers are made

with the women."[23] Combined with the increased education and the opportunity for ownership of economic assets and increased income, this is surely a step toward empowerment.

Working Women's Forum, too, organizes poor rural women into groups that can receive bank loans and other government and foundation support in order to create income-generating projects. Like SEWA, the goal of the Forum, while most obviously to improve the women's lives economically, does not stop there; it aims also to develop women's self-confidence and capacity for leadership and to improve their standing in their communities.[24]

Toward these ends, WWF has begun projects in three rural areas that are geared toward their specific economies. In 1979, WWF organized landless women in the drought-prone Dindigul district of Tamil Nadu. In a situation much like that faced by SEWA in Dholka taluka, women agricultural workers were being vastly underpaid—at the average rate of three rupees (24 cents) a day—but organization was difficult because of the lack of any other employment possibilities. With the use of government loans, WWF organized 250 women in three villages into a dairy project. Within five years, 1200 women were involved in the program. Because of the increased income generated through the dairying, the women were able to apply pressure to the landlords to increase agricultural wages. One researcher claims that, as a result of these activities, the women's incomes have tripled.[25]

In 1981, the United Nations' Food and Agriculture Organization invited WWF to create a fish marketing project in Adirampattanam, a village on the coast of Tamil Nadu. As of 1984, this Working Women's Credit Society was granting low-interest credit to some 1500 women, who could for the first time be free of the middlemen who had until then dominated the market.

The third rural project of WWF was also begun at the invitation of an international organization, in this case the Ford Foundation.[26] The area surrounding Narsapur, a town in Andhra Pradesh, has traditionally been home to women artisans who weave lace. The lacemakers, who work at home, had long been financially victimized by the middlemen who served as exporters. Working Women's Forum has organized over 7000 lacemakers into cooperatives through which loans have been administered and exporting conducted directly. In addition, as a result of the new options open to the women, and bargaining by the Forum, private exporters who buy lace from them have been forced to raise their payments by fifty percent.

In all these projects, while the obvious benefit is financial, there is a gain, more generally, in women's empowerment. In addition to the loan programs, the Forum creates other kinds of support services, including day-care centers, skills training, and counseling in health care, birth control, and nutrition. Most important to all of these—the loan programs as well as the training and child-care activities—is that they are controlled and managed by the women themselves. As one observer notes, the result is that "the women gain confidence in their own cooperative power."[27] They gain skills and participate directly in decisions that affect their lives. Again, here, the women are brought onto a larger political, social and economic stage; their horizons and their collective powers are expanded. In addition, their success in these endeavors and their own heightened self-esteem bring them more respect and greater autonomy within their communities.

There are, then, a number of types of organizations that are working to empower women at the rural grass roots. Some work with men and women; others with women exclusively. Some seek out the assistance of the Government of India and of international organizations and enjoy an international reputation; others are very small, committed to remaining unaffiliated with any outside organization, and to building purely from the ground up. Still, all share the belief that services *delivered* to poor women are of little use in creating a sustained transformation. Their interest is in the empowerment of women, not merely their uplift: they are helping women to gain the capacity to make important decisions—financial, social, familial, personal—in their own lives, to have a sense of personal and community efficacy.

Urban Movements

The last two organizations we have examined, SEWA and WWF, are primarily urban-based organizations. Both of them, along with a third urban group, Annapurna Mahila Mandal, have attracted the interest of international organizations and scholars. In-depth studies of each reach overwhelmingly positive conclusions.[28]

Their economic achievements are indisputable. In its first seven years, WWF distributed approximately U.S. $900,000 worth of loans. As a result of the loans, according to Helzi Noponen's study, a large number of women who had worked for extremely low pay as piece workers were able to become better paid, self-employed workers; a significant number of women who were previously unemployed were able to start businesses;[29] and there was a substantial increase in the earnings of women traders, who no longer had to pay off money lenders or exploitative middlemen. In 70 percent of the cases of women who were previously working, Noponen found, the investment of their loans meant an increase in earnings; the average increase was 93 percent. The added income has been used in most cases to purchase more and better food for the women's families (enabling them, in many cases, to eat twice instead of once daily).[30]

Jennifer Sebstad's study of SEWA found that women who take out loans through SEWA similarly increase their incomes as a result. Sixty percent of the 8000 women who had taken loans invested them directly in their businesses; of these, 48 percent realized increased earnings. Of those women who used their loans for some other purpose, many paid off debts to private money lenders; this, Sebstad points out, helped them to break a cycle of indebtedness and thus also holds the promise of a rising income.[31]

In addition to the loan program, other SEWA activities also have resulted in material benefits. Training programs (for carpenters, bamboo workers and hand-block printers, among others) have equipped working women for higher paying jobs; cooperative production units (for example, of *chindi* [quilt] producers) have given women a more secure and regular source of employment; and through SEWA's efforts, self-employed women have gained access to cheaper raw materials and broader markets.[32]

There is less evidence that Annapurna has been successful in increasing the incomes of its *khanawalli* members through its loan programs.[33] Here, many of the loans seem to be used to repay moneylenders or to make home repairs (which, since the home is often the work site, does mean an improvement in working conditions.) Still, the loans have made a positive impact in the women's lives.

The women seem to gain in status and power within their families as a result of their access to the loans, for the money makes a significant contribution to the family's finances. And interviewees have spoken of their heightened self-esteem and the increased respect of their families by virtue of the recognition they have received from Annapurna and the banks; several women told Everett and Savara that they felt they were "somebody" because the banks had given them a loan.[34] The same is true of women in WWF and SEWA: Noponen found that 35 percent of the women in her study experienced a greater role in household decision making as a result of their expanding economic role, while Sebstad, too, remarks that SEWA members have become more assertive and confident in their behavior vis-à-vis their families.[35] Leaders of WWF report a decrease in wife beating among members as women have become organized: "they are walking taller these days, and people have noticed this."[36]

Just as the material improvements aid in advancing the women's self-esteem and empowerment, so too do other aspects of membership. All of the organizations have created programs to teach skills necessary for economic advancement. Each also provides some additional support services including day-care centers, health and family planning classes, and night classes for the children of members (Forum); legal assistance, a health clinic and an overnight shelter for members facing violence at home (Annapurna); and legal aid, life insurance, widowhood assistance, assistance in obtaining medical care during pregnancy, and day care (SEWA).[37]

The process of regularly working and meeting together helps to create a sense of unity and mutual aid among the women. In all three organizations, individuals' loans are guaranteed by a group. If a woman defaults, the entire group is harmed, and so there is considerable peer pressure to toe the line. While surely this serves the banks' purposes, it is also a means of creating links and mutual dependence among the women. The group becomes a supportive unit and provides the individual with a cushion; in times of personal crisis, the group will help cover a woman's payments or share her work until she can catch up.[38]

The loan groups also provide women with emotional support. Women discuss the best ways to solve a variety of business and personal problems, ranging from how to use their loans, operate their businesses, and retain control of their earnings, to how to handle sexual harassment and family violence.[39] The meetings create a space in which women can openly express themselves and in which their opinions count. Some women learn to exercise leadership, starting first within the group and then sometimes gaining broader responsibilities within the organization.[40]

The groups also provide a forum for education about broader political and social issues. Participation in these organizations brings the women into regular contact with a wide range of public institutions and officials: banks, local public officials, law makers and the courts. Members lobby and demonstrate on behalf of programs and policies that are of direct interest to them, such as the creation of better conditions in public markets, the ending of police harassment, and their right to fair wages. Just as the women become economic actors in their own right, so they also become political actors.

Overall, the participation of women in these organizations not only benefits them financially but also educates them and opens up broader social and political horizons. Through the organizations, they are linked, often for the first time, to people outside their families. They understand that they share interests with other women and, most importantly, they are taught the means to effect change both at a personal level and at the level of economic and political institutions. As Sebstad argues with regard to SEWA's members, the women achieve "a new awareness of the world around them and a new sense of control within their lives."[41] This personal empowerment is of utmost importance in its own right; and it is also the prerequisite for the obtaining of greater rights and the exercise of heightened political power for women.

Notes

1. For example, see the discussion of the weekend camps organized by CROSS in *Towards Empowerment*, ed. Kamla Bhasin (New Delhi: FAO, 1985), pp. 87–97; Manoshi Mitra, "Report on SEWA—Mongher, Bihar," (unpublished paper available in the CWDS library, 23 pps, n.d.), pp. 7, 23; and the story of the Chhatra Yuva Sangarsh Vahini in Manimala, " 'Zameen Kenkar? Jote Onkar!' The Story of Women's Participation in the Bodhgaya Struggle," *Manushi* no. 14 (1983), p. 9.

2. Amrita Basu, "Two Faces of Protest: Alternative Forms of Women's Mobilization in West Bengal and Maharashtra," in *The Extended Family*, ed. Gail Minault (Columbia, MO: South Asia Books, 1981), pp. 242–244; Mira Savara and Sujatha Gothoskar, "An Assertion of Womanpower," *Manushi* no. 13 (1982), pp. 33-34; Kashtakari Sanghatana, "Kashtakari Sanghatana (The Warli Uprising Revisited)," in *Agrarian Struggles in India After Independence*, ed. A. R. Desai (Delhi: Oxford Univ. Press, 1986), pp. 433–434.

3. The last was the case with SUTRA (Society for Upliftment through Rural Action) in Himalchal Pradesh in 1986. Subhash Mendhapurkar and Lina, "It's About Changing Our Lives," *Manushi* no. 40 (1987), pp. 28–37. (Part 1 of this article is in *Manushi* no. 39 (1987), pp.29–36.

4. This was the initial attitude of Bhoomi Sena. Gail Omvedt, "Women in Popular Movements: India and Thailand During the Decade of Women" (A report prepared for the UNRISD Popular Participation Programme, 1985), unpublished, p. 36a.

5. As recounted in Kashtakari Sanghatana, pp. 433–434.

6. In Khanapur taluka, Sangli district, Maharashtra, the Mukti Sangharsh, an association of rural workers, found the same thing; there, too, separate women's associations were formed. Gail Omvedt and Nagmani Rao, "Rural Women's Mobilisation: The Khanapur Taluka Experience," *Lokayan* 3:2 (1985), p. 56.

7. Maria Mies, et al., "Landless Women Organize," *Manushi* no. 15 (1983), pp. 11–19, rpt. in Bhasin, pp. 80–97.

8. Omvedt, "Women in Popular Movements," p. 36. For more on Stri Mukti Sanghatana, see also Omvedt, "Adivasi Women and Personal Law," *Manushi* no. 17 (1983), pp. 20–21.

9. For relatively successful outcomes, see Basu, p. 242 and Manimala, p. 9. For less success, see Mendhapurkar and Lina, *Manushi* no. 39, p. 36 and *Manushi* no. 40, p. 34.

10. Of a *shibir* for women organized by Mukti Sangharsh, Omvedt and Rao write: "For the first time they were the centre of attention. They were given opportunities to express their ideas and feelings and they could sit for hours talking, listening, and singing, without having to worry about household responsibilities. Perhaps for the first time, the women began to feel the exhilaration of a common sisterhood. The idea 'we must get organized' began to have a more concrete meaning" (p. 62).

11. Mendhapurkar and Lina, p. 36.

12. For example, Chhatra Yuva Sangharsh Vahini defines itself as struggling for total revolution—"a complete change in the system." (Manimala, p. 2.)

13. Manimala, p. 6 reports that at one point in the Bodhgaya struggle to obtain land ownership, Chhatra Yuva Sangharsh Vahini "got quite a lot of publicity in the press, and help poured in from urban areas."

14. Since 1984, in accordance with the Foreign Contribution Regulation Act. Discussed in Harsh Sethi and Smitu Kothari, "Editorial," *Lokayan Bulletin* 4:3–4 (1986) pp. 1–7.

15. Publications of such apparently benign organizations as the Centre for Women's Development Studies and the YWCA have been affected by this.

16. A *gherao* is a sit-in in which an official is held temporarily captive.

17. Alaka and Chetna, "When Women Get Land," *Manushi* no. 40 (1987) pp. 25–26.

18. For example, Meena Gupta, Director, Ministry of Labor, interview, New Delhi, 24 July 1986.

19. Bhasin, *Towards Empowerment,* p. 77.

20. The information on SEWA is from Jennifer Sebstad, *Struggle and Development Among Self Employed Women: A Report on the Self Employed Women's Association, Ahmedabad, India* (Washington, D.C.: AID, 1982), pp. 141–158; and Marty Chen and Anila Dholakia, "SEWA's Women's Dairy Cooperatives: A Case Study from Gujarat," in *Indian Women: A Study of their Role in the Dairy Movement* (New Delhi: Shakti Books, 1986), pp. 70–106.

21. Sebstad, p. 146.

22. Interview with Anila Dholakia, Director of SEWA-Jaago, in Sebstad, pp. 149–150.

23. Mahalaxmiben, a SEWA organizer, quoted in Sebstad, p. 181.

24. See Helzi Noponen, "Organizing Women Petty Traders and Home-Based Producers: A Case Study of Working Women's Forum, India," in *Invisible Hands: Women in Home-based Production* ed. Andrea Menefee Singh and Anita Kelles-Viitanen (New Delhi: Sage, 1987), pp. 229–249; Nandini Azad, "Reaching Out to Women Workers Through Grassroots Delivery Systems," *Indian and Foreign Review* 21:22 (1984), pp. 11–13, 27–28; and Marty Chen, *The Working Women's Forum: Organizing for Credit and Change* (New York: SEEDS, 1983).

25. Azad, p. 27.

26. Noponen, p. 233. WWF also worked with the ILO and the Government of India's Ministry of Labour and Commerce (Azad, p. 27).

27. Naponen, pp. 232 and 248.

28. For WWF, I will draw here primarily from Noponen's 1987 article, "Organizing Women Petty Traders . . . " which builds upon her doctoral dissertation, *The Gender Division of Labour in the Urban Informal Sector in India,* University of California, Berkeley. For SEWA, see Jennifer Sebstad's study for the Agency for International Development, *Struggle and Development Among Self Employed Women.* Re: Annapurna Mahila Mandal, see Jana Everett and Mira Savara, "Bank Loans to the Poor in Bombay: Do Women Benefit?" *Signs: Journal of Women in Culture and Society* 10:2 (1984), pp. 272–290.

29. In 1981, 35 percent of Forum members had new jobs as a result of the loans. Noponen, p. 244.

30. Ibid., pp. 242–244.

31. Sebstad, p. 207. Noponen found that over half of the WWF loan recipients used their loans entirely for business purposes. Here, too, "the remaining half diverted part of the loan to critical consumption or debt repayment." p. 245.

32. Sebstad, pp. 205–208.

33. Everett and Savara, pp. 281–282; and Sharayu Mhatre, Sulabha Brahme and Govind Kelkar, *Bank Credit to Women: A Study of Khanavals or Working Class Lunch Suppliers* (Bombay: National Institute of Bank Management, 1980), p. 93.

34. See p. 282; also, Mhatre, et al., p. 93.

35. Noponen, p. 244; Sebstad, p. 210.

36. Quoted in Noponen, p. 248.

37. Chen, pp. 12–14; Everett and Savara, "Class and Gender: The Organizational Involvement of Urban Working Class Women in India," paper prepared for Annual Meeting of the Association of Asian Studies, March 1989, p. 10; and Sebstad, pp. 66–75.

38. Noponen, p. 235; Prema Purao and Mira Savara, *Annapurna Mahila Mandal* (Bombay: AMM, 1982), p. 12.

39. Ibid., Everett and Savara, "Class and Gender . . . ," p. 16; and Sebstad, p. 209.

40. Especially in Working Women's Forum, where the group leaders are local, poor women, not staff members.

41. See p. 211.

8

Conclusion: The Future of the Indian Women's Movement

The Indian women's movement has had only very limited success in securing rights and expanding empowerment for women. Changes in laws have been minimal, and enforcement of those laws even more so. Advocates for women's rights confront forces of communalism and, so far, are losing the battle. Hundreds of thousands of women remain mired in terrible poverty and suffer from malnutrition, illiteracy and violence.

Yet the movement has begun a struggle to change consciousness, so that substantive change may become possible. In addition, for the tens of thousands of women who have participated in the movement, it has already added to empowerment and participation more effectively than other political insitutions. The most impressive organizations in the movement constitute important models for the future development of women's status and power.

After a review of why and how the movement emerged, this chapter discusses what has accounted for its successes and failures: What has the women's movement accomplished, what has it failed to accomplish, and why.

Why and How the Movement Emerged

Two types of belief are critical to the birth of a movement. One type focuses on the grievance; the other on the method of redress. Thus for a feminist movement to emerge, one set of ideas must address the question, "why *feminist*," and the other must explain, "why a *movement*." In India, anger about women's limited status and power emerged at a time when the question of how to create change was being increasingly answered with movement politics.

It was the Indian state's incapacity to create political and economic empowerment for India's poor, coupled with its arrogant disregard for human rights during the 1975–1977 emergency, that set the stage for the development of the Indian women's movement. This crisis of the state prompted, in addition to the women's movement, a number of other movements among the poor and powerless that were not explicitly concerned with gender. Movements developed because no other institutional means of redress of grievance existed. The incumbents showed no signs of addressing dramatic problems of poverty and the diminishment of rights, while the political opposition parties appeared to many to be more opportunist than effective.

Movements developed, too, because the problems of poverty and powerlessness were not thought to be solely resolvable by government actions. Movements, their organizers believed, could provide remedies that normal institutional politics could not. Among many of the grassroots organizations, there was an explicit desire to create through movement politics a culture of confidence, self-esteem and participation among people who had been deprived of significant decision-making ability in their own lives. Claiming a civil space through movement activity in which individuals, working collectively, could determine their own futures has been an explicit goal of movements among women, tribals, Dalits, and the rural poor.

In addition, movements developed because there is room within Indian political culture and law for them to develop. With the exception of the period of the emergency, there is freedom of association, free elections, a free press, and access to government officials. India's democracy, like most, provides far too few avenues of participation for its poorest citizens, for minorities and for women. But it is still a democracy. It allows for dissent, and for movements to exist and mobilize openly.

The answer to "why a *women's* movement?" rests in both domestic and international causes. Within India a number of events built awareness and outrage among educated Indian women about the state's failure to protect and expand women's rights. The passionately angry and compelling report of the Indian Committee on the Status of Women; the heightened press sensitivity to dowry death; rises in prices of household necessities that prompted the organization of the Anti-Price-Rise Movement; a Supreme Court decision in the Mathura case that was egregiously contemptuous of women: all of these transformed consciousness and provoked fury.

The desire to empower women at the grass roots also had indigenous roots. Organizers of the rural poor with no prior gender consciousness often found that women were particularly effective and militant participants in movements designed to gain land or improve wages. As they set about encouraging women's ongoing participation, they learned from practice that women have gender-specific needs (for family care, for meeting times when they could get away from domestic responsibilities) necessary to their participation in movement activity. When organizers helped facilitate the organization of women, at first around class issues, they created a space in which women could discuss and discover their shared gender problems. An expanded women's agenda emerged.

In the cities, too, as educated, politically experienced women activists set about organizing poor women, they quickly saw that the tasks of personal and family empowerment were necessary to women's political participation. Consequently, they developed structures, such as loan groups, that were designed not just to facilitate access to economic assets, but to provide moral support, develop group solidarity and political skills, and build consciousness and self-esteem. They recognized a need to create a culture of empowerment, to create an environment within which women would exercise self-determination and leadership.

A feeling of anger and crisis is not enough to create a movement. Resources that allow for organization are also necessary, and they were available within India. Most important were the educated, politically skilled and economically privileged Indian women who have been the leaders of both the rights and empowerment wings of the movement. Women's organizations already in existence which became more politicized when confronted with new issues, and a free and activist press, with representation from feminist journalists, were the other most critical domestic resources. Also important was an aspect of Indian political culture that could be brought to the fore: from the time of the nationalist movement, women's participation in politics has been accepted in principle. Pushing for it in practice has venerable roots.

Both rights and empowerment groups thus had plenty of domestic factors that promoted their organization. But concern for women was also generated by an ideological transformation taking place worldwide that directly influenced India. Western feminist scholarship and theory was well-known to many of the educated Indian women who became activists. In addition, the feminist impact on the United Nations that resulted in International Women's Year and the United Nations Decade for Women also had strong reverberations in India. It was in response to a United Nations call for country studies of women's condition that the Indian government created the Indian Committee on the Status of Women to write *Towards Equality.*

International feminist influence has continued to aid empowerment groups in particular. By the mid-1970s, feminist critiques of existing development practices were becoming increasingly powerful and gaining adherents in international agencies. Western funding and development agencies were putting more women officers in the field, and they were looking for projects whose efforts centered on women's grass-roots development. Indian women's organizations capable of absorbing and responsibly distributing international funding, including Working Women's Forum, SEWA, and Annapurna Mahila Mandal, have benefitted greatly from this ideological and institutional transformation.

Challenges to existing values about the status of Indian women thus came from both domestic and international sources, and so too did the resources that enabled movement organizations to emerge and grow. When a crisis of confidence developed in the Indian state, when it seemed both incapable of and uninterested in advancing the status of women, there were both ideological and practical resources to draw upon to seek women's rights and empowerment.

What Has the Movement Achieved?

Arenas of Influence

In judging a movement's accomplishments, the first question must be: accomplishments with respect to what? In contrast to interest groups and parties, which exist to influence the state, movements have broader agendas. In India, as elsewhere, the sources of women's relative powerlessness with regard to the economy, society, family and politics are not all to be found within the state, and therefore a movement that seeks to empower them should not confine itself to influencing the state. Women's powerlessness is also located within society and the family, and in ideologies and religious traditions that dictate their secondary status.

These areas are important in their own right, and are also relevant to women's relationship to the state: Male power over women in the family and society, and the ideologies that uphold it, limit women's empowerment in everyday life, and in politics. Women are prevented from gaining economic resources and political power by their subservient social and familial position; the male-dominated family stands between women and the state, and serves to control and limit women's participation in the economy and in politics.[1] Women's position of subordination within the family also limits their ability to organize horizontally, as women, apart from the family unit.[2]

A movement that hopes to gain greater rights and economic status for women must then also create sufficient empowerment for women in their family and social lives so that they can engage with the state. In evaluating the success of a women's movement, then, one must ask if the state has yielded more resources and guaranteed, in law and in practice, greater legal rights. But the analyst must also look for signs of personal growth, empowerment within the family, and activated consciousness about women's subordinate status. A women's movement puts pressure on institutions outside itself. But it also creates changes for its members within the context of their participation in the movement. Both arenas are relevant to judging a movement's success.

Chapter 7 shows that some empowerment organizations, notably SEWA, Working Women's Forum, Annapurna Mahila Mandal and CROSS, have successfully fostered their members' self-esteem and increased the power of individual women within their families. These groups have shown how to create forums in which women learn the skills of participation and leadership, while developing group solidarity and personal confidence. These accomplishments, along with their strategies for providing support systems for women such as health education and childcare, and their success in improving, albeit incrementally, the economic rewards their members enjoy, provide useful models. These groups seem able to empower their members socially, while at the same time giving them the skill to participate with relation to the state. While differing local conditions would alter the precise methods of organization employed, these are groups worth emulating.

But given the scale of India's population and size, these organizations reach only a tiny proportion of poor and powerless women. Real sustained progress for women on a national level, both within the family and with relation to the state, will require a substantial and widespread transformation in consciousness. In this effort, both rights and empowerment organizations have made some progress, as evidenced in improved laws regarding violence against women and the participation of tens of thousands of self-employed women in particular organizations. However, given the depth of problems women confront and the vastness of the Indian population, this is not, as yet, much progress.

Resistance to new ideas is hardly surprising given the depth and pervasiveness of cultural and religious justifications for the subordination of women. It would be unrealistic to expect a swift transformation of consciousness. The question is whether the structures of the women's movement provide the promise of gradual change.

Movement Structures

Rights: The Limits of Elite Politics. In the Indian women's movement, those organizations that seek primarily to move the state to guarantee women's rights are hampered by their elite nature. The rights wing of the movement has generated no new political tactics, although they have pressed for new policies.[3] For the most part, rights organizations operate as interest groups: they attempt to influence government policy, whether through legislation, executive action or judicial decision making.

Leaders of large women's organizations have achieved what David Truman describes as the basic objective of interest groups: access. The organizations are hierarchically structured, and this gives their leaders some representative role. They can claim to speak for a constituency, and their power lies in part in their ability to bring that constituency into the streets in support of certain issues. But access is not limited to those with a large membership behind them. The class and education of the leaders of many of the smaller organizations, too (including research centers such as the Centre for Women's Development Studies and the Research Unit on Women's Studies at SNDT University), and their own backgrounds in political parties, social service agencies, academia and the media, give them a status that in turn provides them with access to political decision makers.[4]

As is the case with Indian interest groups in other policy areas, including economic and educational policy, influence derives less from numbers than from technical expertise.[5] Leaders of interest groups provide expert witnesses to government commissions, write studies, and inspire investigative reports. Because there is an international women's movement, complete with numerous international conferences, the articulate and intellectually compelling leaders of Indian women's organizations have been able to cultivate an international attention to the status of women in India and to the state's role in its maintenance or transformation.

Their elite status also gives them access to the press. They can generate media commentary that is sympathetic to their cause and critical of government officials. The power to embarrass the state is meaningful. The heightened attention the press gave to dowry death and to the egregious sexism of the Mathura rape case had an impact on a chastened government.

When meeting little organized resistance, elite groups can have effect. Ending violence against women is a case in point; it is a position that evokes no formal organized opposition. Consequently, in this instance, the movement has been able to exert influence on government decision makers. Demonstrations, media attention, investigations by women's organizations and repeated meetings with government officials have yielded improved laws regarding the prosecution of rape, the giving and receiving of dowry, and violence against women (including murder) in connection with dowry.

However, this achievement constitutes only very limited progress. It is easy for government officials to pass a law, because with the exception of circumstances in which there is an interest group of equal or greater size and passion engaged in the same issue, the costs to them are small. Laws, if they lack implementation, are only symbolic. In India, laws protecting the rights of the less powerful—be they landless or wage laborers or women—frequently remain on paper only. As Chapter 5 shows, the changes in public policy embodied in new laws attacking violence against women so far have been modest in principle and have had little impact on reality.

To achieve the implementation of laws that challenge the prerogatives of entrenched powers is an even more difficult matter. The inability of the rights wing to mobilize vast numbers—to exert electoral pressure or to create more dramatic and persistent disruptions time and time again—limits its effectiveness. Successful implementation or even the mere passage of laws that threaten the cause of more powerful interest groups requires additional mobilization of support.

In the absence of electoral clout, the power to influence through intellectual persuasion and access to decision makers is not enough. Given their small numbers, there are severe limits to the capacities of rights advocates to create meaningful policy changes: as Chapters 5 and 6 demonstrate, access and expertise take you only so far. In seeking advances for women's rights in personal laws, and in deflecting damage to those laws already in place, the women's movement has come up against the far greater political power of organized conservative Muslims. The electoral concentration and strength of this community far surpass those of the women's movement, and the magnitude of its support and its power underscores the limits of elite influence. Particularly in this era of evermore important communalism, in which women's rights have become a pawn for fundamentalists on all sides, the ability of the women's movement to move the state rests on being able to speak with stronger electoral power.

In the short run, then, the rights wing of the movement has not met with much concrete success in reforming personal law or in stemming violence against women. And yet, despite its apparent failures, it would be inaccurate to deny any accomplishments to this part of the movement. For, particularly in the struggle for improved legislation concerning violence, the women's groups have had a strong hand in defining the terms of debate. They have stimulated the process of the public reexamination of ideas about women and violence. Symbolic change, while not enough, is an important beginning.

As innumerable historical examples demonstrate, movements may take a very long time to accomplish their goals. The changing of consciousness in participants as well as in opponents is a critical task. New ideas are essential challenges to the inequality that is embedded in social and economic as well as political structures. Provoking changes in public consciousness, or in the consciousness of even a part of the public, can be a painfully slow step, but it is a necessary one. It is a task to which the rights wing of the movement, with its ability to gain access to bureaucratic, legislative and judicial decision makers, its influence in the media, and its ability to call upon a constituency for the purpose of peaceful and symbolic agitation, is integral.

Accomplishments and Limits of Empowerment. In addition, there is an obvious need to mobilize the unmobilized. Although they presently affect only a small number of women relative to India's population, it is those organizations attentive to social and economic empowerment that provide a model for how to create a broader women's constituency that can more effectively influence the state.

To be sure, not all empowerment groups fit this description. Some of the activists who organize for empowerment hold to a Marxist perspective that identifies all institutions of the state as inherently the enemies of the poor; they are consequently more interested in eroding state power than in participating in it. As a result of this ideological perspective, women organized under the rubric of such movement organizations may gain political power, but only at a local level. Their clout develops typically through protests and strikes aimed at landlords or local government officials. They may learn new skills in decision making and participation, exercise new assertiveness within their families and communities, and achieve a heightened sense of self-esteem. These things are all significant. However, under present political conditions in which the state is not in fact threatened by such movements among the poor, the power so generated is narrowly confined. The empowerment generated by such groups will not have a national impact nor bring women into participation with national or state governmental institutions.

But SEWA, Working Women's Forum, Annapurna and CROSS have been serving as valuable intermediaries between unmobilized, unempowered women and the institutions of government. In channeling government (and international resources) to poor women, and in altering the consciousness and the material conditions of these women, these organizations both empower women locally and foster an interaction between women and the state. In this model, the mobilization of women makes them available for broader political activities in the future. These are the models from which greater women's power can come.

I noted at the outset of this study that the distinction drawn here between the rights and empowerment wings of the movement is less sharp in actuality than has been portrayed. SEWA, Working Women's Forum and Annapurna Mahila Mandal are all examples of this, for in their form and goals they combine aspects of interest group politics and empowerment movements. Each has leadership with expertise in politics and access to government officials. The leaders' high level of sophistication about the workings of government has allowed for the acquisition and then distribution of needed financial resources. The professionalized character of the leadership of these mass organizations has been a prerequisite to their emergence and growth.

Still, SEWA, WWF and Annapurna work primarily at the grass roots. Here, the organizational structures are hundreds of small groups uniquely suited to mobilizing women with little power and little autonomy. The groups resonate to local needs, particularly economic ones, not ideological abstractions or the electoral goals of political parties. There is a flexibility and responsiveness to individual goals and problems, and this provides an added incentive for participation. Because the groups address issues of immediate concern in a concrete, material fashion, they have enjoyed impressive success in mobilizing women who have heretofore been excluded from participation in any economic or political collectivity.

Participation is facilitated by the small size of the groups. These are non-intimidating forums that allow the women access to direct participation in discussions and, although not in every instance, decision making. The small scale promotes the building of confidence and assertiveness in individuals and provides a setting for the creation of mutual assistance and group power. By engaging women in discussion about daily problems, the groups also become mechanisms for the development of consciousness about gender issues.

The organizations of urban self-employed women have increased the incomes of their members. Although the increases are modest, they have a positive impact not only on the material lives of the women and their families, but also on the women's autonomy and status within the family. The material benefits also help to weaken resistance against women's political participation on the part of their male relatives.

Because the local groups are linked together into a larger whole with a professional leadership, the needs of the members can be aggregated and then articulated to government institutions. Although the mobilization occurs at the grass roots, groups on the model of SEWA, Working Women's Forum and Annapurna are at the same time integrating women into a broader governmental system. Local participation translates into the involvement of poor and powerless women in state and national political institutions.

Thus mobilization at the grass roots need not end there. Far from representing a threat to the state, this form of movement politics in fact heightens participation in institutional politics by integrating a population whose interests have been underrepresented or ignored by existing institutions. Because of the relative superficiality of the organizing efforts of political parties, it is here that they fail and movements may succeed. Rather than mobilizing women as voters only, the empowerment movements bring them into a wider range of political activities and into contact with more institutions of government. Thus, far from signifying a necessarily harmful attack on the democratic system, movements may on the contrary play a critical role—particularly in less developed polities—in integrating those who have been kept out of politics into purposeful political action.[6]

The Interrelatedness of Movement Structures. For women to be able to move the state to work for the protection or furthering of their rights, the mobilization of larger numbers is critical. Raising issues and perhaps consciousness about women at the elite level is an important task, but if heightened debate is to translate into the passage and particularly the implementation of laws more favorable to women, greater organized power is necessary. For the rights wing of the movement to be successful, the empowerment wing of the movement must be successful.

The task of empowerment is vital, though, not only for this purpose. Empowerment is most necessary because the power of the state is limited. Moving the government is part of the means, not the total goal of the women's movement. Success for the women's movement will not be measured in laws passed, nor in access to political power alone. The transformation of women's lives requires, in addition, increased access to economic power and material well-being, and greater social power, marked by increased equality within the family, access to decision making, and freedom from violence. These are tasks that are appropriate to the empowerment wing of the movement.

A proliferation of movement organizations—each free to create new ideas about what is needed and what can work locally, each able to allow women to exercise leadership and organizational skills outside the family structure—is critical to transforming the lives of the mass of Indian women. The state alone does not have the capacity (even if it had the will) to reform the myriad of social structures that perpetuate women's secondary status. Empowerment must come first, not at the level of the state, but at the level of the individual, the family and the community.

The best hope for the success of the women's movement, then, is to deepen the cooperation that already exists between the rights and empowerment wings of the movement. The mobilization of women under the empowerment wing can enhance the political clout of those pursuing governmental changes. In turn, the pursuit of necessary resources for empowerment can be facilitated by the organizations of the rights wing. They can serve as an additional link between women at the grass roots and government decision makers. With resources flowing from above, and ideas about grass-roots development being generated from below, it is possible for the two branches of the movement to work in symbiosis.

An example of this can be found in successful efforts by both wings of the movement to heighten the commitment of government officials to greater economic assistance for women, particularly women in the informal sector. In 1980, after Indira Gandhi's return to office, a new draft five year plan was drawn up. As recounted in Chapter 4, women's organizations received word that the draft made barely any mention of women. Representatives of women's groups vigorously lobbied the Planning Commission and, as a result, a chapter entitled "Women and Development" appeared for the first time in a five year plan.[7]

The Planning Commission again included a plan for women's development in the *Seventh Five Year Plan (1985–90)*. In addition, in 1987 the government established two separate, high-profile commissions to suggest ways to improve economic development for women. The Department of Women and Child Development of the Ministry of Human Resource Development created a group headed by Margaret Alva, Minister of State, to write the *Draft National Perspective Plan for Women 1988–2000 A.D.* The actual preparation of *DNPPW* took place under the supervision of Dr. Nandini Azad, who is the daughter of Jaya Arunachalam of Working Women's Forum. The same Department also appointed the National Commission of Self-Employed Women, chaired by Ela Bhatt of SEWA, to make a comprehensive study of women workers in the informal sector and to "suggest measures . . . for removing the constraints which adversely affect the integration of self-employed women in the national development process."[8]

The two studies differ in their conclusions as to what role the government should play. *DNPPW* adopts more of a "rights" philosophy: It endorses technical improvements in the existing top-down approach of government to women's development, and improvements in law, including the passage of a Uniform Civil Code, the implementation of laws protecting women, and the reservation of thirty percent of seats in local government for women.[9] *Shramshakti* rejects this "beneficiary approach" in favor of what it terms the "involvement [or empowerment] approach." Its authors urge the government to support the organizing efforts of poor women at the grass roots.[10]

Concrete progress in direct response to the five-year plans and to these two studies has so far been modest.[11] Yet the documents signal the increased visibility of women and women's economic development needs on the government's agenda, and testify to the extraordinary access and influence the leaders of women's organizations have so far achieved.[12] Moving the government beyond debate and into action will require still greater success in the mobilization of women.

The Future of the Movement

Whether and how movements can use state and outside resources without becoming coopted has been a subject of considerable dispute, both within Indian women's organizations, and within other movements to increase the power of the powerless. This study has shown that the use of state and international resources is vital both to the success of the women's movement and to its expansion.

Some activists (and scholars) maintain that the Indian state is so controlled by dominant castes and bourgeois classes that only socialist revolution will create empowerment for the poor. In the absence of such a revolution, the poor and powerless must organize in militant opposition to the state wherever possible. Any cooperation with the capitalist state will lead not to empowerment but to continued domination.[13]

Others, however, while acknowledging the power of dominant castes and classes, see the Indian state as an arena in which conflict for resources can occur, and in which the organized poor can make some gains.[14] Acceptance of this modest proposal is essential if the women's movement is to increase its power both with respect to the grass roots and in its ability to influence the state. For it is only through cooperation with the state that essential resources can be tapped. Failure to gain access to these resources would doom the movement to irrelevancy for any but an infinitesimal percentage of women.

This is not to say that cooperation with the state is without cost to the effort to create autonomy and empowerment. In recent years, the Government of India has paid increasing attention to movement organizations, and has moved toward increasing regulation of them in return for state funding or for permission to receive funding from international sources. This may be seen as an ironic tribute to the potential of movements, for it is an acknowledgment that movements are generating significant changes at the grass roots, and that these have been taking place outside of state control.

Since the passage in December 1984 of the Foreign Contribution Regulation Act, organizations that receive grants from abroad must register with the Ministry of Home Affairs. The necessity to conform to government regulations and thus, to some extent, operating procedures, inevitably involves some loss of autonomy. Similarly, in the Seventh Five Year Plan, the Government of India promised increased support for autonomous organizations, but simultaneously introduced steps to regulate them.[15] The government also proposed a Council for Rural Voluntary Agencies, complete with a code of conduct and regulatory powers.

These developments appear to represent an attempt by the state to control those who will cooperate with it and isolate those who will not.[16] This creates nervousness and anger among most movement activists. The most radical argue that movements must retain total autonomy from the state: any actions that allow for state control or that, through the cooperation of movement organizations, legitimize the state, are not in the long-term interests of women or the poor.[17]

And yet, this insistence on total organizational autonomy is ultimately self-defeating. The socialist revolution desired by many of those who argue for autonomy is simply not in India's foreseeable future. The empowerment achieved by purely autonomous movements is too localized and limited to transform any but those most directly affected, and the movements themselves are too few and too small to have widespread impact. While their doctrine is the most uncompromised, their accomplishments must by necessity be very narrow.

The state controls the resources that are necessary to any widespread empowerment or transformation in women's lives. There is evidence that an organization that uses state resources is the most effective in gaining resources and autonomy for those it organizes. In addition to the numerous studies of SEWA, Working Women's Forum and Annapurna cited in Chapter 7, a more recent comparison of five Bombay organizations of women in the informal sector has found that those organizations with greater access to external resources are better able to improve economic conditions, as well as solidarity among the women they organize, than those with less access.[18]

Surely there are limits to the magnitude of change that may be made within present state structures. Organizations of poor women in the informal sector improve their economic condition, but only marginally. But revolutionary transformation is not a viable alternative, and while militant, autonomous grass-roots movements do obtain resources and sometimes protection from the government against rural elites, more energy is expended with less result than is the case with broader-based movements headed by elites who have access to decision makers and thus greater access to resources. I have argued elsewhere that autonomous grass-roots movements have the potential to make a dramatic impact on the state's distribution of resources, but only if their numbers are vastly greater than they are at present.[19] That argument still holds. Local grass-roots movements are simply too few and too disparate to alone effect any but the narrowest change; they will not alter the structure of the Indian state any more than reformist movements will.

Empowerment movements need to use whatever resources they can wrest from the state to build alternative structures that empower in civil society and open up participation within the state. Empowerment can be developed locally by confronting the state; but it can be achieved more broadly, affect more women, by utilizing the resources yielded by some cooperation with the state.

The Indian Women's Movement
and Theories of New Social Movements

A school of movement theory that developed in Europe in the 1970s identified "new social movements" as a product of postindustrial society.[20] In these feminist, human rights, environmental and peace movements (among others), middle-class people with adequate time and resources to expend in political activity seek to create a politics within civil society that is characterized by participatory democracy and unencumbered by the bureaucratization characteristic of the advanced capitalist state. These individuals object to the expanded capacity of the state to penetrate all areas of life, and seek to reclaim a civil space apart from state interference within which they can construct a more satisfying culture. Some of the values compelling movement participants include advocacy of personal autonomy, decentralized decision making, participatory democracy and self-help. The movements themselves attempt to organize and operate in a fashion that is consistent with these values. Thus, the organization itself becomes a model of how society might better be organized and political decision making and action pursued.

The new social movement theorists acknowledge that the values embraced by the new movements—such as autonomy, identity, human rights, peace and ecology—are not new. But, they argue, the way in which they are linked together *is* new.[21] Thus, a clean environment requires peace; peace is impossible without human rights; human rights are less valuable in a polluted environment. The linkage, they argue, is a reaction to conditions created by the post-industrial state: The values proclaimed by "modern" society clash with these other, more important values. Thus technical "progress" may destroy the environment, private property defeat human rights.

This study of the Indian women's movement reveals that these values and linkages are "new" only to Western movements. Many of the thoughts and activities that new social movement theorists believe to be uniquely post-industrial are in fact present in economically "backward" India in movements of the poor and powerless. Indian movement organizations are politicizing precisely those issues that Western theorists have labeled a product of advanced capitalist society. These issues include human rights (with emphasis on the rights to health, adequate nutrition, and education), women's rights specifically, and environmental balance.

As in the "new" Western movements, many of these movements particularly insist on local autonomy and community decision making; they share the same desire "to open alternative political spaces outside the usual arena of party and government . . . to redefine the very content of politics." Furthermore, like the Western movements, Indian organizations are "providing new linkages with segments of people's lives that had hitherto remained isolated and specialized: culture, gender and age, technology, ecology, health and nutrition, education and pedagogy."[22]

The Indian movements and those deemed "new" in the West call for the creation of a political sphere directly controlled by the community rather than the state, and share the belief that the way in which change is pursued will largely determine the result. But in India these concerns are anything but new. The Indian movements draw in part on a tradition of Gandhian anarchism that has long emphasized the central importance of the connection between means and ends, and has extolled community self-sufficiency and self-governance.

The values expressed are similar. But the political function of the Indian movements is different than that suggested by new social movement theorists. The theorists see the creation of a politicized sphere of action between the public, political world and the private world as a step that protests institutional politics; it is an attempt to *reclaim* politics. But in India, occurring as they do among those who are not well integrated into the mainstream of institutional political life, the secular nonparty movements serve a different function. As a result of becoming empowered through their participation in small, local groups, poor and relatively powerless individuals may for the first time become available for participation in institutional politics.

For Indian women, who suffer a lack of esteem and power in both the public and private spheres, participation in movements can enable them to gain the skills, self-esteem and mutual support needed to engage in more formal political activities. In fact, the same may be true for the movement participation of women in the West. Contrary to new social movement theory, many women in the West have not been reclaiming politics, but, instead, entering it, in much the same way as Indian women, through a process of local empowerment and the subsequent ability to actively engage the state.

Thus, new social movement theory needs to expand beyond its limited geographical boundaries to reassess what causes particular values to emerge, and to better explore the relationship between gender and politics. Values and ambitions embraced by middle-class movements in advanced capitalist societies are not unique to these societies; they are equally present in movements among the poor and powerless in the developing world. For women, whether women of the middle class in advanced capitalist society or the poorest women in India, participation in movements may be the first step toward empowerment in civil society and toward a more powerful engagement with the state.

Notes

1. Prof. Barnett Rubin suggests that in its mediating role between the individual woman and the state, the family serves a similar function for women as patron-client networks play for poor peasants. Personal correspondence, 23 August 1991.

2. So, too, does women's identification with their ethnic, caste, religious or other social subdivision.

3. In addition to those analyzed in Chapters 5 and 6, these include police action against the perpetrators of violence against women; improved access to education and to the training necessary for employment in the organized sector; greater government expenditure on health care for women and infants; implementation of minimum wage laws, the Equal Remuneration Act (1976), and the Child Marriage Restraint Act (1929, amended in 1978); job reservations for women; and guaranteed employment.

4. In his study of U.S. interest groups, *The Governmental Process* 2nd ed. (New York: Knopf, 1971), Truman remarks that "perhaps the most basic factor affecting access is the position of the group or its spokesman in the social structure." (See pp. 264-265.) The same is true in India.

5. See Lloyd I. Rudolph and Susanne Hoeber Rudolph, *In Pursuit of Lakshmi* (Chicago: Univ. of Chicago Press, 1987), pp. 231–232 and Part 4.

6. As the Rudolphs rightly point out in *In Pursuit of Lakshmi*, p. 237, and as our examples have shown, Samuel Huntington's argument in *Political Order in Changing Societies* (New Haven: Yale University Press, 1968) that participation outside of formal political processes is dangerous to the state is not necessarily true.

7. Interview, Vina Mazumdar, New Delhi, 23 June 1986. Sharma, p. 1462. See Government of India, Planning Commission, *Sixth Five Year Plan 1980–85*, pp. 423–429.

8. *Shramshakti: Report of the National Commission on Self Employed Women and Women in the Informal Sector* (1988), p. 2. Arunachalam was appointed a member of this Commission, but attended few of its meetings and refused to sign the report on the grounds that it was redundant of the *DNPPW*. See "Note of Dissent," in *Shramshakti*, p. 330, and a response by Ela Bhatt, p. 331.

9. *Draft National Perspective Plan for Women 1988–2000 A.D.*, pp. 77–79. See also Jana Everett and Mira Savara, "Class and Gender: The Organizational Involvement of Urban Working Class Women in India," paper delivered at the 1989 Annual Meeting of the Association for Asian Studies, Washington, D.C., p. 2.

10. *Shramshakti*, pp. 245–248.

11. See "Women's Perspective Plan: Skirting the Issue," *India Today*, 30 Sep. 1989, p. 44.

12. Indeed, Ela Bhatt has been both a member of the Rajya Sabha, the upper house of Parliament, and of the Indian Planning Commission.

13. See a summary of these points in Jana Everett, "Incorporation versus Conflict: Lower Class Women, Collective Action, and the State in India," in *Women, the State, and Development* ed. Sue Ellen Charleton, Jana Everett and Kathleen Staudt (Albany: State University of New York Press, 1989), pp. 156–160.

14. See, for example, Rudolph and Rudolph, *In Pursuit of Lakshmi*, and Francine Frankel, *Indian's Political Economy* (Princeton: Princeton Univ. Press, 1978).

15. See Government of India, Planning Commission, *Seventh Five Year Plan, 1985–90,* pp. 68–70, "Involvement of Voluntary Agencies."

16. See Kalpana Sharma, "Neutralizing Voluntary Agencies," *Indian Express,* August 3, 1986; and Rajesh Tandon, "Regulating NGOs: New Moves," in *Lokayan Bulletin* 4:3–4, 1986, pp. 37–42.

17. See, for example, Bharat Patankar and Gail Omvedt, "The Bourgeois State in Post-Colonial Social Formations," *Economic and Political Weekly,* 31 Dec. 1977, pp. 2165–2177; and P.M. Mathew, "Women's Industrial Employment in Kerala, India," *Bulletin of Concerned Asian Scholars* 18:3 (1986), pp. 43–58, cited in Everett, pp. 156-159.

18. See Everett and Savara, "Class and Gender."

19. Calman, *Protest in Democratic India* (Boulder, CO: Westview, 1985).

20. See Chapter 1, note 11.

21. Claus Offe, "New Social Movements: Challenging the Boundaries of Institutional Politics," *Social Research* 52 (1985), pp. 849–850.

22. Rajni Kothari, "Party and State in Our Times: The Rise of Non-Party Political Formations," *Alternative* 9 (1984), pp. 551–553.

Glossary

bandh	strike
chipko	to hug; name of a movement to prevent deforestation
dalits	the oppressed; members of scheduled castes (formerly called untouchables or harijans [children of god])
dharna	demonstration
gherao	a sit-in demonstration that detains an official
Janata	people; name of a political party
Lok Sabha	House of the People; elected lower house of Parliament
mela	fair
sabha	society, association
saheli	sister; name of a women's group in New Delhi
samiti	association, committee
sarkar	government
sarvodaya	the welfare of all; the name of a non-violent movement to gain land and rights for the poor
taluka	a subdivision of a district

Acronyms

AICCWW	All India Coordinating Committee of Working Women
AIDWA	All India Democratic Women's Association
AIWC	All India Women's Conference
CITU	Centre of Indian Trade Unions
CPC	Criminal Procedure Code
CPI	Communist Party of India
CPI(M-L)	Communist Party of India (Marxist-Leninist)
CPM	Communist Party of India (Marxist)
CROSS	Comprehensive Rural Operations Service Society
CSP	Congress Socialist Party
DGSM	Dashauli Gram Swarajya Mandal (a Sarvodaya group)
DMK	Dravida Munnetra Kazhagam (a political party powerful in the southern state of Tamil Nadu)
DVCM	Dahej Virodhi Chetana Manch (Forum to Combat the Dowry Menace)
EPW	*Economic and Political Weekly*
ILO	International Labor Organization
MDS	Mahila Dakshata Samiti (Women's Vigilance Committee)
NFIW	National Federation of Indian Women
SEWA	Self Employed Women's Association
WWF	Working Women's Forum
YWCA	Young Women's Christian Association

Bibliography

Agarwal, Bina. *Cold Hearths and Barren Slopes: The Woodfuel Crisis in the Third World.* New Delhi: Allied Publishers, 1986.

Agarwal, Bina and Afshar, Haleh, eds. *Women, Poverty and Ideology in Asia.* Houndmills, Basingstoke, Hampshire: Macmillan, 1989.

Alvarez, Sonia. *Engendering Democracy in Brazil.* Princeton: Princeton University Press, 1990.

Andreas, Carol. *When Women Rebel: The Rise of Popular Feminism in Peru.* Westport, CT: Lawrence Hill and Co., 1985.

Anklesaria, Shahnaz. "Women, and Rape: Defenceless Before Laws and Man." *Himmat,* 7 March 1980, pp. 13–18.

————. "Women in Gujarat: Behind the Facade." *Eve's Weekly,* 26 Feb. 1981.

Anthony, M.J. *Women's Rights.* New Delhi: Dialogue Publications, 1985.

"At the New Delhi Women's Center." *Off Our Backs,* Jan. 1985.

Austin, Granville. *The Indian Constitution: Cornerstone of a Nation.* Oxford: Oxford University Press, 1966.

Azad, Nandini. "Reaching Out to Women Workers Through Grassroots Delivery Systems." *Indian and Foreign Review,* 21:22 (1984).

Basu, Amrita. "Grass Roots Movements and the State: Reflections on Radical Change in India." *Theory and Society,* vol. 16 (1987), pp. 647–674.

Basu, Amrita. "Two Faces of Protest: Alternative Forms of Women's Mobilization in West Bengal and Maharashtra." *The Extended Family.* Ed. Gail Minault. Columbia, MO: South Asia Books, 1981.

Beneria, Lourdes, ed. *Women and Development: The Sexual Division of Labor in Rural Societies.* New York: Praeger/ILO, 1982.

Bhate, Kamakshi, et al. *In Search of Our Bodies.* Bombay: Shakti, 1987.

Bhattacharjea, Ajit. *Jayaprakash Narayan: A Political Biography.* Delhi: Vikas Publishing, 1975.

Bhatty, Zarina. "Status of Muslim Women and Social Change." *Indian Women: From Purdah to Modernity.* Ed. B.R. Nanda. New Delhi: Vikas, 1976.

————. *The Economic Role and Status of Women in the Beedi Industry in Allahabad, India.* Saarbrucken, Germany: Breitenbach, 1981.

Bondurant, Joan. *Conquest of Violence.* Berkeley: University of California Press, 1969.

"Born to Die." *India Today,* 15 June 1986, pp. 10–17.

Boserup, Ester. *Women's Role in Economic Development.* New York: St. Martin's Press, 1970.

Brijbhushan, Jamila. *Muslim Women: In Purdah and Out of It.* New Delhi: Vikas Publishing House, 1980.

Brown, Judith. *Gandhi's Rise to Power: Indian Politics 1915–1922.* London: Cambridge Univ. Press, 1972.

Butalia, Subhadra. "Karmika Demands Abolish Humiliating Cross Examination, Place the Onus of Consent on Accused." *How,* 4:2–3 (1981), p. 30.

Butalia, Urvashi. "Indian Women and the New Movement." *Women's Studies International Forum,* 8:2 (1985).

————. "Indian Women Fight On." *Inside Asia,* no. 1 (1984), pp. 25–26.

"Caged: A Survey of India." *The Economist,* 4 May 1991.

Calman, Leslie J. *Protest in Democratic India: Authority's Response to Challenge.* Boulder, CO: Westview Press, 1985.

————. "Women and Movement Politics in India." *Asian Survey,* 29:10 (1989), pp. 947–948.

Caplan, Patricia. *Class and Gender in India: Women and their Organizations in a South Indian City.* London: Tavistock, 1985.

Carden, Maren Lockwood. "The Proliferation of a Social Movement: Ideology and Individual Incentives in the Contemporary Feminist Movement." *Research in Social Movements, Conflicts and Change,* vol. 1 (1978), pp. 179–196.

Charlton, Sue Ellen, Jana Everett and Kathleen Staudt, eds. *Women, the State and Development.* Albany, New York: SUNY Press, 1989.

Chattopadhayay, Kamaledevi. *Indian Women's Battle for Freedom.* New Delhi: Abhinav Publications, 1983.

Chen, Marty. *The Working Women's Forum: Organizing for Credit and Change.* New York: SEEDS, 1983.

————, et al. *Indian Women: A Study of their Role in the Dairy Movement.* New Delhi: Shakti Books, 1986.

Cohen, Jean L. "Strategy or Identity: New Theoretical Paradigms and Contemporary Social Movements." *Social Research,* no. 52 (1985), pp. 663–716.

Dalton, Dennis. "Gandhi's Styles of Leadership." *Leadership in South Asia.* Ed. B.N. Pandey. New Delhi: Vikas, 1977.

Dasgupta, Biplab. *The Naxalite Movement.* Bombay: Allied, 1974.

Desai, A.R. "Women's Movement in India: An Assessment." *Economic and Political Weekly,* 8 June 1985, pp. 992–995.

Desai, Anita. "India: The Seed of Destruction." *New York Review of Books,* 27 June 1991.

Desai, Neera. *Woman in Modern India.* Bombay: Vora, 1977.

de Silva, G.V.S. et al. *Bhoomi Sena: A Struggle for People's Power.* Bombay: National Institute of Bank Management, 1978.

————and Krishna Raj, Maithreyi. *Women and Society in India.* Delhi: Ajanta Publications, 1987.

————and Patel, Vibhuti. *Indian Women: Change and Challenge in the International Decade 1975–85.* Bombay: Popular Prakashan, 1985.

Dhanagare, D.N. "Agrarian Reforms and Rural Development in India." *Research in Social Movements, Conflicts and Change,* 7 (1984), pp. 177–201.

Donati, Paolo R. "Organization Between Movement and Institution." *Social Science Information,* 23 (1984), pp. 837–859.

"The Dowry Prohibition Act, 1961: Struggling for an Amendment." *Samya Shakti*, 1:2 (1984), pp. 131–134.

"Dowry: Spreading Among More Communities." *Manushi*, no. 16 (1983) pp. 31–32.

Durkheim, Emile. *The Division of Labor in Society*. New York: Free Press, 1933.

Eldridge, Philip. "The Political Role of Community Action Groups in India and Indonesia: In Search of a General Theory." *Alternatives*, 10 (1984–85), pp. 401–434.

Elections in India: Data Handbook on Lok Sabha Elections, 2nd ed., 1952–85. Ed. V.B. Singh and Shankar Bose. Beverly Hills, CA: Sage, 1986.

Engineer, Asghar Ali. "Does the Quran Discriminate Against Women?" *Onlooker*, 8–22 Sept. 1985, pp. 41–42.

Everett, Jana. "Approaches to the 'Woman Question' in India: From Maternalism to Mobilization." *Women's Studies International Quarterly*, 4 (1981), pp. 169–178.

_____ . "The Upsurge of Women's Activism in India." *Frontiers*, 7 (1983), pp. 18–26.

_____ . "We Were in the Forefront of the Fight: Feminist Theory and Practice in Indian Grass-roots Movements." *South Asia Bulletin*, no. 6 (1986).

_____ . *Women and Social Change in India*. New Delhi: Heritage, 1981.

_____ and Mira Savara. "Bank Loans to the Poor in Bombay: Do Women Benefit?" *Signs*, 10:2 (1984), pp. 272–290.

_____ and Mira Savara. "Class and Gender: The Organizational Involvement of Urban Working Class Women in India." Paper presented at the Annual Meeting of the Association for Asian Studies, Washington, D.C., March 1989.

Fireman, Bruce and William A. Gamson. "Utilitarian Logic in the Resource Mobilization Perspective." *The Dynamics of Social Movements*. Ed. Mayer N. Zald and John D. McCarthy. Cambridge, MA: Winthrop Publishers, Inc., 1979.

Fisher, Jo. *Mothers of the Disappeared*. Boston: South End Press, 1989.

Flavia. "The Relationship Between Women's Institutions and Social Movements." Paper presented at the workshop Institutional Approaches to Helping Women in Distress, organized by the Women's Centre (Bombay) and Nirmala Kiketan. Bombay, 1984.

Forbes, Geraldine H. "Caged Tigers: 'First Wave' Feminists in India." *Women's Studies International Forum*, 5 (1982), pp. 525–536.

_____ . "From Purdah to Politics: The Social Feminism of the All-India Women's Organizations." *Separate Worlds*. Ed. Hanna Papanek and Gail Minault. Delhi: Chanakya Publications, 1982.

_____ . "The Indian Women's Movement: A Struggle for Women's Rights or National Liberation?" *The Extended Family*. Ed. Gail Minault. Columbia, MO: South Asia Books, 1981.

Frankel, Francine R. *India's Political Economy, 1947–1977*. Delhi: Oxford University Press, 1978.

Freeman, Jo. "A Model for Analyzing the Strategic Options of Social Movement Organizations." *Social Movements of the Sixties and Seventies*. Ed. Jo Freeman. New York: Longman, 1983.

_____ . "On the Origins of Social Movements." *Social Movements of the Sixties and Seventies*. Ed. Jo Freeman. New York: Longman, 1983.

_____ . *The Politics of Women's Liberation*. New York: David McKay, 1975.

Gamson, William A. *The Strategy of Social Protest*. 2nd ed. Belmont, CA: Wadsworth, 1990.

Gandhi, Manju. "National Federation of Indian Women (NFIW): Work and Issues Taken Up During the Decade." Paper presented at the National Seminar on a Decade of Women's Movement in India: A Review of Achievements and Issues. Research Unit on Women's Studies, SNDT Women's University, Bombay, 8–10 January 1985.

Gandhi, Nandita. "The Emergence of Autonomous Women's Groups." *Lokayan Bulletin*, 4:6 (1986), pp. 84–90.

———— . "When the Rolling Pins Hit the Streets." Paper presented at National Conference on Women's Studies. Punjab University, Chandigarh, 1–4 October 1986.

———— . "Women's Movement in India: Proposing an Alternative Perspective." New Delhi: Lokayan paper, n.d.

Ganguly, Arati. "A Decade of Women's Organizations." Paper presented at National Seminar on A Decade of Women's Movement in India: Review of Achievements and Issues. SNDT University, Bombay, 8–10 January 1985.

Geertz, Clifford. *The Interpretation of Cultures*. New York: Basic Books, 1973.

Gotoskar-Kanhare, Sujata. "Organising Working Class Women." *HOW*, 5:1 (1982), pp. 11–14.

Government of India, Ministry of Education and Social Welfare. *Towards Equality: Report of the Committee on the Status of Women in India*. New Delhi, 1974.

———— , Ministry of Social and Women's Welfare. *Women in India: Country Paper*. New Delhi, 1985.

Gulati, Leela. *Fisherwomen on the Kerala Coast*. Geneva: International Labour Office, l984.

Gupta, Shekhar. "The Muslims: A Community in Turmoil." *India Today*, 31 Jan. 1986.

Gupta, Sunil and Kumar, Ashish. "Gays in India: Closetted by Caste and Class." *Inside Asia*, nos. 3–4 (1985), pp. 45–47.

Gurr, Ted. *Why Men Rebel*. Princeton: Princeton University Press, 1970.

Gusfield, Joseph R. "Social Movement and Social Change: Perspectives of Linearity and Fluidity." *Research in Social Movements, Conflicts and Change*, 4 (1981), pp. 317–339.

Haithcox, John Patrick. *Communism and Nationalism in India: M.N. Roy and Comintern Policy, 1920-1939*. Princeton: Princeton University Press, 1971.

Haksar, Nandita. *Demystification of Law for Women*. New Delhi: Lancer Press, 1986.

Hardgrave, Robert L. Jr. *India Under Pressure*. Boulder, CO: Westview Press, 1984.

———— and Kochanek, Stanley A. *India: Government and Politics in a Developing Nation*. 4th ed. New York: Harcourt Brace Jovanovich, 1986.

Hoffer, Eric. *The True Believer*. New York: Harper and Row, 1951.

In Search of Our Bodies: A Feminist Look at Women, Health and Reproduction in India. Bombay: Shakti, 1987.

Invisible Hands: Women in Home-Based Production. Ed. Andrea Menefee Singh and Anita Kelles-Viitanen. New Delhi: Sage, 1987.

Jacobson, Doranne and Susan S. Wadley. *Women in India: Two Perspectives*. New Delhi: Manohar, 1986.

Jaggar, Alison. *Feminist Politics and Human Nature.* Totowa, N.J.: Rowman and Allanheld, 1983.

Jain, Devaki. *Women's Quest for Power.* District Ghaziabad: Vikas, 1980.

Jain, Shobhita. "Women and People's Ecological Movement: A Case Study of Women's Role in the Chipko Movement in Uttar Pradesh." *Economic and Political Weekly,* 13 October 1984, pp. 1788–1794.

Jaising, Indira. "The Politics of Personal Law." *The Lawyers,* Feb. 1986, pp. 6–8.

Jaquette, Jane. "Women and Modernization Theory: A Decade of Feminist Criticism." *World Politics,* 34:2 (1982), pp. 267–284.

Jenkins, J. Craig. "Resource Mobilization Theory and the Study of Social Movements." *Annual Review of Sociology,* 9 (1983), pp. 527–553.

—————— and Charles Perrow. "Insurgency of the Powerless: Farm Worker Movements (1946-1972)." *American Sociological Review,* 42 (1977), pp. 249–268.

Jhabvala, Renana. *Closing Doors: A Study of the Decline in Women Workers in the Textile Mills of Ahmedabad.* Ahmedabad: SETU, 1985.

——————. "Women's Struggle in the Informal Sector: Two Case Studies from Sewa." Paper read at National Conference on Women's Studies. Punjab University, Chandigarh, 1–4 October 1986.

Johnson, Chalmers. *Revolutionary Change.* Boston: Little, Brown and Co., 1966.

Joshi, Sharmila. "The Awakening Feminists." *Imprint,* April 1986, pp. 66–71.

Kannabiran, Vasanth and Veena Shatrugna. "The Relocation of Political Practice—The Stree Shakti Sangathana Experience." *Lokayan Bulletin,* 4:6 (1986).

Karkal, Malini. "How the Other Half Dies in Bombay." *Economic and Political Weekly,* 24 August 1985.

Kashtakari Sanghatna. "Kashtakari Sanghatna (The Warli Uprising Revisited)." *Agrarian Struggles in India after Independence.* Ed. A.R. Desai. Delhi: Oxford University Press, 1986.

Katzenstein, Mary Fainsod. "Organizing Against Violence: Strategies of the Indian Women's Movement," *Pacific Affairs.* 62:1 (1989), pp. 53–71.

Katzenstein, Mary Fainsod. "Towards Equality? Cause and Consequence of the Political Prominence of Women in India." *Asian Survey,* 18 (1978), pp. 473–486. Rpt. in *The Extended Family.* Ed. Gail Minault. Columbia, MO: South Asia Books, 1981.

Kelkar, Govind. "Women and Structural Violence in India." *Women's Studies Quarterly,* 12:3–4 (1985) pp. 16–18.

Kishwar, Madhu. "Introduction." *In Search of Answers: Indian Women's Voices from Manushi.* Ed. Madhu Kishwar. London: Zed Press, 1984.

Kochanek, Stanley A. "Mrs. Gandhi's Pyramid: The New Congress." *Indira Gandhi's India.* Ed. Henry C. Hart. Boulder, CO: Westview, 1976.

Kohli, Atul, ed. *India's Democracy: An Analysis of Changing State-Society Relations.* Princeton: Princeton University Press, 1988.

Kothari, Rajni. "Communalism in India: The New Face of Democracy." *Lokayan Bulletin,* 3:3 (1985), pp. 3–21.

——————. "End of An Era." *Seminar,* no. 197 (1976), pp. 22–28.

——————. "Party and State in Our Times: The Rise of Non-Party Politcal Formations." *Alternatives,* 9 (1984), pp. 541-564.

_____ . "The Non-Party Political Process." *Economic and Political Weekly*, 4 Feb. 1984.

Kulkarni, Sharad. "Social Mobilisation Groups: A Review." New Delhi: Lokayan, n.d. Mimeographed.

Kumar, Ajay. "Muslim Women Bill: the Gathering Storm." *India Today*, 31 March 1986, pp. 14–17.

_____ "The Muslims: Anger and Hurt." *India Today*, 15 March 1986.

Lateef, Shahida. "Indian Women Caught in a Time Warp." *Indian Express Sunday Magazine*, 30 March 1986.

Lawyers Collective. *Recent Changes in Laws Relating to Women*. Bombay: Lawyers Collective, 1985.

Liddle, Joanna and Rama Joshi. *Daughters of Independence: Gender, Caste and Class in India*. London: Zed Press, 1986.

"Lokayan: A Six Year Report." *Lokayan Bulletin*, 3:6 (1985), pp. 3–54.

Loutfi, Martha F. *Rural Women: Unequal Partners in Development*. Geneva: International Labour Office, 1985.

McCarthy, John D. and Mayer N. Zald. "Resource Mobilization and Social Movements: A Partial Theory." *American Journal of Sociology*, 82 (1977), pp. 1212–1241.

"Madhu Interviewed," *Spare Rib*, [London] no. 145 (1984).

Mahanta, Aparna. "The Women's Movement: Perspectives and Future Strategy." Paper presented at National Conference on Women's Studies. Punjab University, Chandigarh, 1–4 October 1986.

Mahila Dakshata Samiti. *Report of Seminar on Amendment to the Prohibition of Dowry Act and Protection of Abandoned Women and Children*. New Delhi: MDS, 1979.

_____ . *Biennial Report, 1984–85: Report of the Workshop on Relevance of Law to Women*. New Delhi: MDS, 1985.

Manimala, "'Zameen Kenkar? Jote Onkar!' The Story of Women's Participation in the Bodhgaya Struggle." *Manushi*, no. 14 (1983).

"Manushi." *Lokayan Bulletin*, 3:3 (1985), pp. 58-72.

"Margaret Alva on Indian Women and Changing Society." *Choice*, 2:12 (1985) pp. 3–11.

Mazumdar, Vina. "The Role of Research in Women's Development: A Case Study of the ICSSR Programme of Women's Studies." *Samya Shakti*, 1:1 (1983), pp. 24–42.

_____ . "The Social Reform Movement in India—From Ranade to Nehru." *Indian Women: From Purdah to Modernity*. Ed. B.R. Nanda. New Delhi: Vikas, 1976.

Melucci, Alberto. "An End to Social Movements?" *Social Science Information*, 23 (1984), pp. 819–835.

_____ . "The Symbolic Challenge of Contemporary Movements." *Social Research*, 52 (1985), pp. 789–816.

Mendhapurkar, Subhash and Lina. "It's About Changing Our Lives." *Manushi*, no. 39 (1987) and no. 40 (1987).

Mhatre, Sharayu, Sulabaha Brahme and Govind Kelkar. *Bank Credit to Women: A Study of Kanavals or Working Class Lunch Suppliers*. Bombay: National Institute of Bank Management, 1980.

Mies, Maria. *Indian Women and Patriarchy*. New Delhi: Concept Publishing, 1980.

_____ . "Landless Women Organize." *Manushi,* no. 15 (1983), pp. 11–19.

Miller, Barbara. *The Endangered Sex: Neglect of Female Children in Rural North India.* Ithaca: Cornell University Press, 1981.

Minault, Gail. "Sisterhood or Separatism? The All-India Muslim Ladies' Conference and the Nationalist Movement." *The Extended Family.* Ed. Gail Minault. Columbia, MO: South Asia Books, 1981.

Mody, Nawaz. "The Press in India: The Shah Bano Judgement and Its Aftermath." *Asian Survey,* 27:8 (1987), pp. 935-953.

Mohanty, Chandra T., et al., eds. *Third World Women and the Politics of Feminism.* Bloomington: Indiana University Press, 1991.

Mohanty, Manoranjan. *Revolutionary Violence: A Study of the Maoist Movement in India.* New Delhi: Sterling, 1977.

Mukhopadhyay, Maitrayee. *Silver Shackles: Women and Development in India.* Oxford, England: Oxfam, 1984.

Mumtaz, Khawar and Farida Shaheed. *Women of Pakistan.* London: Zed Press, 1987.

"Muslim Personal Law: Evading the Issue." *Economic and Political Weekly,* 30 Nov. 1985.

Nandy, Ashis. "Culture, State and the Rediscovery of Indian Politics." *Economic and Political Weekly,* 8 December 1984, pp. 2078–2083.

Narayan, Jayaprakash. *Prison Diary, 1975.* Bombay: Popular Prakashan, 1977.

_____ . *Towards Revolution.* New Delhi: Arnold-Heinemann, 1975.

_____ . *Towards Total Revolution.* 4 vols. Bombay: Popular Prakashan, 1978.

National Federation of Indian Women. *For Equality: For a Just Social Order.* New Delhi: NFIW, 1984.

"National Federation of Indian Women." *HOW,* 4:2-3, p. 14.

Oakley, Peter and David Marsden. *Approaches to Participation in Rural Development.* Geneva: International Labour Office, 1984.

Oberschall, Anthony. *Social Conflicts and Social Movements.* Englewood Cliffs, NJ: Prentice Hall, 1973.

Offe, Claus. "New Social Movements: Challenging the Boundaries of Institutional Politics." *Social Research,* 52 (1985), pp. 817–868.

Olson, Mancur. *The Logic of Collective Action.* New York: Schocken, 1971.

Omvedt, Gail. *We Will Smash This Prison: Indian Women in Struggle.* London: Zed Press, 1980.

_____ "Women in Popular Movements: India and Thailand During the Decade of Women." A report prepared for the UNRISD Popular Participation Programme, June 1985. Mimeographed.

_____ and Rao, Nagmani. "Rural Women's Mobilisation: The Khanapur Taluka Experience." *Lokayan Bulletin,* 3:2 (1985), pp. 50–67.

"On Threats to the Non-Party Political Process." *Lokayan Bulletin,* 3:2 (1985), pp. 37–49.

Ostergaard, Geoffrey and Melville Currell. *The Gentle Anarchists: A Study of the Sarvodaya Movement for Non-Violent Revolution in India.* Oxford: Clarendon, 1971.

Papanek, Hanna and Gail Minault, eds. *Separate Worlds: Studies of Purdah in South Asia.* Delhi: Chanakya Publications, 1982.

Patel, Vibhuti. "Emergence and Proliferation of Autonomous Women's Groups in India (1974 -1984)." Paper presented at National Seminar on A Decade of Women's Movement in India: A Review of Achievement and Issues. SNDT Women's University, Bombay, 8–10 January 1985.

_____ . "Ideological Debates Among Autonomous Women's Groups in India." Paper presented at National Conference on Women's Studies. Punjab University, Chandigarh, 1–4 October 1986.

_____ . "Impact of Autonomous Women's Organisations." *Lokayan Bulletin,* 4:6 (1986), pp. 90–103.

_____ . "Indian Women on Warpath." *Reaching for Half the Sky.* Baroda: Antar Rashtriya Prakashan, 1985.

_____ . "Women's Liberation in India." *New Left Review, no.153 (1985), pp. 74–86.*

Pendse, A., A.K. Roy, and H. Sethi. "People's Participation: A Look at Non-Party Political Formations in India." New Delhi: Lokayan, n.d. Mimeographed.

People's Union for Democratic Rights. *Inside the Family: A Report on Democratic Rights of Women.* 2nd edition. New Delhi: PUDR, 1986.

Perrow, Charles. "The Sixties Observed." *The Dynamics of Social Movements.* Ed. Mayer N. Zald and John D. McCarthy. Cambridge, MA: Winthrop Publishers, Inc., 1979.

"Providing 'Compensatory Justice': Draft National Perspective Plan for Women." *Economic and Political Weekly,* 16 July 1988, pp. 1461–1462.

Purao, Prema. "Annapoorna Mahila Mandal." *How,* 4:2–3 (1981), pp. 11–13.

_____ and Mira Savara. *Annapurna Mahila Mandal.* Bombay: AMM, n.d.

Puri, Balraj. "Muslim Personal Law." *Economic and Political Weekly,* 8 June 1985, pp. 987–991.

Rajaram, Indira. "Economics of Bride-Price and Dowry." *Economic and Political Weekly,* 8 February 1983, pp. 275-279.

Randeria, Shalini and Leela Visaria. "Sociology of Bride Price and Dowry." *Economic and Political Weekly,* 14 April 1984, pp. 648–652.

Reaching for Half the Sky: A Reader in Women's Movement. Baroda: Antar Rashtriya Prakashan, 1985.

Report of the National Conference on Women's Studies. Bombay: SNDT Women's University, 20–24 April 1981.

Report, National Conference: Perspectives for the Autonomous Women's Movement in India. Bombay, December 1985.

Roy, Asish Kumar. *The Spring Thunder and After.* Calcutta: Minerva, 1975.

Rubin, Barnett R. "The Civil Liberties Movement in India: New Approaches to State and Social Change." *Asian Survey,* 27:3 (1987), pp. 370–392.

Rudolph, Lloyd I. and Rudolph, Susanne Hoeber. *The Modernity of Tradition.* Chicago: Univ. of Chicago Press, 1967.

_____ . *In Pursuit of Laksmi: The Political Economy of the Indian State.* Chicago: Univ. of Chicago Press, 1987.

Saheli. *Saheli: The First Four Years.* New Delhi: 1985.

_____ . "Wife Battering: Issues Facing the Women's Movement." Paper presented at National Conference on Women's Studies. Punjab University, Chandigarh, 1–4 October 1986.

_____ . "Women's Organisations: A Perspective." Paper presented at National Conference on Women's Studies. Punjab University, Chandigarh, 1–4 October 1986.

Sarkar, Lotika. "Jawaharlal Nehru and the Hindu Code Bill." *Indian Women: From Purdah to Modernity.* Ed. B.R. Nanda. New Delhi: Vikas, 1976.

Savara, Mira and Sujatha Gothoskar. "An Assertion of Womanpower." *Manushi,* no. 13 (1982).

Sebstad, Jennifer. *Struggle and Development Among Self Employed Women: A Report on the Self Employed Women's Association, Ahmedabad, India.* Washington, D.C.: AID, 1982.

Sen, Amartya and Sunil Sengupta. "Malnutrition of Rural Children and the Sex Bias." *Economic and Political Weekly,* May 1983, pp. 855–864.

Sen, Gita and Caren Grown. *Development, Crises and Alternative Visions: Third World Women's Perspectives.* New York: Monthly Review Press, 1087.

Sen Gupta, Bhabani. *CPI-M: Promises, Prospects, Problems.* New Delhi: Young Asia, 1979.

Sethi, Harsh. "Groups in a New Politics of Transformation." *Economic and Political Weekly,* 18 February 1984, pp. 305–316.

_____ . "The Immoral 'Other': Debate Between Party and NonParty Groups." *Economic and Political Weekly,* 23 February 1985, pp. 378–380.

_____ . "Some Dilemmas Facing Non-Party Political Groups: A Response to the Party-Based Critiques." *Lokayan Bulletin,* 2:2 (1984), pp. 17–26.

Shah, Ganshyam. "The Upsurge in Gujarat." *Economic and Political Weekly,* 9:32–34 (1974).

Shah Bano. Ed. Janak Raj Jai. New Delhi: Rajiv Publications, 1986.

The Shah Bano Controversy. Ed. Ashgar Ali Engineer. Bombay: Orient Longman, 1987.

Sharma, Kalpana. "Neutralizing Voluntary Agencies." *Indian Express,* 3 August 1986.

Sharma, Kumud, Balaji Pandey and Kusum Nautiyal. "The Chipko Movement in the Uttarkhand Region, Uttar Pradesh, India: Women's Role and Participation." *Rural Development and Women: Lessons from the Field.* Ed. Shimwaayi Muntemba. Geneva: International Labour Office, 1985, pp. 173–193.

Sharma, Ursula. *Women, Work and Property in North-West India.* London: Tavistock Publications, 1980.

Sherwani, Madeeha. "Why More Women Entering Work Force?" *Yojana,* 28 (1984), pp. 23–25, 33.

Sheth, D.L. "Grass-roots Initiatives in India." *Economic and Political Weekly,* 11 February 1984.

_____ . "Grass-Roots Stirrings and the Future of Politics." Alternatives 9 (1983), pp. 1–24.

Shramshakti: Report of the National Commission on Self Employed Women and Women in the Informal Sector. New Delhi: Government of India, 1988.

Skocpol, Theda. *States and Social Revolutions.* New York: Cambridge University Press, 1979.

Smelser, Neil. *The Theory of Collective Behavior.* New York: Free Press, 1951.

Srivastava, T.N. *Women and the Law.* New Delhi: Intellectual Publishing House, 1985.

The State of India's Environment 1984–85: The Second Citizens' Report. New Delhi: Centre for Science and Environment, 1985.

Stein, Dorothy. "Burning Widows, Burning Brides: the Perils of Daughterhood in India." *Pacific Affairs,* 61:3 (1988).

Symbols of Power: Studies on the Political Status of Women in India. Ed. Vina Mazumdar. Bombay: Allied Publishers, 1979.

Tandon, Rajesh. "Regulating NGOs: New Moves." *Lokayan Bulletin,* 4:3–4, 1986, pp. 37–42.

Tilly, Charles. "Does Modernization Breed Revolution?" *Comparative Politics,* 5:3 (1973).

———. *From Mobilization to Revolution.* Reading, MA: Addison-Wesley, 1978.

Tinker, Irene and Michele Bo Bramson, eds. *Women and World Development.* Washington, D.C.: Overseas Development Council, 1976.

Touraine, Alain. "An Introduction to the Study of Social Movements." *Social Research* 52 (1985), pp. 749–788.

Towards Empowerment. Ed. Kamla Bhasin. New Delhi: FAO, 1985.

Truman, David. *The Governmental Process.* New York: Knopf, 1951.

Turner, Ralph H. "Collective Behavior and Resource Mobilization as Approaches to Social Movements: Issues and Continuities." *Research in Social Movements, Conflicts and Change,* 4 (1981), pp. 1–24.

Useem, Bert. "Solidarity Model, Breakdown Model and the Boston Anti-Busing Movement." *American Sociological Review,* 45 (1980), pp. 357–369.

Vanita, Ruth. "The Bills to Amend the Rape and Dowry Laws—Mending or Marring?" *Manushi,* no. 16 (1983), pp. 27–30.

——— and Madhu Kishwar. "A Woman's Home is Not Her Own." *Indian Express,* 8 June 1986.

Veigas, Savia and Shrabani Basu. "Like a Bridge Over Troubled Waters." *Femina,* 8–22 September 1984.

Weiner, Myron. *India at the Polls: The Parliamentary Elections of 1977.* Washington, D.C.: American Enterprise Institute for Public Policy Research, 1978.

———. "The 1971 Elections and the Indian Party System." *Asian Survey,* 11 (1971), pp. 1153–1166.

Women in Contemporary India and South Asia. Ed. Alfred de Souza. New Delhi: Manohar, 1980.

Wood, John R. "Extra-Parliamentary Opposition in India: An Analysis of Populist Agitations in Gujarat and Bihar." *Pacific Affairs,* Fall 1975, pp. 313–325.

Zald, Mayer N. and Roberta Ash. "Social Movement Organizations: Growth, Decay and Change." *Social Forces,* 44 (1966), pp. 327–340.

Zald, Mayer N. and John D. McCarthy. "Introduction." *The Dynamics of Social Movements.* Ed. Mayer N. Zald and John D. McCarthy. Cambridge, MA: Winthrop Publishers, Inc., 1979.

"'Zameen Kenkar? Jote Onkar!' The Story of Women's Participation in the Bodhgaya Struggle." *Manushi,* 3:2 (1983), pp. 2–16.

About the Book and Author

Analyzing Indian women's groups as one sector of a complex of new grass-roots, non-party political movements, Dr. Calman considers why and how a women's movement evolved in India when it did. She describes the nature, origins, and meanings of the movement for Indian women and discusses the movement's significance for Indian politics in general as well as for understanding the nature of movement politics worldwide. She outlines the women's achievements so far and concludes with an assessment of their future prospects for bettering their lives through participation in the movement.

Leslie J. Calman is director of the Barnard Center for Research on Women and lecturer in political science at Barnard College. She is the author of *Protest in Democratic India: Authority's Response to Challenge.*

Index

Gandhi and, 22–35, 48, 63
  human rights and, 51
  proclaiming, 30–34
  women's movement and, 74, 94, 184
Emergency Proclamation, 30, 32
Employment, 13
  discrimination in, 12, 58, 59
  press and, 85
  women's, 57–58
Empowerment, 10–14, 18(n10), 22, 36, 40,
    50–51, 73, 107(n4), 163, 168, 176–179,
    197
  economic, 3, 4, 137, 139, 170, 183, 190
  grass-roots, 17, 88–90, 140, 171, 177,
    184–185, 192
  key to, 168
  limited, 91, 183, 186, 190–192
  personal, 9, 185, 192
  psychological, 5, 137, 139, 167, 170
  rural organizing for, 92
  seeking, 16, 17, 173, 186, 187, 195
  social, 4, 15, 190
  See also Power
Empowerment wing, 9, 89, 91, 94, 97, 137,
    190, 192
  goals of, 15–17
  leaders of, 185
  priorities of, 16
  See also Rights wing
Environmental movement, xvi, xviii, 3, 9,
    22, 93–94, 196
Equal pay. *See* Wages
Equal protection of the law, 151
Equal Remuneration Act (1976), 71(n19),
    96–97, 198(n3)
Equal rights, xiv, 5, 108(n27)
Ethnic divisions, xv, xxii(n9)
Eve teasing. *See* Harassment, sexual

Faizal Ali, S.M.: on rape, 119
Family
  laws pertaining to, 140, 147
  religious law and, 53, 147
  role of, 12, 50, 198(n1)
  status within, 5, 10, 11, 118, 124, 186, 191,
    192
Family courts, 80
Family planning, 52, 178
  fight for, 104
  WWF and, 103
  See also Birth control
Family Planning Foundation, funding from,
    102
Family violence, 13, 140
  counseling on, 77
  curbing, 12, 14, 87, 179

  police and, 77, 124
  See also Violence
FAO. *See* Food and Agriculture
    Organization
Feminist Network, 82, 84, 108(n35)
Feminists, 6, 8, 80, 86, 183, 196
  dowry and, 56, 129
  dowry death and, 129
  influence of, 87, 92, 185
  marital rape and, 121–122
  violence and, 129
  women's rights and, 163
  See also International feminism; Women's
    movement
Fernandes, George, 29
Fertility rate, 61–62
Firestone, Shulamith, 86
Five year plans, 80, 193, 194
Food and Agriculture Organization (FAO)
    (UN)
  funding from, 95, 102
  WWF and, 176
Ford Foundation, 111(n79), 113(n110)
  funding from, 16, 87, 95, 102, 105, 176
Foreign Contribution Regulation Act, 194
42nd Amendment, 32, 34
Forum Against Rape, 69, 83
Forum Against the Oppression of Women,
    38, 69, 139
Forum to Combat the Dowry Menace,
    dowry deaths and, 129
Freeman, Jo, 83
Freire, Paulo: conscientization and, 40
Fundamentalists
  human rights and, 148
  pressure by, 157, 161
  uniform civil code and, 156–158
  women's rights and, 189
Fundamental Rights, 53, 150, 151
Funding
  international, 87–88, 94–95, 168, 186, 194
  regulation of, 171, 194
  significance of, 87–88, 120
  sources of, 16, 87–88, 90, 94–95, 102, 104,
    105, 168, 171, 176, 186, 194

Gandhi, Indira, 60, 75, 77
  Bihar movement and, 28, 29
  corruption and, 26, 31
  CPI and, 38, 44(n61)
  deinstitutionalization by, 33, 37
  Emergency and, 22–35, 48, 63
  five year plan and, 193
  J.P. movement and, 30
  popularity of, 23, 24, 35
  populist goals of, 24, 25, 32